Visual and Multimodal Research in Organization and Management Studies

This volume brings together two hitherto disparate domains of scholarly inquiry: organization and management studies on the one hand, and the study of visual and multimodal communication on the other. Within organization and management studies it has been recognized that organizational reality and communication are becoming increasingly visual, and, more generally, multimodal, whether in digital form or otherwise. Within multimodality studies it has been noted that many forms of contemporary communication are deeply influenced by organizational and managerial communication, as formerly formal and bureaucratic types of communication increasingly adopt promotional language and multimodal document presentation.

Visual and Multimodal Research in Organization and Management Studies integrates these two domains of research in a way that will benefit both. In particular, it conceptually and empirically connects recent insights from visual and multimodality studies to ongoing discussions in organization and management theory. Throughout, the book shows how a visual/multimodal lens enriches and extends what we already know about organization, organizations, and practices of organizing, but also how concepts from organization and management studies can be highly productive in further developing insights on visual and multimodal communication.

Due to its essentially interdisciplinary objectives, the book will prove inspiring for academics and scholars of management, the sociology of organizations as well as related disciplines such as applied linguistics and visual studies.

Markus A. Höllerer is Professor of Public Management and Governance at WU Vienna University of Economics and Business, Austria, and Professor of Organization Theory at UNSW Business School, Australia.

Theo van Leeuwen is Professor at the Department of Language and Communication at the University of Southern Denmark.

Dennis Jancsary is Assistant Professor at the Institute for Organization Studies at WU Vienna University of Economics and Business, Austria.

Renate E. Meyer is Professor of Organization Studies at WU Vienna University of Economics and Business, Austria, and part-time Professor of Institutional Theory at Copenhagen Business School, Denmark.

Thomas Hestbæk Andersen is Associate Professor at the Department of Language and Communication at the University of Southern Denmark.

Eero Vaara is Professor of Organization and Management in the Department of Management Studies at Aalto University School of Business, Finland. He is a permanent Visiting Professor at EMLYON Business School, France, and a Distinguished Visiting Scholar at Lancaster University, UK.

Routledge Studies in Management,
Organizations and Society

This series presents innovative work grounded in new realities, addressing issues crucial to an understanding of the contemporary world. This is the world of organised societies, where boundaries between formal and informal, public and private, local and global organizations have been displaced or have vanished, along with other nineteenth-century dichotomies and oppositions. Management, apart from becoming a specialized profession for a growing number of people, is an everyday activity for most members of modern societies.

Similarly, at the level of enquiry, culture and technology, and literature and economics, can no longer be conceived as isolated intellectual fields; conventional canons and established mainstreams are contested. **Management, Organizations and Society** addresses these contemporary dynamics of transformation in a manner that transcends disciplinary boundaries, with books that will appeal to researchers, student and practitioners alike.

Recent titles in this series include:

Corporate Social Responsibility, Social Justice and
The Global Food Supply Chain
Towards An Ethical Food Policy For Sustainable Supermarkets
Hillary J. Shaw & Julia J. A. Shaw

Organizational Identity and Memory
A Multidisciplinary Approach
Andrea Casey

Organizational Theory and Aesthetic Philosophies
Antonio Strati

Visual and Multimodal Research in Organization and
Management Studies
Markus A. Höllerer, Theo van Leeuwen, Dennis Jancsary, Renate E. Meyer, Thomas Hestbæk Andersen, and Eero Vaara

For more information about this series, please visit: www.routledge.com/Routledge-Studies-in-Management-Organizations-and-Society/book-series/SE0536

Visual and Multimodal Research in Organization and Management Studies

Markus A. Höllerer, Theo van Leeuwen,
Dennis Jancsary, Renate E. Meyer,
Thomas Hestbæk Andersen, and
Eero Vaara

First published 2019
by Routledge
52 Vanderbilt Avenue, New York, NY 10017

and by Routledge
2 Park Square, Milton Park, Abingdon, Oxon, OX14 4RN

Routledge is an imprint of the Taylor & Francis Group, an informa business

© 2019 Taylor & Francis

The right of Markus A. Höllerer, Theo van Leeuwen, Dennis Jancsary, Renate E. Meyer, Thomas Hestbæk Andersen, and Eero Vaara to be identified as authors of this work has been asserted by them in accordance with sections 77 and 78 of the Copyright, Designs and Patents Act 1988.

All rights reserved. No part of this book may be reprinted or reproduced or utilised in any form or by any electronic, mechanical, or other means, now known or hereafter invented, including photocopying and recording, or in any information storage or retrieval system, without permission in writing from the publishers.

Trademark notice: Product or corporate names may be trademarks or registered trademarks, and are used only for identification and explanation without intent to infringe.

Library of Congress Cataloging-in-Publication Data
A catalog record for this title has been requested

ISBN: 978-1-138-21057-8 (hbk)
ISBN: 978-1-315-45501-3 (ebk)

Typeset in Sabon
by Apex CoVantage, LLC

Contents

List of Figures x
List of Tables xii
Acknowledgements xiii
Preface xiv

PART I
Introduction 1

1 Purpose of This Volume 3

   1.1 Aims and Objectives 3
   1.2 Different Fields, Similar Interests—Exploring Intersections Between Organization and Multimodality Research 5
      1.2.1 Visual and Multimodal Turn in Organization Studies 6
      1.2.2 Organizational Turn in Multimodality Studies 8
      1.2.3 Intersections and Opportunities 9
   1.3 Recent Developments at the Intersection of Organization and Multimodality Research 10
      1.3.1 Visuality: Making Organization 'Visible' 10
      1.3.2 Materiality: Making Organization 'Tangible' 12
      1.3.3 Further Extensions of the Communicative Construction of Organization and Organizing 14
   1.4 Roots and Inspirations for Multimodal Organization Research 15
   1.5 Approaches to the Study of Multimodality in Organizations 19
   1.6 Case Studies and Applications 22
   1.7 Conclusion 23

2 A Social Semiotic Approach to Multimodality 24

2.1 What Is Social Semiotics? 25
2.2 The 'Social' in Social Semiotics 25
2.3 The 'Semiotic' in Social Semiotics 27
  2.3.1 System and Instantiation 27
  2.3.2 Metafunctions 30
  2.3.3 Stratification 35
2.4 Another Look at Mode and Multimodality 39
  2.4.1 Mode Revisited 39
  2.4.2 Multimodality Revisited 41
2.5 Conclusion 44

PART II
Strategies for Multimodal Scholarly Inquiry 47

3 Approaches, Methods, and Research Agenda: An Overview 49

4 The Archaeological Approach 52

4.1 Core Ideas 52
4.2 Aspects of Organization 53
4.3 Methods 55
4.4 Exemplary Studies 56
4.5 Implications of Different Modes for Archaeological Research 58
4.6 Specific Challenges and Opportunities Regarding Multimodality 60

5 The Practice Approach 62

5.1 Core Ideas 62
5.2 Aspects of Organization 63
5.3 Methods 65
5.4 Exemplary Studies 66
5.5 Implications of Different Modes for Practice Research 67
5.6 Specific Challenges and Opportunities Regarding Multimodality 69

6 The Strategic Approach 71

6.1 Core Ideas 71
6.2 Aspects of Organization 71
6.3 Methods 73
6.4 Exemplary Studies 74

6.5 Implications of Different Modes for Strategic Research 77
6.6 Specific Challenges and Opportunities Regarding Multimodality 77

7 The Dialogical Approach — 79

7.1 Core Ideas 79
7.2 Aspects of Organization 80
7.3 Methods 82
7.4 Exemplary Studies 83
7.5 Implications of Different Modes for Dialogical Research 85
7.6 Specific Challenges and Opportunities Regarding Multimodality 86

8 The Documenting Approach — 88

8.1 Core Ideas 88
8.2 Aspects of Research 88
8.3 Exemplary Studies 90
8.4 Implications of Different Modes for Documenting Research 92
8.5 Specific Challenges and Opportunities Regarding Multimodality 94

9 Summary: Towards Multi-Approach Studies in Multimodal Organization Research — 97

PART III
Application — 99

10 Introduction to Four Case Studies — 101

10.1 Case Selection 101
10.2 Case Presentation 102

11 The Power of Diagrams — 104

11.1 Some Characteristics of Diagrammatic Communication 105
11.2 Aspects of the Grammar of Diagrams 111
11.3 Analysing Diagrams 118
11.4 Resources for Producing Diagrams: Microsoft SmartArt 122
11.5 Conclusions 127

12 The Use of Logos in Post-Merger Identity Construction at Aalto University   129

12.1 *Identity-Building in Mergers and Acquisitions 129*
12.2 *Logos in Identity-Building 130*
12.3 *The Aalto Merger: Key Events 132*
12.4 *Aalto University's Visual Identity 133*
12.5 *Use of the Logo in Intentional Identity Construction in Internal and External Arenas 135*
12.6 *Reactions and Use of the Logo 137*
12.7 *Conclusions 139*

13 Multimodal Meaning-Making in Online Shopping   140

13.1 *Multimodal Meaning-Making in Zalando's Online Shop 141*
    13.1.1 *An Overview of zalando.co.uk 142*
    13.1.2 *Register Variation at zalando.co.uk 142*
    13.1.3 *The Catalogue 144*
    13.1.4 *The Product Sheet 144*
    13.1.5 *Retail Register 146*
    13.1.6 *Advertising Register 149*
    13.1.7 *Fashion Magazine Register 150*
    13.1.8 *Meaning-Making at zalando.co.uk—In a Nutshell 154*
13.2 *The Practice of Shopping on www.zalando.co.uk 155*
13.3 *Customer Motivation 158*
13.4 *Conclusions 160*

14 Multimodal Legitimation and Corporate Social Responsibility (CSR)   162

14.1 *Multimodal Legitimation 162*
14.2 *Corporate Social Responsibility as a Response to Issues of Legitimacy 164*
14.3 *Corporate Social Responsibility in Austrian Corporate Reporting 166*
    14.3.1 *Data and Sampling 167*
    14.3.2 *Analytical Procedures 168*
    14.3.3 *Central Findings 171*
14.4 *Implications of Multimodality for Legitimacy Research 177*

*14.5 Other Research Approaches to Multimodal
    Legitimation 178*
14.6 Conclusions 179

PART IV
Discussion 181

15 The Way Ahead: Discussion and Conclusion 183

*15.1 Taking Stock: Ongoing Progress in Multimodal
    Organization Research 183*
  *15.1.1 Growing Realization About the
      Multimodality of Contemporary
      Organization(s) 184*
  *15.1.2 Engagement With a Broad Spectrum of
      Topics and Issues 184*
  *15.1.3 Increasing Sophistication in the
      Conceptualization of Modes 185*
  15.1.4 Doing Research Multimodally 186
*15.2 Unrealized Potentials and Avenues for Future
    Research 187*
  *15.2.1 More Sophisticated Understandings of
      Modal Orchestrations/Amalgamations 187*
  *15.2.2 Developing Systematic Methodologies
      to Tackle Multimodality 188*
  *15.2.3 Systematizing the 'Omelette' of Concepts
      and Theories 189*
  *15.2.4 Acknowledging the Cultural Construction
      of Modes 189*
  *15.2.5 Avoiding 'Cherry-Picking' of Modes Under
      Study 190*
15.3 Towards a Joint Way Forward 191
15.4 Implications for Organizational Practice 192
  15.4.1 Increasing Attention and Literacy 192
  *15.4.2 Expanding the Communicative
      Toolbox 193*

References 195
Index 223

Figures

2.1	System Network of Timing	28
2.2	The Instantiation of Systemic Choices in Text	29
2.3	Parametric System of Voice Quality	31
2.4	An Architect Reading Blueprint	32
2.5	Stratification (Language) Embedded in Context	35
8.1	Illustration of Multimodal Support in the Research Process: (a) Arranging Print-Outs on the Floor; (b) Enhancing Photographs Through Software; (c) Creating a Conceptual Map	95
11.1	Research KPIs in an Australian University	106
11.2	(Reconstructed) Apple Organization Chart	110
11.3	'The British Used Guns'	112
11.4	A Likeness of a Cybernetic Diagram	113
11.5	Shannon and Weaver's Communication Model	114
11.6	A Likeness of a Flowchart for Medical Consultation	115
11.7	The Three Voices of XBS	116
11.8	After 'Friendships in a Bank Wiring Observation Room'	118
11.9	A Likeness of a University Funding Model	119
11.10	Organization Chart of a University Faculty	121
11.11	SmartArt 'Hierarchy List' Template	123
11.12	SmartArt 'Opposing Arrows' Template	124
11.13	SmartArt 'Random to Result' Template	124
11.14	SmartArt 'Upward Arrow' Template	125
11.15	SmartArt 'Half-Circle Organization Chart' Template	126
11.16	SmartArt 'Continuous Block Process' Template	126
12.1	Aalto University's Official Logo in Nine Variants	134
12.2	Colours Used in Aalto University's Official Logo	134
12.3	Guidelines for the Use of Aalto University's Official Logo	135
12.4	Logos of the Three Merger Partners	136
12.5	Use of Aalto's Logo in Criticism and Resistance	138
13.1	Sitemap (Reduced)	143

13.2	Screen Shot of Catalogue Page	145
13.3	Screen Shot of Product Sheet	146
13.4	Screen Shot of the Catalogue Page for 'Women's Blouses and Tunics'	147
13.5	Eye-Tracking in Check-Out Phase	148
13.6	Catalogue Pictures and Fashion Pictures	150
13.7	Screen Shot of Catalogue Page for 'Women's Heels'	152
13.8	Screen Shot of the Menu 'Style Notes'	153
13.9	Screen Shot of Feature About Carly Rowena	154
13.10	Trajectory of Experimental Subjects Making Zalando Purchases	157
13.11	Trajectory of Customer A and B; Each Number Represents an (Inter)action Sequence on a Particular Part of the Website	159
14.1	Children Playing at a Fountain	168
14.2	Examples for Authorization	172
14.3	Examples for Moral Evaluation	173
14.4	Examples for the Scrutinizing Gaze Towards Ecological Impact	174
14.5	Example for the Partner-Like Gaze on Management	175
14.6	Example for the Benevolent Gaze Towards the Human 'Other'	176

Tables

3.1	Different Approaches to Multimodal Artefacts	50
4.1	Selection of Further Readings (Archaeological Approach)	59
5.1	Selection of Further Readings (Practice Approach)	68
6.1	Selection of Further Readings (Strategic Approach)	76
7.1	Selection of Further Readings (Dialogical Approach)	84
8.1	Selection of Further Readings (Documenting Approach)	93
10.1	Illustrative Cases Described Along a Variety of Parameters	103

Acknowledgements

Renate E. Meyer, Markus A. Höllerer, and Dennis Jancsary wish to thank SCANCOR for providing an excellent and supportive working environment. The authors also express their gratitude to Anna Maaranen and Miikka Kareinen for helping with the analysis of the Aalto merger, and to Ines Kuric, Birgit Schüber, and Nikolai Staudinger for their support with the finishing touches in compiling the manuscript.

Preface

The cross-fertilization between the scholarly domains of organization and management theory, on the one hand, and multimodality studies, on the other, has been on our minds for years. Both research areas have been very prolific within their own broader academic communities. However, it was not until recently that organization and management theory has developed a more genuine interest in the different modes that constitute communication in and around organizations—and multimodality researchers, in turn, have started to regard organizational and managerial contexts as being more than merely another research setting.

Back in 2013, Renate, Markus, Dennis, and Theo were able to publish a review piece in the *Academy of Management Annals* (Meyer, Höllerer, Jancsary, & van Leeuwen, 2013), a leading academic outlet in organization and management studies. In their article, they systematically laid out how research in organization theory has drawn on insights from different strands of theories on the visual, and how such agenda could further be strengthened. As the article was generously received in the community of organizational researchers, we were encouraged to pursue this agenda further, eventually expanding our interest from visuality to multimodality.

Two factors were strongly influential for the genesis of this book. First, the cooperation between organizational scholars and multimodality scholars for the 2013 article was both inspiring and challenging at times. It became clear very soon that integrating the different perspectives—despite shared backgrounds in the phenomenological sociology of knowledge and discourse studies—meant more than simply borrowing a few concepts or compiling insights. Rather, it meant genuinely engaging with each other's points of view, conceptual underpinnings, and ideas about relevant research questions, not to mention writing styles and forms of creating arguments. After this valuable experience, we all felt that such collaboration outside our respective 'comfort zones' was extremely generative and should definitely continue. Second, we were approached by Routledge in late 2015 about a possible extension of our 2013 article into a full-fledged research book. This was a great opportunity to continue from what we had already compiled and both update and extend the scope of the original review and the insights we gained from it. We gratefully accepted the offer and—after being joined by Thomas and Eero as additional distinguished experts in multimodality studies and organization theory, respectively—we agreed to create a monograph that, on the one hand, builds on the published article in the *Academy of Management Annals*, but also extends and deepens its insights in substantial ways.

First, whereas the article clearly targeted an audience of organization and management scholars, we hope that the book will prove to be a valuable resource for researchers in *both* the areas of organization and management theory and multimodality studies. Second, the book provides a much more detailed conceptual introduction into multimodality studies, particularly from a social semiotic perspective (Chapter 2). This is primarily meant to equip organizational scholars with a solid conceptual 'toolkit' for doing multimodal organizational research—although, of course, it is only one potential perspective among others. Third, our literature review (Chapters 4–8), while drawing on the original 'approaches' identified in the *Academy of Management Annals* article, both updates and extends the previous review of literature and introduces and discusses a number of studies integrating modes beyond the visual. All approaches are also discussed in more detail both conceptually and methodologically. Fourth, and finally, Chapters 11–14 contain four quite different in-depth case studies that provide hands-on advice for dealing with multimodal data, and what this can contribute to the study and understanding of a variety of organizational topics and issues.

We sincerely hope that this book will prove to be an equally inspirational source for scholars and students of both organizations and multimodality and—eventually—facilitate interdisciplinary collaborations and research projects between these two disciplines. Our own experiences with writing this book have clearly confirmed our initial impression that such interdisciplinary work is extremely enriching and has the potential to expand insights in both fields of research. We are looking forward to future research at the interface of the two disciplines that further pushes the boundaries of knowledge creation.

Vienna/Odense/Sydney/Helsinki, September 2018

Part I
Introduction

1 Purpose of This Volume

1.1 Aims and Objectives

Organization studies is a fertile and expansive field of research since its beginnings in the early twentieth century. Its roots go back to the classical work of Max Weber and Robert Michels, who studied the role of the then new organizational form in an increasingly rationalized society, and to Henri Fayol and Frederick Taylor, who focused on the design of its structures and processes, both regarding production and its management and administration (for an overview of the development of organization research, see, for instance, Adler, Du Gay, Morgan, & Reed, 2014; Du Gay & Vikkelsø, 2017; Hinings & Meyer, 2018; Pugh & Hickson, 2007). Current organization research encompasses a variety of topics related to organizational design, such as governance, leadership, decision-making, innovation and strategy, structure, and process. In addition, much attention has also been given to the human, social, and cultural aspects of organizations, such as communication and rhetoric, identity and identification, organizational culture, power and authority, emotion, and aesthetics. Furthermore, the interfaces between organizations and their environment have been studied intensively, for instance with regard to inter-organizational relationships, legitimacy, the spread of ideas and practices, the creation of novel categories, and, more broadly, the embeddedness of organizations in society and their role with regard to societies' grand challenges.

In terms of theory, organization research borrows from a variety of traditions, most prominently sociology, (social) psychology, and economics. However, much insight has also been gained by drawing on ideas from philosophy, history, political science, linguistics, and even the arts. What all of these approaches share is a preoccupation with the social construct of 'organization', although theories differ vastly in terms of their ontological and epistemological assumptions. In this volume, we apply a more sociologically oriented lens to issues of organization and management, and engage less with more economic or applied approaches. In this sense, the version of organization and management theory suggested in this book is not restricted to the study of how (formal) organizations can be optimized and managed efficiently, but extends to broader social issues, of which organizing and multiple organizational forms are central aspects.

'Multimodality', on the other hand, refers to the phenomenon that contemporary communication uses a multiplicity of modes, but equally refers to a particular approach to studying these modes, which has its roots in linguistics. Other approaches study the same phenomenon from the vantage point of other disciplines and under slightly different names, for example, 'multisensoriality', which takes a cultural-historical approach (Classen, 1993), 'intermediality' (Elleström, 2010), which could be seen as a multimodal extension of the concept of 'intertextuality', and 'multimediality', which is a more technical and practically oriented approach focusing on (digital) media rather than on modes of communication. It is these modes of communication, defined as more or less systematically organized resources for making meaning (Halliday, 1978; van Leeuwen, 2005), together with the ways they are used in multimodal texts in specific social and cultural contexts, which are at the heart of the 'multimodal' approach.

Historically, there have been three main approaches to multimodality. The first was the Prague School of the 1930s and 1940s, which focused on literature, the theatre, and the arts (see Garvin, 1964; Matějka & Titunik, 1976), although it also included studies of other modes such as dress (Bogatyrev, 1971 [1937]). It was a functional approach which placed great emphasis on the 'aesthetic' or 'poetic' function of communication, something which, today, has become of renewed relevance, as even everyday organizational communication has to 'look good' (van Leeuwen, 2015). The second was the Paris school of the 1960s, in which Roland Barthes was a particularly pivotal figure (1967, 1973). Theoretically, it focused on the underlying structures of communicative modes rather than on their uses, but this was balanced by the social topicality of the fields it studied, which included popular culture (Barthes, 1973), press and advertising images (Barthes, 1977; Durand, 1970), comic strips (Fresnault-Deruelle, 1977), film (Metz, 1974), fashion (Barthes, 1983), and many other types of text, as can be seen in the special issues of its excellent journal, *Communications*. With the exception of an interest in advertising, Paris school semiotics did not engage with organization and management studies, but, as discussed in more detail later in this chapter, it nevertheless had considerable influence on multimodal work in that field.

The third approach was inspired by the social semiotic linguistics of Michael Halliday (1978), which takes its inspiration from Malinowski rather than Saussure and from anthropological rather than structuralist linguistics. Theoretically, it focuses on the social functions and social and cultural contexts of communication and sees communication as playing a key role in the social construction of reality (Halliday & Matthiessen, 1999). Its multimodal extensions adopt the same social semiotic approach in studying a range of modes as meaning-making resources, including the visual mode, the moving image, colour, sound and music, material objects and three-dimensional space, as well as the ways in which these resources are used in specific cultural and social contexts (Hodge & Kress, 1988; Kress, 2010; van Leeuwen, 2005).

These three approaches are of course closely tied to the development of contemporary multimodal communication, which started in the early twentieth century as a movement in avant-garde art, was then taken up in popular culture and the mass media of print, broadcasting and film, and more recently, in the digital era, extended to many other spheres of life, including education and a wide range of organizational communicative practices.

How does an interest in multimodality fit into the vast 'jungle' of scientific approaches to, and perspectives on, the phenomena summarized under the term of organization? We suggest that multimodality should be at the core of scholarly engagement with organizations. In particular, such an agenda corresponds excellently with perspectives on organization that emphasize the communicative construction of social reality, building on the work of Thomas Luckmann (2006; Berger & Luckmann, 1967) that has been quoted frequently by social semioticians, including Halliday (1978) and van Leeuwen (2008a). If organizations are constituted communicatively and discursively (see, for instance, Cornelissen, Durand, Fiss, Lammers, & Vaara, 2015), then the different modes and media through which this is achieved should be at the front and centre in theorizing about organizations. Recent advances in exploring the distinct role of visuality and multimodality in organizational contexts (Bell & Davison, 2013; Bell, Warren, & Schroeder, 2014; Meyer, Höllerer, Jancsary, & van Leeuwen, 2013) have already started to acknowledge this. Within multimodality research, on the other hand, there is a need to engage with the increasing influence of organizations and their communication on the semiotic landscape generally.

The volume is innovative in bringing together these two hitherto disparate domains of scholarly inquiry. We aim at enhancing organizational and management studies with the theoretical and methodological insights of contemporary multimodality research, and enriching multimodality research through application to the multiplicity of conceptual issues and empirical phenomena modern organization and management studies deal with and through the sociological insights it has to offer. In this opening chapter, we will bring forward arguments to encourage engagement with research at the interface of these two traditions and highlight the benefits that will result from this endeavour.

1.2 Different Fields, Similar Interests—Exploring Intersections Between Organization and Multimodality Research

Whereas research on organizations is increasingly acknowledging the crucial role of multimodal communication in the constitution of organizations and institutions (Bell et al., 2014; Meyer et al., 2013; see also the Special Issues in *Organization Studies* [Vol. 39, Issue 5–6] and *Research in the Sociology of Organizations* [Vol. 54 A&B]), research in social semiotics is turning to the study of organizations as central 'building blocks' of societies. But although the overlaps and potential synergies between the two fields of study are substantial, cross-fertilization has been hampered by different theoretical foundations and distinct technical vocabularies which impede research collaborations and cross-disciplinary reception and refinement of ideas. In this section, we provide an overview of trends in both disciplines that reveals several opportunities for convergence. We conclude with a brief assessment of the potential contributions enabled by a stronger and more substantial cooperation.

1.2.1 Visual and Multimodal Turn in Organization Studies

The potential of multimodality research for organization and management theory is particularly strong in strands of research that take a more social-scientific stance towards organizations. Much has been written about the 'linguistic', 'discursive', and 'cultural' turns in the social sciences (see, for instance, Rorty, 1967), and in organization research in particular—in fact, they are already pretty much taken for granted (Deetz, 2003). As Alvesson and Kärreman (2000, p. 137) suggest, the shared assumptions of researchers taking the linguistic turn is that "the proper understanding of societies, social institutions, identities, and even cultures may be viewed as discursively constructed ensembles of texts". Or, even more concretely, "speech and other forms of symbolic interactions are not just seen as expressions or reflections of inner thoughts or collective intentions but as potentially formative of institutional reality" (Cornelissen et al., 2015, p. 11). In fact, language and text are omnipresent in and around organizations, and they have been studied in similar yet distinct ways from the traditions of discourse analysis (Phillips, Lawrence, & Hardy, 2004; Phillips & Oswick, 2012), narrative theory (Czarniawska, 1997; Rowlinson, Casey, Hansen, & Mills, 2014; Vaara, Sonenshein, & Boje, 2016), rhetoric (Green, 2004; Green, Li, & Nohria, 2009; Sillince & Barker, 2012), and research on vocabularies (Loewenstein, Ocasio, & Jones, 2012; Mills, 1940). These theoretical approaches span a wide range of applications, including research on frames (Meyer & Höllerer, 2010), logics (Friedland & Alford, 1991; Thornton, Ocasio, & Lounsbury, 2012), identities (Creed, Scully, & Austin, 2002; Gioia, Patvardhan, Hamilton, & Corley, 2013), theorization (Strang & Meyer, 1993), translation (Boxenbaum, 2006; Czarniawska & Joerges, 1996; Wedlin & Sahlin, 2017), and power and resistance (Deetz, 1992; Mumby, 2004).

However, the linguistic turn has never been, and is still not, monolithic. There have always been different ways of understanding both communication and organization, and the relationship between them. Putnam,

Phillips, and Chapman (1996), for instance, distinguish seven metaphor clusters that direct or guide research: conduit, lens, linkage, performance, symbol, voice, and discourse. Each directs attention to different aspects of organization, and also incorporates a particular understanding of how communication and organization are related. Cornelissen et al. (2015) further advance such conceptual thinking and summarize approaches to communication and organization into three categories. In the *conduit* model, communication is described as simple transmission with a negligible role in explaining organizational processes. The *rhetorical* model, on the other hand, suggests a performative relationship between communication and organization, meaning that communication is seen as a generative force that creates organizations and institutions through cognitive reactions in audiences. While organization and communication are mostly discrete, such a perspective links them in a relation of mutual influence (Ashcraft, Kuhn, & Cooren, 2009). Finally, a *communicative* model stresses ongoing interactions and moment-by-moment dialogue. The dividing line between communication and organization is largely abandoned here, which creates equivalency between the two: organization is communication (Ashcraft et al., 2009).

Surprisingly enough, despite such a prominent line of research on communication, discourse, and rhetoric, organization theory has, so far, been largely restricted to verbal language, and multimodal aspects of meaning construction have remained rather neglected. There is, by now, a broad acknowledgement within the scientific community that discourse encompasses verbal, as well as visual, material, and/or embodied representations (in discourse analysis in general, see Fairclough, 1992; Hodge, 2017; Hodge & Kress, 1988; Wodak & Meyer, 2016; in organization studies, see Cornelissen, Holt, & Zundel, 2011; Grant, Hardy, Oswick, & Putnam, 2004; Phillips et al., 2004). Additionally, first calls for a more thorough integration of visual data have existed for more than 25 years (see Meyer, 1991) and have been reiterated and intensified more recently (Bell & Davison, 2013; Meyer et al., 2013). Furthermore, organization researchers increasingly stress the importance of materiality for understanding organizations and institutions (Elsbach & Pratt, 2007; Jones, Boxenbaum, & Anthony, 2013; Orlikowski & Scott, 2008). However, given the vast amount of research conducted on organizations and organizing, it is astonishing that most studies have almost exclusively focused on verbal text.

This is unfortunate, since communication is not 'mono-modal', but increasingly combines and integrates multiple modes into elaborate orchestrations (Kress, 2010). By focusing on the verbal mode exclusively—or also by treating other modes as if they worked in the same way as the verbal—organization research ignores empirical material that is readily available and misrepresents the actual life-worlds of actors in and around organizations. More than that, such neglect also impoverishes

8 *Introduction*

our conceptual understandings of organizations and organizing. Jones, Meyer, Jancsary, and Höllerer (2017), for instance, detail a catalogue of central topics in organizational institutionalism that would strongly benefit from a consideration of multimodality. Boxenbaum, Jones, Meyer, and Svejenova (2018) explore the potential of a visual and material turn in organization research. Höllerer, Daudigeos, and Jancsary (2018) review research that explicitly considers the role of multimodality in the constitution of meaning(s) and institutions in and around organizations. The first objective of this book, consequently, is to more systematically argue the value and potential of multimodality for a more thorough understanding of what is going on in organizations and in processes of organizing.

1.2.2 Organizational Turn in Multimodality Studies

We do not wish to create the impression, however, that research through a multimodal lens is completely novel to, or absent from, the social sciences *per se*. On the contrary, a vibrant community dedicated to this topic has emerged during the last two decades, with two dedicated journals, *Multimodal Communication* and *Visual Communication*, a bi-annual international conference, a dedicated series of monographs (*Routledge Studies of Multimodality*, edited by Kay O'Halloran), and a range of edited books (Bowcher, 2012; Djonov & Zhao, 2014; Jewitt, 2014; LeVine & Scollon, 2004; Norris, 2012; Norris & Jones, 2005; O'Halloran & Smith, 2006; Unsworth, 2008; Ventola, Charles, & Kaltenbacher, 2004), including a 4-volume anthology edited by Sigrid Norris (2016).

The field has built up an impressive array of frameworks for the analysis of specific modes such as visual communication (Bateman, 2008; Kress & van Leeuwen, 2006; O'Toole, 1994; Painter, Martin, & Unsworth, 2013), typography (van Leeuwen, 2006), colour (van Leeuwen, 2011), visual metaphor (Forceville, 1996), film (Bateman & Schmidt, 2012; Tseng, 2013; Wildfeuer, 2013), material artefacts (Björkvall, 2009; Djonov & van Leeuwen, 2011; van Leeuwen & Caldas-Coulthard, 2004); space (Ravelli & McMurtrie, 2016; Stenglin, 2009), and music (Machin, 2010; van Leeuwen, 1999; Way & McKerrell, 2017), as well as frameworks for analysing how these modes are orchestrated into multimodal texts (Baldry & Thibault, 2006; Bateman, 2014; Martinec & Salway, 2005; van Leeuwen, 2005). These frameworks have been applied to texts from a range of fields, including education (Jewitt, 2006; Kress, Jewitt, Ogborn, & Tsatsarelis, 2001), critical discourse analysis (Djonov & Zhao, 2014), media studies (Caple, 2013; Knox, 2007), and new media studies (Djonov, 2008; Kvåle, 2016; Zappavigna, 2016). And although only 7 of the 107 papers in the 2016 International Conference on Multimodality dealt with topics of direct relevance to organizational studies, as opposed to 55 papers dealing with educational topics (ICOM,

2016), papers on organizational topics have recently increased in number (Aiello, 2017; Aiello & Dickinson, 2014; Graakjaer, 2012; Ledin & Machin, 2016; Roderick, 2016; van Leeuwen, 2017).

This is important, because just as organization and management studies can benefit from drawing on multimodality research, so can multimodality studies gain from insights within organization and management studies. Interconnecting the two can align fine-grained multimodal analysis with the socially significant themes on the agenda of organization studies, such as legitimation, power, identity, and innovation, so making multimodal analysis more meaningful and relevant. In short, multimodality studies need not only to be multimodal but also multidisciplinary. Just as a meaningful theory of visual semiotics needs to draw on linguistically inspired semiotic theory as well as on art and design theory, so a meaningful *social* semiotic analysis needs to engage with theories of social organization as well as with theories of the discourses that construct, and are being constructed by, organizations that play a crucial role in contemporary society.

1.2.3 Intersections and Opportunities

The social semiotic study of multimodality is grounded in anthropological and social theory, as we will discuss in detail in Chapter 2, but multimodal research has often focused on applying its analytical frameworks, rather than on developing its theory or bringing relevant ideas from cultural and social theory to bear on the phenomena it investigates. With some exceptions (Kress, 2010), it can therefore be said that multimodality has mainly focused on methodology and text analysis rather than on theory.

By contrast, the field of organization and management studies has a distinct theoretical trajectory and a clear agenda with respect to the themes and social issues it seeks to address. However, it has not developed a systematic and detailed framework to the analysis of multimodal communication, so that papers on multimodal topics from within organization and management studies have tended to draw on perhaps all too wide a range of approaches, as we will map later in this chapter, and in the second part of the book. This can make it difficult to compare and contrast their findings in any detail.

Thus, the key theoretical concerns of the two disciplines converge. Both see organized social practices as constituted, legitimated, and changed in and by discourse, and as increasingly shaped by the digital resources which organize almost all aspects of social life. But the approaches of the two disciplines differ. We therefore aim to bring together the theoretical strength of organization and management studies, that is, its emphasis on major themes such as legitimation, identity, power, and innovation, with the empirical strength of multimodal discourse analysis, namely,

10 *Introduction*

its ability to show how these themes are materialized and embodied in actual organizations and organizing practices.

1.3 Recent Developments at the Intersection of Organization and Multimodality Research

To date, whereas there are some intersections between the two disciplines, these are rather unsystematic and focus on individual modes more than actual multimodality. However, recent broader developments in organization and management research make multimodality an increasingly interesting and vital area of study. In organization studies, the topics of *visual* and *material* aspects of organizations and institutions have received the most attention, which can be understood as an acknowledgement of the fact that there is not only an increasing quantity but also a novel quality to the usage of multimodal communication. Beyond these two modes, there is also a growing engagement with *digitalization*, and a somewhat hesitant acknowledgement of communication through sound and smell. We argue that these developments make the intersection of research on organizations and research on multimodality equally interesting for both groups of researchers alike.

1.3.1 Visuality: Making Organization 'Visible'

An emerging literature in organization and management theory focuses on the particular performance of 'visual language', drawing for instance on Kress and van Leeuwen (2006) and Mitchell (1994). The basis of such engagement can be found in the fact that various scholars in cultural and social sciences have proclaimed an 'iconic' (Boehm, 1994; Maar & Burda, 2004), 'imagic' (Fellmann, 1995), or 'pictorial' turn (Mitchell, 1994). Consequently, a number of studies in organization theory (Graves, Flesher, & Jordan, 1996; Hardy & Phillips, 1999) have begun to pay closer attention to the 'visualization' of and within their field of study. However, despite an increasing prominence of the visual mode in organization research, manifested, for instance, through a growing number of special issues in scholarly journals (for instance, in the *Accounting, Auditing & Accountability Journal* in 2009, *Qualitative Research in Organizations and Management* in 2012, and *Organization Studies*, 2018), edited books (Bell, Warren, & Schroeder, 2014; Margolis & Pauwels, 2011; Puyou, Quattrone, McLean, & Thrift, 2012), and review articles (Bell & Davison, 2013; Kunter & Bell, 2006; Ray & Smith, 2012), a clear and broadly shared research agenda has yet to emerge. In addition, existing research has most commonly acknowledged the usefulness of visual artefacts as additional sources of data. However, as Meyer et al. (2013) stress, images and visual artefacts are more than simple add-ons to verbal texts: They have their very own way of constructing, maintaining, and transforming meaning (Kress & van Leeuwen, 2001; Raab, 2008). Still, the specific performativity of visuals and visual discourse, as well as their interaction with other modes of meaning construction is only insufficiently recognized in organization studies.

We suggest that a great deal can be gained on exactly these issues from multimodality studies. Combining the strengths of these two approaches, therefore, holds ample potential. Some pioneering work on the particular performance of the visual and its relationship to the verbal exists with regard to processes of institutionalization (Meyer, Jancsary, Höllerer, & Boxenbaum, 2018), legitimation (Lefsrud, Graves, & Phillips, 2013, 2018), and the theorization and encapsulation of multiple distributed phenomena in a single coherent concept (Höllerer, Jancsary, & Grafström, 2018). However, efforts to create a systematic engagement with multimodality have so far been rather fragmented and explorative, and have yet to engage with the detailed frameworks for analysing multimodal texts that the multimodal literature has made available, and with recent theoretical developments in multimodality which stress that visuality is no longer only about images, but also about diagrams and other abstract visualizations, and also about the way visual composition integrates text, images, colour and typography into new forms of writing that combine words into messages through a visual rather than a linguistic syntax (Djonov & van Leeuwen, 2013; van Leeuwen, 2008b). Since the foundational work of Kress and van Leeuwen (2006) and O'Toole (1994), semiotic theories and methods for the study of visuality have extended into a number of new directions, often in relation to specific kinds of texts, such as picture books (Painter et al., 2013), press photography (Caple, 2013), online news (Knox, 2007), or social media (Zappavigna, 2016). The multimodal study of visuality has also moved into the area of the moving image (Bateman & Schmidt, 2012; Boeriis, 2009; Tseng, 2013; van Leeuwen, 2005; Wildfeuer, 2013), including kinetic typography (Djonov & van Leeuwen, 2015) and animation (Leão, 2013), and has engaged more closely with aspects of social practice theory, such as social actor theory (van Leeuwen, 2008a), legitimation (van Leeuwen, 2018a), and with dynamic processes of resemiotization (Iedema, 2001, 2003a), which will be discussed in more detail in Chapter 2. Many of these will be highly relevant to organization and management studies, and conducive to enriching key themes in this field. Visual social actor theory, for instance, can throw new light on the way leaders, employees and customers can be, and are, portrayed in multimodal organizational communication.

In this book, we therefore aim to systematically and substantially integrate insights from organization studies and multimodality research to avoid what Pauwels (2010) criticizes in visual sociology: A lack of integrative efforts can easily lead to a constant 'reinvention' of knowledge about the visual and its particular performativity. We therefore stress the

12 Introduction

importance of consolidating lessons learned, and use them as a starting point for an even more fertile research agenda within the domain of multimodal organization and management theory.

1.3.2 Materiality: Making Organization 'Tangible'

The role of material properties of objects in organizations and processes of organizing has rapidly increased in pace after the mid-1980s, specifically in organization and management theory (Jarzabkowski & Pinch, 2013). As Jones et al. (2017) note, materiality is what constitutes the reality of our everyday life. It refers to physical objects and their properties, which already appear objectified and embedded in social reality by means of particular vocabularies. Materiality is omnipresent in and around organizations, whether we are talking about the physical environment in organizations (Elsbach & Pratt, 2007), the sociomateriality of technology and work (Orlikowski & Scott, 2008), the relative permanence of institutions (Jones, Boxenbaum, & Anthony, 2013), the aesthetic properties of innovations (Eisenman, 2013), the political properties of organizational spaces (Wasserman & Frenkel, 2011), the material codes used to create new categories and collective identities (Jones, Maoret, Massa, & Svejenova, 2012), the material dimensions of legitimacy through proper accounts (Puyou & Quattrone, 2018), or the symbolic properties of organizational dress (Rafaeli & Pratt, 1993), among other relevant topics.

The study of objects and their role in the construction of social reality and organizations has found particularly fertile communities in the fields of science and technology studies (STS; see, for instance, Biiker, Hughes, & Pinch, 1987; Felt, Fouché, Miller, & Smith-Doerr, 2017; Pinch & Swedberg, 2008) and actor-network theory (ANT; see, for instance, Latour, 2005). These traditions acknowledge that material objects are also performative, that is, they 'take part' in the constitution, transformation, and stabilization of social reality. However, one challenge of research on materiality is that it is an inherently polysemic concept (Carlile, Nicolini, Langley, & Tsoukas, 2013; Leonardi, 2012; Oliveira, Islam, & Toraldo, 2018), and researchers have used the label to refer to considerably different things and ideas.

Within multimodality studies, several frameworks for analysing material objects and architectural space have been developed and applied to a range of areas, including the kinetic design of toys and other artefacts (van Leeuwen & Caldas-Coulthard, 2004), and the design of furniture, including office furniture (Björkvall, 2009; Roderick, 2016), office space (van Leeuwen, 2005), the interior decoration of Starbucks coffee shops (Aiello, 2017; Aiello & Dickinson, 2014), exhibitions (McMurtrie, 2017), and libraries (Ravelli & McMurtrie, 2016). As a matter of fact, during the first wave of multimodal studies, the Prague School scholar Veltruský

(1964 [1940]) already wrote about theatrical sets, costumes, and props as signs that provide setting and characterization as well as take part in the action, concluding that the theatre, in this way, restores "the link between man and his environment" (Veltruský, 1964 [1940], p. 91).

One research area in which ideas from STS and ANT about materiality have found particularly fertile ground is studies on the sociomateriality of technology (see, for instance, Orlikowski & Scott, 2008). Such literature asks what technology implies for organizations, their norms, structures, and capabilities. Sociomateriality research regards the social and the material as inherently inseparable, and therefore proposes a relational ontology. In essence, it constitutes "a move away from focusing on how technologies influence humans, to examining how materiality is intrinsic to everyday activities and relations" (Orlikowski & Scott, 2008, p. 455). Such perspective implies that material artefacts inhere a certain 'performativity', which means a potential for the enactment and constitution of social reality (Callon, 1998). In organization research, sociomateriality has, for instance, been successfully applied as a lens to strategy-making (Balogun, Jacobs, Jarzabkowski, Mantere, & Vaara, 2014). Multimodality research is developing in a similar direction, with work that analyses 'semiotic technologies' such as Word and PowerPoint as resources for meaning-making that both facilitate and constrain what users can do in ways that are increasingly modelled on corporate genres and styles of communication (Kvåle, 2016; Zhao, Djonov, & van Leeuwen, 2014). This builds on Fairclough's work on the marketization of public discourse, the adoption of genres and styles of communication that originated in advertising by many other domains of public communication.

In institutional theory, it has been recognized since the very beginning that different institutional spheres are co-constituted by a duality of both symbolic and material aspects (Friedland & Alford, 1991; Thornton et al., 2012). However, this kind of materiality, so far, has mostly been understood as the materiality of practices (Friedland, Mohr, Roose, & Gardinali, 2014). Stigliani and Ravasi (2012, p. 1233) talk about "materialization" in the sense of practices related to material artefacts, and claim that artefacts are "constitutive elements of the broader sociomaterial practices through which organizational processes are accomplished". Jones, Anthony, and Boxenbaum (2013), on the other hand, understand materiality more in terms of the attributes of physical objects. They suggest that the material has two core dimensions: Durability relates to properties like tensile and compressive strength, as well as to symbolic constructions of such properties. Transferability refers to the mobility of physical artefacts and may, for instance, be relevant for the ways in which meanings and ideas are shared and translated. Jones et al. (2017) emphasize that from an institutionalist perspective materiality is conceptualized as a means for revealing and consolidating institutions. Within

14 *Introduction*

multimodality studies, a recent social semiotic study of texture (Djonov & van Leeuwen, 2011) has proposed ways of analysing such material properties, and also discussed how they are remediated in digital media that cannot directly utilize the affordances of texture and must translate the tactile into the visual.

Thus, there are obvious connecting points between organization and management research and multimodality research. Both acknowledge differences between the material and other modes of communication as a basis for a better understanding of the materiality of multimodal resources and texts. We strongly argue, therefore, that an engagement with materiality as a complex of semiotic modes, as well as a closer look at how it may be distinguished from and integrated with, and how it interacts more generally with other modes, should be highly valuable for organization and management theory more broadly.

1.3.3 Further Extensions of the Communicative Construction of Organization and Organizing

In general, we observe a distinct—if somewhat hesitant—desire to extend our understandings of how organizations and organizing are communicatively constructed through a broad variety of semiotic resources and their orchestrations. A recent topic of research is the increasing digitalization of organizations and their management. This prompts interesting insights into the specific 'materiality'—or absence thereof—of digital resources (Dourish & Mazmanian, 2012). In the context of the 'semiotic technology' approach within multimodality research, new research is beginning to focus on the digital remediation and resemiotization of educational and other social practices, with work on online learning resources that seek to supplant classroom learning (van Leeuwen & Iversen, 2017), online resources that remediate, and thereby transform, academic communication, such as ResearchGate (Djonov & van Leeuwen, 2018), and work on online shopping (Andersen & van Leeuwen, 2017). The latter will be presented in detail in Chapter 13 of this book.

As discussed in Section 1.2.2, multimodal research has provided detailed analytical frameworks for a range of semiotic modes, including visual communication, film and video, objects and architectural space, as well as sound and music. To this can be added an increasing interest in diagrams and other abstract visualizations (Kvåle, 2016; Martinec & van Leeuwen, 2009), and a renewed interest in a social semiotic rather than psychological approach to 'non-verbal communication' (Hood, 2011), which picks up from Martinec's earlier work (2001, 2004). But other modes remain relatively unexplored, for instance smell (although there is extensive work on this in the field of 'multisensoriality'; see, for instance, Classen, Howes, & Synnott, 1994). Smell as semiotic mode is also largely absent from organization theory (Gümüsay,

Höllerer, & Meyer, 2018), with the exception of recent investigations into scent-innovation (Islam, Endrissat, & Noppeney, 2016), transfer of tacit knowledge through specific scent (Gümüsay, 2012), and office smell (Riach & Warren, 2015). Animation, and its increasingly important role in abstract visualizations, also remains relatively unexplored (Leão, 2013), despite a range of multimodal approaches to film and video. Video research is one facet of multimodality that has also been acknowledged in organization studies and is currently theorized more systematically. One application of video methods is strategy research (Gylfe, Franck, Lebaron, & Mantere, 2016; Vesa & Vaara, 2014) or video ethnography (Hassard, Burns, Hyde, & Burns, 2018; Llewellyn & Hindmarsh, 2013). Even more recently, in 2018, a special issue in *Organizational Research Methods* has been exclusively dedicated to the intricacies of video research, for instance, its utility in reconstructing 'elusive' knowledges (Toraldo, Islam, & Mangia, 2018).

As for the orchestration of different modes, there has been a good deal of work on the relation between the verbal and the visual mode, both in static modes (Baldry & Thibault, 2006; Bateman, 2014; Martinec & Salway, 2005; van Leeuwen, 2005) and in time-based modes (Tseng, 2013; van Leeuwen, 2005), building on Barthes' seminal work in this area (1977) as well as on Martin's system of conjunction (1992). Van Leeuwen (2005, 2016) has proposed a range of principles for the integration of modes in multimodal texts, including genre, rhythm, visual composition, conjunction, and dialogue structure, and more recently explored a parametric approach for the integration of different material aspects of texts and communicative events.

Again, research on the relationships between modes in organization research is still in its infancy. However, the topic is gaining traction, as can be seen, for instance, in the recent volume of *Research in the Sociology of Organizations* on "Multimodality, Meaning, and Institutions" (Höllerer, Daudigeos, & Jancsary, 2018) and a Special Issue in *Organization Studies* (Boxenbaum et al., 2018). Some of these recent studies will be discussed in greater detail in Part II of this book.

1.4 Roots and Inspirations for Multimodal Organization Research

As we have outlined in Chapter 1.3, multimodal research has started to take root in organization and management studies primarily with regard to the inclusion of the visual mode. We suggest that this engagement with visual aspects of organizations may be seen as a fertile starting point for a broader development towards multimodal organization research. Accordingly, the visual has become a 'baseline' of understanding the concept of mode in organization studies. Such research has drawn heavily from adjacent disciplines in which visuality has had a long and colourful

16 *Introduction*

history. We here briefly summarize the acknowledgement of such work in Meyer et al. (2013) in an attempt to outline the intellectual spaces from which any engagement with multimodality may draw inspiration before focusing more specifically on a social semiotic perspective in the following chapter. Of necessity, this overview can only be an acknowledging 'tip of our hat' towards research in other disciplines, since the volume of contributions is simply too large for any systematic discussion.

A first source of intellectual inspiration for the engagement with multiple modes—particularly the visual one—is *art history*. In fact, the study of art has provided an important basis for more social-scientific approaches to visuality (Berger, 1972; Gombrich, 1960; Mitchell, 1980, 1994; Panofsky, 1939). Despite the challenge of translating methodologies from art history for organization research, visual analysis has drawn quite strongly on insights developed especially by German art historians Panofsky and Imdahl (Christmann, 2008; Müller-Doohm, 1997; Rose, 2012). The influence of Panofsky on Bourdieu, for instance, can clearly be seen in Panofsky's (1957) notion of habitus which was later picked up and further developed by Bourdieu. Both Bohnsack's (2008) documentary analysis and Müller-Doohm's (1997) structural-hermeneutical symbolic analysis draw on Panofsky, and his iconology is part of the standard repertoire of recent handbooks on visual methods (Müller, 2011; Rose, 2012; van Leeuwen & Jewitt, 2001).

Philosophy provides a substantial amount of insight into the visual and has strongly influenced other disciplines. However, few philosophical positions are directly relevant for organization and management theory, and many have not yet been translated into the social sciences, for instance in the fields of sociology, psychology, semiotics, or cultural studies. Foucault (1979) provides interesting ideas about visuality in his treatment of the 'gaze' and the panopticon as 'seeing machine'. Such thinking has inspired critical management studies which focus on reconstructing and deconstructing the grand disciplinary regimes that give rise to particular forms and ways of seeing. Still, there is more on visuality to be discovered in his writings. Similarly, there is much to gain from engaging with the work of other prominent philosophical scholars like Sartre (1940), Derrida (1987, 1993), or Merleau-Ponty (1964, 1968). In a similar way, management scholars might also draw inspiration from research in the field of *theology*, which might shed additional light on issues like religious and spiritual symbolism in organizations (Tracey, 2012), spiritual aspects of visualization, and visual taboo.

Sociology has recognized the value of the visual very early on, in particular with regard to ethnography and photo-documentation. Visual anthropology (see, for instance, Collier & Collier, 1986; Pink, 2001) has had a strong influence on methodologies. Becker's (1974, 1998) societal analysis through photographs can be considered the start of a genuinely visual sociology which uses visual data in sociological research (Banks, 2001;

Chaplin, 1994; Grady, 1996; Rose, 2012; Wagner, 2002; for an overview, see Bolton, Pole, & Mizen, 2001; Pauwels, 2010). Work by renowned sociologists such as Bourdieu (1990, 2004) or Latour (1986) has been revisited by organization and management scholars with regard to their insights about the visual construction of meaning. The phenomenological sociology of knowledge (Berger & Luckmann, 1967) has been taken up by Raab (2008) and adapted to include visual knowledge more systematically, or by Couldry and Hepp (2017) in their book on the 'mediated' construction of reality. Furthermore, the sociological study of visual culture provides an extensive methodological toolbox. Photo-documentation techniques require researchers to collect visual evidence actively via recordings (either photographs, films, or sketches). An array of non-participatory visual methods, like content analysis, compositional interpretation, semiotic analysis, or visual discourse analysis (see Rose, 2012), allows for the reconstruction of meanings and meaning patterns in pre-existing visual and multimodal artefacts in the field. Finally, photo elicitation techniques are a powerful tool that uses visual texts as triggers to elicit more holistic and comprehensive information from interviewees to better understand their individual life-worlds as well as broader social and cultural phenomena (Collier, 1957; for an overview, see Harper, 2002).

Psychology informs us about how we process multimodal information and the consequences of this for both cognition and affect. Cognitive approaches, for instance, have a considerable tradition in researching how visual information is differently perceived and processed from verbal and aural information (Arnheim, 1974; Elkins, 2000; Livingstone, 2002; Massironi, 2002), focusing on the cerebral processes related to the perception of visual information (Barnhurst, Vari, & Rodríguez, 2004). Yantis (2001) provides a review of such cognitive research on vision. Another focus of immediate interest for organization and management research is the psychology of affect and emotion. Although research in this area has provided mixed and partially contradictory findings, there is a common conviction that visuals have particular ways of communicating and eliciting emotional reactions in viewers (Müller & Kappas, 2010) through colour (Labrecque, Patrick, & Milne, 2013; Mariarcher, Ring, & Schneider, 2013; Valdez & Mehrabian, 1994), image content (Bernat, Patrick, Benning, & Tellegen, 2006), and style (Bambauer-Sachse & Gierl, 2009). Psychologically inspired research that focuses on the persuasive potential and rhetorical effect of visual artefacts is commonly utilized in organization and management research in the area of marketing, advertising, and consumer research (McQuarrie & Mick, 1999; McQuarrie & Phillips, 2005; Phillips, 2000; Scott, 1994). Finally, visual approaches drawing on psychoanalysis (Aaron, 2007; Hall, 1999; Pollock, 2006) utilize Freud, Lacan, or Kristeva to conduct deep psychoanalytical readings of visuals (Matilal & Höpfl, 2009; Pollock, 2006), for instance in feminist and gender studies, as well as queer theory (see Rose, 2012).

The news media—whether printed or online—are a field in which the shift from verbal to visual text has been particularly dramatic. Accordingly, there is a vast body of literature on multimodality and visuality in *communication and media studies* (for an overview, see, for instance, Barnhurst et al., 2004). Such research borrows from a variety of other academic fields and traditions and, accordingly, has developed a multiplicity of research streams. Of particular relevance for organization and management theory is research on the performative and rhetorical power of visuals in the public media, since this is the area where organizational issues are commonly debated and framed, and therefore where organizational reality is socially constructed. Research in this area has used the label of 'visual framing' (for an overview, see Rodríguez & Dimitrova, 2011). It builds on the prominent assertion of Messaris and Abraham (2001) that visual messages are often more easily and readily received than verbal messages alone. The research agenda in visual framing literature has primarily focused on issues of war (Parry, 2010; Schwalbe, Silcock, & Keith, 2008), terrorism (Fahmy, 2010), or disasters (Borah, 2009; Fahmy, Kelly, & Kim, 2007). Modern information and communication technologies have also made websites a particularly important outlet for communication with audiences. With growing global and local engagement with visual and multimodal communication, particular conventions of visual design are beginning to emerge (Knox, 2007).

Semiotic approaches to visual meaning often refer to the seminal work of the Paris school, specifically that of French philosopher and literary theorist Roland Barthes (1973, 1980, 1982). Also, the heritage of the Prague school is commonly acknowledged. To some extent, the two schools resemble each other, as they are both anchored in a structuralist tradition, drawing on Saussure's ideas about semiology, and emphasizing the centrality of the sign. Whereas the Prague school primarily focused on fine arts (such as literature and the theatre), Barthes broadened the semiotic endeavour. His work has been used, for instance, in research on accounting (Davison, 2008), marketing (Scott, 1994), and rhetoric (Hill & Helmers, 2004). More critical approaches in semiotics focus on uncovering visual arrangements and show how the manipulation of symbols opens up particular readings. Such critical engagement also includes sign-makers and their intentions as a central part of analysis (Kress, 2010; Kress & van Leeuwen, 2006). Barthes (1975) also draws attention to intertextuality, stressing that the interpretation of images is shaped by the stock of cultural knowledge in which individuals are embedded. A major advantage of semiotic theory is that it makes no major distinction between 'high art' and everyday visual depiction (Bell & Davison, 2013), which makes its concepts and tools relevant for a broad variety of research endeavours.

A specific variant of semiotic theory—*social semiotics*—builds on, but at the same time transcends, Barthes' approach (see, for instance,

Kress & van Leeuwen, 2001, 2006). It can therefore be understood as the third, most recent approach within semiotic multimodality research. To the concern of the Paris School of semiotics with the 'lexis' of visual and multimodal design, that is, with the denotative and connotative meanings of the people, places, and objects depicted, the social semiotic approach adds the idea of a visual 'grammar' which points at the ways in which the elements within a visual artefact are linked and combined into meaningful wholes that are greater than the sum of their respective parts (Kress & van Leeuwen, 2006). This approach borrows extensively from systemic functional linguistics (Halliday, 1978) as well as from the visual theory of Arnheim (1974, 1982). Whereas Barthes saw the visual and the verbal mode as realizing separate 'messages', Kress and van Leeuwen (2001) argue that, in our modern, more strongly multimodal Western societies, they have become increasingly merged, so that complete messages can only be assessed by analysing the interaction between the modes, since neither can be fully understood separately. Given its cultural and multimodal focus, we argue that the social semiotic approach provides an excellent basis for multimodal organization research. We will therefore elaborate its conceptual underpinnings more systematically and in more detail in Chapter 2.

1.5 Approaches to the Study of Multimodality in Organizations

The study of visuality and multimodality in organization research has revolved around five different approaches, of which each assumes a different role for multimodal text and is dedicated to a distinct area of scholarly inquiry (Meyer et al., 2013). We briefly introduce these five approaches and their central characteristics here in the introduction and will provide a more detailed outline of research within these traditions in Part II of this book.

First, an *archaeological* approach to the study of multimodality derives its name from the fact that researchers 'dig' for traces of sedimented social knowledge in multimodal artefacts and reconstruct the socially constructed meanings inherent in them. Multimodal artefacts, accordingly, are seen as a 'storage' of social stocks of knowledge, and as a form of 'cultural memory'. Accordingly, researchers in this tradition do not produce their own data (i.e., take pictures, or construct artefacts), but focus on natural data created by field actors. Methodologies in this tradition cast the researcher as main interpreter and often follow content or discourse analytical strategies which are well-suited for uncovering such crystallized meanings. However, depending on the mode (or combination of modes) under scrutiny, methods and analytical tools have to be adapted accordingly. Exemplary research includes, for instance, Höllerer, Jancsary, Meyer, and Vettori's (2013) study on how local understandings of corporate social responsibility (CSR) become instantiated in the visual parts of Austrian CSR reports, and which institutional orders were reproduced in this way, or Puyou and Quattrone (2018) who study the visual and material dimensions of bookkeeping and their implications for legitimacy from Roman times to modernity. Van Leeuwen (2017) in turn discusses how corporate identities and related values are expressed by sound and music. He focuses specifically on 'sonic logos' and shows how these announce a product, service, or organization ('heraldic' function) and convey the identity of that product, service, or organization ('expressive' function).

Second, the *practice* approach focuses on the study of multimodal artefacts *in situ*. Whereas it is also acknowledged that such artefacts constitute carriers of social knowledge, the focus lies on their use—and, consequently, their performativity—in networks of agencies. Studies focus on how artefacts are constructed, how they impact on specific understandings in and around organizations, and how they display a certain 'career' from production to eventual destruction. Akin to archaeological studies, practice studies also rely on natural data produced by field actors, but researchers are not the sole 'arbiters' of meaning. Rather, interactions with actors in the field are a common way of ascertaining the role and meaning of artefacts. Research in this tradition often draws on conceptual and methodological insights from STS or ANT, and it focuses on affordances and inscriptions of multimodal artefacts in the social world. Such research is well exemplified, for instance, by Justesen and Mouritsen's (2009) research on how 3-D visualizations as artefacts mediate social worlds and activities, such as reporting, design, marketing, construction, and accounting. Similarly, Henderson (1995) follows what she calls the 'political career' of a design prototype and argues that such artefacts exhibit sufficient 'plasticity' to mediate between local needs and global identities.

Third, multimodal artefacts are also employed in what Meyer et al. (2013) have termed a *strategic* approach. Such approach constitutes a more instrumental take on the meaning-making power of different modes and is primarily focused on the aim of eliciting specific responses from audiences. In this vein, the strategic approach focuses on the sensory, embodied, and affective impact of modes and their orchestrations. This approach differs from the two previously discussed approaches in that a deliberate manipulation of the research situation is a common feature. Multimodal stimuli are most often artificially created by the researchers, although some studies also utilize naturally occurring ones. Interpretation of multimodal artefacts usually occurs on two levels: First, study subjects process and react to the stimuli presented to them as multimodal artefacts. The researchers then interpret the audiences' response to these stimuli. Unsurprisingly, such studies primarily draw from (cognitive) psychology and employ (field) experiments as their main methodological tool. A broad variety of studies—particularly in the field of marketing—has studied the persuasive potential of visual text. For instance, Houston, Childers, and Heckler (1987) investigate how multimodal messages (containing both verbal and visual cues) in advertisements enhance memorability. To a lesser degree, such studies have also been applied to other modes. Spangenberg, Grohmann, and Sprott (2005), for instance, show the combined effect of olfactory and musical stimuli on individuals' evaluations of shopping experiences.

A fourth approach is even more clearly directed towards the meaning constructions of field actors. Meyer et al. (2013) call this the *dialogical* approach. In this tradition, multimodal artefacts are utilized to start a 'dialogue' with actors in the field, and to engage in a conversation on (subjectively) ascribed meanings. Multimodal artefacts assume the role of both 'triggers' and media that allow access to, as well as expression of, knowledge and feelings that the verbal mode alone cannot reach or express adequately. Multimodal artefacts may be either provided by the researcher, produced on the spot by research subjects, or be pre-existing in the relevant field. However, the primary interpreters of these artefacts are field actors; their understandings guide the research process. Methods include ethnographical designs and specific forms of multimodal interviewing techniques. For instance, Warren (2005) argues that the use of visuals in interviews lowers the power distance between researcher and participants and grants more 'voice' to participants. Less commonly, the materiality of artefacts, in addition to their visuality, has been harnessed in dialogical research. Heracleous and Jacobs' (2008) study of strategy-making involving participants crafting physical artefacts can serve as a fitting example of research situated between a practice and a dialogical approach.

Fifth, and finally, the *documenting* approach, while least common in organization and management studies, draws from a substantial history in visual anthropology and ethnography. Similarly, but still different from the dialogical approach, multimodal artefacts are not mainly understood as primary data to be analysed, but rather as tools for organizing the research process. The most common use of multimodal artefacts in this approach is as 'field notes'—as non-verbal storage of impressions and insights gained during the study. Stowell and Warren (2018), for instance, use photos taken by the researchers during an ethnographic study to capture the experiences and feelings of suffering. Due to their multimodal nature, they can be argued to provide a more 'complete' capturing of such impressions (Kunter & Bell, 2006; Ray & Smith, 2012). Multimodal artefacts may, consequently, also be used to make findings and interpretations more transparent (Czarniawska, 2010) or to present and discuss results in a non-traditional way. A less explored application is the use of visuals to develop theory (Swedberg, 2016). As this approach mostly sees multimodal artefacts as supplementary rather than core to the research process, no elaborate methods or conceptual frameworks exist of it yet. However, multimodal text thus produced and collected can be utilized flexibly, and in accordance with other approaches. For instance, photographs taken by researchers to document certain spatial and visual properties of the research case can either be content analysed or used in dialogical conversations with field actors afterwards.

1.6 Case Studies and Applications

Thus, the potential interface between research on organizations and research on multimodality is substantial, and addressing their intersections more systematically in both theoretical and empirical research promises to provide significant new insights into both areas. The core of this volume (Part III), will therefore present a number of case studies to illustrate such potential. Whereas the literature review in Part II is meant to provide an overview of realized intersections and overlaps, Part III gets into the nitty-gritty of how to do multimodal research.

To provide a broad exemplification with a limited number of case studies, we have selected the cases according to a number of parameters that span the space of both multimodality and organizations. First, we focus on various *communicative relations* organizations are commonly embedded in, including communication with the broader societal environment, inter-organizational communication, intra-organizational communication, and communication to specific customer groups. Second, we focus on specific *conceptual issues* that can be regarded as 'classics' of organization research: the management of legitimacy, organizational identity, power and authority, and control. Third, we position our cases in the context of diverse *organizational phenomena* such as organizational structure and hierarchy, mergers and acquisitions (M&As), CSR, and design of the point-of-sale. Fourth, we relate these contextual and conceptual concerns to the concrete multimodal *texts and media* that realize them—texts as diverse as reports, websites, organizational space, logos, and diagrams. Fifth, and finally, through our choice of texts, we cover a variety of different modes, such as the verbal and visual mode, spatial layout, colour, materiality, and diagrammatic resources.

The *first case* focuses on the role of diagrams and charts in representing—and constructing—organizational structure and processes. In this context, we provide insights into the relevance and characteristics of diagrammatic communication and exemplify these conceptual points through the analysis of several diagrams. The *second case* explores multimodal organizational logos and their relevance for organizational identity. A single empirical case—that of the Aalto University Merger—is used to illustrate how visual identity can be analysed in a detailed manner. The *third case* takes digital 'resemiotization' (Iedema, 2001, 2003a) as its starting point and discusses how multimodal meaning is constructed in the context of online shopping. We show how multimodal websites create relationships between organizations and customers and present an analysis of Zalando's online shop to illustrate the different multimodal registers of the website. The *fourth case*, finally, explores how multimodality provides resources for organizations to establish legitimacy and illustrates such mechanisms by drawing on two empirical studies of CSR in Austria.

1.7 Conclusion

In this introduction, we hope to have established that there is a natural and substantial overlap between the research agendas of organization theory and multimodal studies, and that the strengths of each will complement the other. So far, the two have mostly operated separately and without realizing the potential of mutual engagement with each other's insights. It is therefore the explicit aim of this book to start a conversation between the two communities, and to do so by proposing particularly promising avenues for engagement. In doing so we focus especially, although not exclusively, on the social semiotic approach to multimodality, and we therefore present a brief outline of this approach in the following chapter.

The second part of the book, then, is dedicated to an overview of the different approaches to multimodal artefacts common to organization and management studies. For each approach, we will introduce its core ideas and most common methods the aspects of organization it tends to address, and a number of exemplary studies. Additionally, we discuss in depth what the acknowledgement of different modes means for research taking a specific approach, and we particularly expand on the challenges and potentials of true multimodal research, that is, research that takes an integrative view on the combination of multiple modes in organizational communication.

Part III introduces the four case studies meant to provide a more 'hands-on' access to multimodal organization research. Within each case, we illustrate the relevance of multimodal artefacts for different organizational domains and provide detailed methodological advice on how to empirically grasp multimodality in and around organizations. Finally, Part IV closes the book with a discussion of the main learnings, a presentation of potentially fruitful avenues for future research, and some implications for practitioners.

2 A Social Semiotic Approach to Multimodality

The term multimodality designates both a field of research, that is, the phenomenon to be studied, and a particular approach to the study of the phenomenon. As a field of research, multimodality is the phenomenon that all communication integrates a range of meaning-making resources, that is, images, words, sound, etc. Different meaning-making resources make up different modes, so we can talk about a visual mode, a verbal mode, an aural mode. These modes can be further subdivided into other modes, such as a mode for colour, a mode for light, a mode for speech, or a mode for writing, and on an even more concrete level, we can talk about, for example, a mode for photography, a mode for paintings, or a mode for graphic symbols. The concept of mode, in other words, is somewhat fuzzy. However, on an abstract level, a mode can be understood as a system of meaningful contrasts between forms that can be used for meaning-making in a community; this meaning-making will always combine three strands of meaning: ideational meaning (i.e., some representation of the goings-on), interpersonal meaning (i.e., some enactment of the relationship between the interactants in the meaning-making process), and textual meaning (i.e., some construal of a coherent message). In all communicative practices, we encounter the integration of different modes—hence the phenomenon of multimod(e)ality.

In this chapter, we shall approach the phenomenon of multimodality from a social semiotic angle. As already outlined in Chapter 1, social semiotics has in recent years developed into a widely used theoretical and methodological approach to the study of multimodality. Influenced both by Prague School functional linguists such as Mathesius and by Malinowski's anthropological theory of language, social semiotics was developed by Halliday (1978), further elaborated by linguists such as Lemke, Martin, and Matthiessen (Andersen, Boeriis, Maagerø, & Tønnesen, 2015), and extended into the study of multimodality by Hodge, Kress, van Leeuwen, and others (Hodge & Kress, 1988; Kress, 2010; Kress & van Leeuwen, 2001; van Leeuwen, 2005). In what follows, we shall approach the phenomenon of multimodality from the point of view that no mode is *a priori* more important than others, although in specific communicative artefacts, one or a few modes might play a more significant role than other potentially actualized modes.

2.1 What Is Social Semiotics?

The 'social' in social semiotics emphasizes that meaning is a supra-individual concept, intersubjectively negotiated and institutionalized in various practices and cultural settings, while 'semiotics' signals the resulting organization of meaning according to semiotic principles of different kinds. Such organized meaning systems then constitute resources for communication in specific contexts. Social semiotics therefore involves three closely interrelated activities: describing semiotic resources and their histories; describing how these resources are used in specific contexts and how such uses are, with greater or lesser degrees of freedom, regulated by normative discourses, taught, legitimated, critiqued, further developed, etc.; and exploring how, on the basis of semiotic insights, new resources and new ways of using existing resources can be developed (van Leeuwen, 2005). In our discussion of key social semiotic concepts, we will, in each case, start with the linguistic concepts from which they originated, to then move to the way they have been taken up in social semiotic accounts of multimodal communication.

2.2 The 'Social' in Social Semiotics

The fundamental difference between social semiotics and the structuralist semiotics that preceded it lies in the notion of context. It is this what makes social semiotics a 'branch of sociology' (Halliday, 1978). Saussure's view of 'semiology' was also social, but, influenced by Durkheim, he saw society as unified by a national language and a 'collective consciousness'. Halliday stresses variety. For him, for the purpose of laying out grammars and compiling dictionaries, or methods of textual analysis, language can be seen as an overall resource, but this is ultimately a construct. What exists is what people say and write in specific 'contexts of situation', where particular social practices require specific uses of language, or 'registers':

> We do not simply 'know' our mother tongue as an abstract system of vocal signals, or as if it was some sort of a grammar book with a dictionary attached. We know it in the sense of knowing how to use it; we know how to communicate with other people, how to choose forms of language that are appropriate to the type of situation we find ourselves in, and so on.
>
> (Halliday, 1978, p. 13)

This notion of 'context of situation' is derived from the work of Malinowski (1923, 1935), who showed that meaning not only stems from 'signs' which have a fixed, pre-existing link between form and meaning, but also from the context in which these signs are used. In other words, signs and sign systems have meaning *potentials,* which get actualized in particular contexts, where their *actual* meanings will be motivated by the needs and interests that prevail in that context. In Halliday's words, the context of situation covers

(1) the social action: that which is 'going on', and has recognizable meaning in the social system; typically a complex of acts in some ordered configuration, and in which the text is playing some part; and including 'subject-matter' as one special aspect,
(2) the role structure: the cluster of socially meaningful participant relationships; both permanent attributes of the participants and role relationships that are specific to the situation; including the speech roles, those that come into being through the exchange of verbal meanings,
(3) the symbolic organization: the particular status that is assigned to the text within the situation; its function in relation to the social action and the role structure; including the channel or medium and the rhetorical mode.

(Halliday, 1977, p. 55)

The uses of the meaning potentials in specific contexts of situation are regulated in some way or other. In this respect there has been, in social semiotics, a gradual move away from a relatively deterministic view in which *types* of contexts of situation constrain what we can say and do, to a view which accords sign-makers greater individuality and agency and sees them as using the semiotic resources that happen to be available in the context to make meaning on the basis of the sign-makers' needs and interests: "sign-makers choose forms for the expression of what they have in mind, forms which they see as most apt and plausible in the given context" (Kress & van Leeuwen, 2006, p. 13). However, both these points of view may be too absolute. What people can and cannot say and do in different contexts of situation will be regulated by 'normative discourses' (van Leeuwen, 2005, 2008a), but to different degrees and in different ways. Normative discourses can be explicit, whether in the form of strict rules or guidelines or advice that leaves more room for choice. They can also remain implicit, for instance in the case of taken-for-granted customs or traditions. In such cases, normative discourses may once have existed, but subsequently have been forgotten, in what Bourdieu has called 'genesis amnesia' (1977), or what is regarded as 'background' programs in the case of fully institutionalized knowledge (Berger & Kellner, 1984).

Along with the idea of 'context of situation', Halliday also followed Malinowski in adopting the idea of 'context of culture' (Malinowski,

1923, 1935). Semiotic resources develop in particular cultural and historical contexts, and if we want to explain why they are as they are, we must look for an answer in the beliefs and values that constitute this 'context of culture'. The multimodal turn in communication can itself be seen as an example. In today's consumer culture, affect and emotion, rather than rationality, are increasingly seen as the main motivation for people's decisions, so communication must increasingly appeal to all the senses, and foreground aesthetic qualities.

> A social reality (or a 'culture') is itself an edifice of meanings—a semiotic construct. . . . This in summary is what is intended by the formulation 'language as social semiotic'. It means interpreting language within a sociocultural context, in which the culture itself is interpreted in semiotic terms.
> (Halliday, 1996, p. 89; see also Halliday, 1984b; Hasan, 2005)

This also means that social semiotics sees meaning not as arising from the individual's cognitive capabilities, but within and for social practices. As Lemke (1995, p. 9) puts it:

> Instead of talking about meaning-making as something that is done by minds, I prefer to talk about it as a social practice in a community. It is a kind of doing that is done in ways that are characteristic of a community, and its occurrence is part of what binds the community together and helps to constitute it as a community. In this sense, we can speak of a community, not as a collection of interacting individuals, but as a system of interdependent social practices: a system of doings, rather than a system of doers.

This is of evident importance for organizational communication or field-level communication. Organizations are complexes of social practices, of specific contexts of situation. Organizational communication, increasingly multimodal, both constructs and is constructed by these contexts, in a way that is regulated by normative discourses in different ways and to different degrees. But for these various practices to cohere, they must ultimately be informed by common beliefs and values, by a 'context of culture'.

2.3 The 'Semiotic' in Social Semiotics

2.3.1 System and Instantiation

In social semiotics, 'semiotic' focuses on meanings rather than 'signs' (Halliday, 1995). The Saussurean concept of the sign, as a combination of a 'signifié' with a 'signifiant' (see Saussure, 1949), is abandoned in favour of the concept of the semiotic system. A semiotic system is "a systemic resource for meaning" (Halliday, 1985b, p. 193), and social semiotics is a systemic semiotics, where meaning is described in terms of systemic, paradigmatically organized relations of similarity and difference. Here is an example from the social semiotics of music (van Leeuwen, 1999), showing part of the system of rhythm:

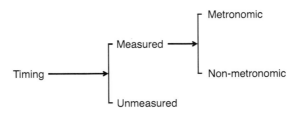

Figure 2.1 System Network of Timing

Unmeasured sounds have no rhythmic structure. They are ongoing, sustained sounds which do not have a regular beat. Special instruments have been designed to produce such sounds, such as church organs, didgeridoos, and today, electronic instruments. The ongoing sounds of such instruments cannot normally be produced by human voices since humans have to breathe from time to time, although special techniques such as 'circular breathing' can overcome this. For this reason, their meaning potential is 'non-human'. In context this can then become, for instance, the 'divine', or 'nature', or 'outer space'. As mentioned before, the binary choices of such systems have a definite meaning *potential*, whether because of what they literally are or do (in this case the sustained nature of unmeasured sound) or because of the history of their use, but they do not acquire actual meaning until they are used in a specific context.

Unlike unmeasured time, measured time has a definite 'beat', a rhythm you can tap your foot to or dance on. This rhythm may be very precise ('metronomic') or not, and this meaning potential can then be filled in differently in different contexts. It can come to stand for military regimentation or the mechanical rhythm of the machine, for instance. Non-metronomic time then becomes freedom from, or revolt against, such regimentation. Philip Tagg (1990, p. 112) has described the timing of rock music in this way, as an attempt to "gain control over time through musical expression" in contexts where mechanical time remains dominant "at work and in other official realms of power". The example shows that quite abstract semiotic choices can relate to very concrete social phenomena.

Technically, the example shows how meanings are contrasted in a system, and how the idea of 'choice' (see Halliday, 1985b; Fontaine, Bartlett, &

A Social Semiotic Approach to Multimodality 29

O'Grady, 2015) is central. Any semiotic system has an 'entry condition', which is specified, that is, sub-categorized, in two or more choices, and each of these choices can then function as a new entry condition with further choices to it, and so on. In Figure 2.1, 'timing' is the entry condition, 'measured' and 'unmeasured' being the first sub-categorization, whereas 'measured' becomes the entry condition for a further sub-categorization (between 'metronomic' and 'non-metronomic'). Theoretically, the figure demonstrates the importance of paradigmatic organization in social semiotics: "A system is . . . a representation of relations on the paradigmatic axis, a set of features contrastive in a given environment" (Halliday, 1966, p. 110).

When we exchange meanings as texts, we do not actualize all the choices the relevant systems allow. We actualize meaning-making with parts from various semiotic systems, for instance visual parts together with verbal parts together with graphical parts when posting on Instagram, but never the whole, as shown in Figure 2.2. The term 'instantiation' is then used to refer to "text as actualized potential; it is the actual seen against the background of the potential" (Halliday, 1978, p. 40). This is a crucial aspect of social semiotics. Social semiotics focuses on semiotic resources and their meaning potential as well as on texts and other semiotic artefacts and the meanings they actualize—it looks at the two in relation to each other. System and text "are not two separate phenomena; they are the same phenomenon seen by different observers, observing from different time depths" (Halliday, 1998, p. 382).

The choices systems make available can be realized in different material forms. Unmeasured time, for instance, can be realized by a church

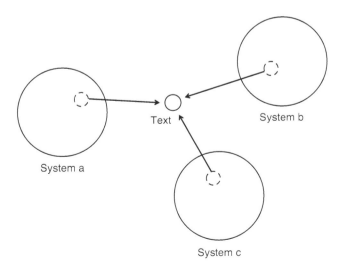

Figure 2.2 The Instantiation of Systemic Choices in Text

organ, an electronic instrument, or a singer or didgeridoo player who has mastered the technique of circular breathing. Such material forms themselves contribute to meaning. Unmeasured time performed on a church organ does not mean the same thing as unmeasured time produced by a synthesizer. The meanings of such material forms do not derive from binary systems of choices, but from parametric systems in which a number of parameters are all simultaneously present but used to different degrees. The sound of an instrument or a singing voice, for instance, will always have to have some value on the scale from tense to lax, *and* the scale from high to low register, *and* the scale from loud to soft, *and* the scale from wavering (vibrato) or plain, *and* the scale from rough or smooth, and so on (van Leeuwen, 2014), but it may, for instance combine a high level of tension with a low volume. The overall timbre then results from all the parameters together, in their various proportions, and each of the parameters contributes to the meaning potential of the whole. We can understand this meaning potential on the basis of experience. We know from experience, for instance, that our voice starts to waver when we get emotional for one reason or another. Hence wavering can, in context, come to mean fear (for instance in the music of a horror film) or love (for instance in the music, played by strings, of a romantic scene in a movie). Figure 2.3 represents this as a parametric system, with the curly bracket indicating simultaneous choices and the double-headed arrows indicating that the choice is not an 'either/or' choice, but a matter of degree.

2.3.2 Metafunctions

Halliday's social semiotics is above all a *functional* semiotics: "Language is as it is because of what it has to do" (1978, p. 19), and this applies to other semiotic modes as well. In his metafunctional theory three metafunctions, three overall communicative functions, are simultaneously at work in every act of communication: the ideational, the interpersonal, and the textual metafunction.

The *ideational metafunction* organizes the resources we use when we construct representations of reality. It is

> concerned with the content of language [or any other mode], its function as a means of the expression of our experience, both of the external world and of the inner world of our own consciousness—together with what is perhaps a separate sub-component expressing certain basic logical relations.
>
> (Halliday, 1973, p. 66)

As can be seen from this quote, Halliday distinguishes between two aspects of the ideational metafunction, two 'sub-metafunctions', namely the experiential and the logical metafunction. The experiential

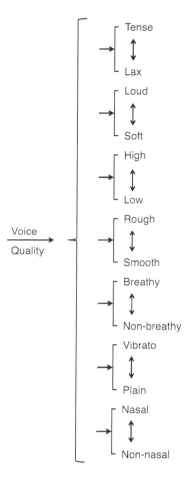

Figure 2.3 Parametric System of Voice Quality

metafunction constructs units of experiential meaning by relating a process (e.g., 'reads') with one or more participants (e.g., 'the architect' and 'the blueprint') and circumstances (e.g., 'on the third floor' or 'today'). Together, these components constitute the representation of an action or event ('the architect reads the blueprint on the third floor'). The same schema has been applied to other semiotic modes, that is, to visual images (Kress & van Leeuwen, 2006). Figure 2.4 shows two participants (main 'volumes'), the architect and the blueprint, as well as a circumstance (the location) and the process of reading, here indicated by the vector formed by the eye line that connects the architect and the blueprint. In other words, the visual mode allows the same construction of reality as the verbal mode, but it does so by different means: volumes and vectors, foreground and background, rather than nominal groups, verbal groups, and

Figure 2.4 An Architect Reading Blueprint
Source: Used under license from Getty Images

prepositional phrases. And whereas the functional concepts (e.g., 'participant' and 'process') are taken from Halliday, the realizational concepts ('volume' and 'vector') are taken from the work of the art theorist Arnheim (1974, 1982)—multimodality also needs to be multidisciplinary.

The logical metafunction describes the temporal, spatial, and logical connections between events and construes meaning in a more abstract way than the experiential metafunction: Whereas a direct reference to things and state of affairs in 'real life' is at play in the experiential metafunction, logical relations are "independent of and make no reference to things" (Halliday, 1979, p. 73). Social semiotics has developed a range of systems to map the possible relations between visually represented events, and between visually and verbally represented events in multimodal texts (Martinec & Salway, 2005; van Leeuwen, 2005). This brings out some crucial differences between language and visual communication in terms of the logical relations they can realize. Conditional and causal relationships cannot currently be realized visually, for instance. But visuals are better at realizing intricate spatial relationships.

The *interpersonal metafunction* concerns the way language *enacts* interactions and relationships. Following on from the speech act theorists, social semiotics recognizes that communication not only constructs representations of reality, but also acts in the world. The interpersonal metafunction also concerns the communication of attitudes to what it is being represented. In other words, the interpersonal metafunction functions as

> the mediator of role, including all that may be understood by the expression of our own personalities and personal feelings on the one hand, and forms of interaction and social interplay with other participants in the communication situation on the other hand.
>
> (Halliday, 1973, p. 66)

In verbal language, interpersonal meaning is realized in several ways: through the mood system, which can create basic 'speech functions' such as statement, question, and command; through forms of address (e.g., systems of personal pronouns) that can realize different degrees of formality; but also through choices that are "distributed like a prosody throughout a continuous stretch of discourse" (Halliday, 1979, p. 66). This, too, has been applied to other semiotic modes, where, again, comparable meanings can be exchanged, but by different means. Images, too, can either directly address the viewer, by having a depicted person look directly at the viewer, or not, and they can enact relationship between viewers and what is depicted in an image, through 'point of view', through the angle at which we see a person or place or thing (from above or from below, frontally or from the side, and so on), and through the distance from which we see these (the range from 'close shot' to 'long shot'). We will give some examples in the case on CSR in Chapter 14.

Another important interpersonal system is modality, the system for expressing 'as how true' a representation is meant to be taken. In verbal language, this is typically expressed through the modal auxiliary verbs (e.g., *may, will*, and *must*) and through modal adverbs such as *maybe, certainly*, and *usually*. But it can also be expressed in other ways (Halliday, 1994). In visual images, it can be expressed, for instance, by the degree of detail shown, the use of perspective, and so on. But context needs to be taken into account. The cartoons on the opinion pages of newspapers may not use perspective and show relatively little detail. This then signifies that they are to be taken as 'opinions', in contrast to the claim of factuality attached to news photographs. But in scientific drawings, the lack of detail and perspective can make austere line drawings more real, in scientific terms, as their abstract nature can suggest that they reveal a more general truth (Kress & van Leeuwen, 2006). Modality can also be realized in other semiotic systems, such as sound and music (van Leeuwen, 2005). This again shows that the same kind of communicative function, the expression of degrees of truth and factuality, can be realized in different semiotic modes, albeit in different ways.

The last of the three metafunctions, the *textual metafunction*, organizes the ideational and interpersonal resources we use to create cohesive and contextually functional texts. The textual metafunction "is the component that enables speakers to organize what they are saying in such a way that it makes sense in the context and fulfils its function as a message" (Halliday, 1973, p. 66). Textual meaning is not realized by constituency or by prosodic structure, but by the thematic organization of the different parts of discourse, from clauses, to paragraphs and larger sections and whole texts:

> What the textual component does is to express the particular semantic status of elements in the discourse by assigning them to the

boundaries . . . ; this marks off units of the message as extending from one peak of prominence to the next.

(Halliday, 1979, p. 69)

In formulating his metafunctional theory, Halliday recognized the influence of Whorf, Malinowski, and Mathesius: Whorf's work inspired the idea of the ideational metafunction, Malinowski's work the idea of the interpersonal metafunction, and Mathesius' work the idea of the textual metafunction:

> For Malinowski, language was a means of action; and since symbols cannot act on things, this meant as means of interaction—acting on other people. Language need not (and often did not) match the reality; but since it derived its meaning potential from use, it typically worked. For Whorf, on the other hand, language was a means of thought. It provided a model of reality; but when the two did not match, since experience was interpreted within the limitations of this model, it could be disastrous in action. . . . Mathesius showed how language varied to suit the context. Each sentence of the text was organized by the speaker so as to convey the message he wanted at that juncture, and the total effect was what we recognize as discourse. Their work provides the foundation for a systemic functional semantics.
>
> (Halliday, 1984a, p. 311)

Social semiotics has also taken up Jakobson's theory of the functions of language (Jakobson, 1960a). Some of Jakobson's functions are similar to Halliday's metafunctions. His 'referential function' can be compared to Halliday's ideational function, his 'conative function' to one aspect of Halliday's interpersonal function, language as a means of action, and his 'expressive function' to another aspect of the interpersonal function, the expression of attitudes. But Jakobson also recognizes the 'poetic' function, which, like the other metafunctions, has its own verbal realizations—alliteration, assonance, rhyme, and so on. In a time when aesthetic considerations become increasingly important in many forms of written communication, whether print or electronic, this is of renewed importance, and now beginning to be taken up in multimodality studies as well (van Leeuwen, 2015).

The metafunctional theory remains of central importance in social semiotics—both theoretically and methodologically, reminding us that we need to understand semiotic resources as resources for the construction of reality as well as for the enactment of social practices and their attendant relationships, and that both these dimensions need to be kept in focus in the analysis of texts and semiotic artefacts. As there is, in many domains, an increasing focus on formats, templates, and genres rather than on content, this is particularly important, as is attention to the division of labour between semiotic modes in this respect, both in the culture at large, and in specific contexts.

2.3.3 Stratification

According to Halliday, language is stratified, organized in four layers: the 'content strata' of semantics and lexicogrammar, and the 'expression strata' of phonology and phonetics. The relationship between the strata is one of realization (see Figure 2.5). Context, the social world, is realized in semantics, the meaning system of language, which is then realized in lexicogrammar, the 'wording' system of language, which is then realized in phonology, the sound system of language, which is then realized in phonetics, the actual sounds. The realizational relationship has a progressive scope, meaning that context is realized not only in semantics but in the sum of all the linguistic strata as well, that is, in all the strata below context (Halliday, 1992), so that there is a progression from meaning to its concrete utterance.

In a system consisting of simple signs, which are signs that combine a meaning with a form, or a *signifié* with a *signifiant* (see Halliday, 1992), there can only be as many meanings as there are signs. But when we expand from a 'bi-stratal' semiotic system into a 'tri-stratal' semiotic system (such as e.g., verbal language, which has phonology, lexicogrammar, and semantics), a limited number of sounds or other basic units can be used to produce an infinite (and ever growing) number of meanings as

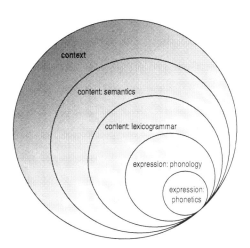

Figure 2.5 Stratification (Language) Embedded in Context

Source: Published originally as Figure 1–10 in Halliday & Matthiesen [2014]. Halliday's introduction to functional grammar [4th ed.; p. 26]. Routledge

the limited number of speech sounds (or letters) can be combined into a large number of words, using phonological combination rules, whereas words, in turn, can be combined into an even larger number of utterances. As Halliday states,

> [I]t is typical of semiotic systems that the different strata are not isomorphic; there is no relation of bi-uniqueness (one-one correspondence) between one level and the next. This is bound to be the case in a system such as language, where the coding not only converts elements of one kind into elements of another kind—meanings into wordings into sounds—but also reduces both the size and the inventory of the basic components. By any usual definition of linguistic units, units of speech sound are both smaller than and fewer than units of form; and units of form are both smaller than and fewer than units of meaning.
>
> (Halliday, 1979, p. 58)

Certain other modes, including the visual, have long been regarded as bi-stratal. Both late medieval books of emblems and contemporary source books for graphic designers have the format of a dictionary, a collection of examples. *The Dictionary of Visual Language* (Thompson & Davenport, 1982) contains some 1,500 entries, alphabetically arranged pictures with brief explanations ('Abacus', 'Acorn', 'Acrobat', 'Aerial', etc.). Designers can then use these as a source of inspiration, for instance by using an abacus as a symbol for thinking or reasoning. It has been one of the achievements of social semiotics to propose grammars where previously none existed, so contributing to semiotic change in ways that were at the same time pursued by software designers, for instance in the development of tri-stratal systems of emojis—emojis which can be combined into complex messages rather than only used as standalones.

What is the difference between (and the relation between) semantics and lexicogrammar, and why does Halliday combine grammar and lexicon into a single term? The difference is, first, that semantics is about meaning and lexicogrammar about wording. Semantics organizes "the flux of experience" (Halliday, 1998, p. 379), that is, all human experience in certain ways. It transforms reality into meaning, and this can be done in different ways. In the Wintu language of Northern California, for instance, it is not possible to distinguish between subjectivity and objectivity. One cannot say "This is bread"—this would have to be expressed as "I see this as bread" or "I call this bread" (Lee, 1954, p. 9), that is, in ways we would regard as subjective. Some social semioticians have therefore argued that semantics does not belong to language but to the culture as a whole. Different semiotic modes can then express different parts of the semantic system, sometimes overlapping, so that things can, for instance, be expressed both verbally and visually, or both verbally and musically, sometimes not, so that something can only be expressed verbally or only visually, and so on (Kress & van Leeuwen, 2001). Such divisions of labour between semiotic modes differ between cultures, and also historically, as is shown, for instance, by the great iconoclasms, which violently replaced religious images with words.

According to Halliday, the relation between semantics and lexicogrammar is not arbitrary, in other words if the semantics makes a distinction between objective and subjective, then the lexicogrammar will have the resources for wording it, for instance through the distinction between mental process verbs such as 'feel', 'see', and 'know' and relational process verbs such as 'have' and 'be'. The same distinction can be realized through visual grammar. In films, for instance, certain standard devices can make a shot subjective, seen from a character's point of view. When these devices are absent, the shot is objective.

By using the term 'lexicogrammar', Halliday indicates that both grammar and lexicon play a role in 'wording' meaning—grammar at a more general level, and the lexicon at a more 'delicate' level. 'Actor', for instance is a grammatical role that realizes a participant as 'doing' something at a general level. 'Architect' also realizes someone doing something, but at a much more specific level. As van Leeuwen has shown (2008a), the same distinction can be made in the realization of visual 'actors'.

Language—and indeed any other semiotic system—is context-sensitive, in the sense that its categories are motivated by the social context in which it functions, and in the sense that its categories reflect back on context by imposing a certain understanding of reality. Halliday therefore embeds the four linguistic strata in a stratum of context as illustrated in Figure 2.5 above. There is again a relation of realization. To Halliday, context can be understood in terms of three variables, field, tenor, and mode. Field is

> the social action: that which is 'going on', and has recognizable meaning in the social system; typically, a complex of acts in some ordered configuration, and in which the text is playing some part; and including 'subject-matter' as one special aspect.
>
> (Halliday, 1978, p. 55)

Tenor is

> the role structure: the cluster of socially meaningful participant relationships; both permanent attributes of the participants and role relationships that are specific to the situation; including the speech roles, those that come into being through the exchange of verbal meanings.

And mode is "the symbolic organization: the particular status that is assigned to the text within the situation; its function in relation to the social action and the role structure; including the channel or medium and the rhetorical mode" (Halliday, 1978).

These contextual variables are then related to the metafunctions in the following way: Field is associated with the experiential metafunction, and from there with specific lexicogrammatical systems such as transitivity (the relation between processes, participants, and circumstances); tenor is associated with the interpersonal metafunction, and from there with grammatical system of mood and modality; and mode is associated with the textual metafunction, and from there with the system of theme (see Caffarel, 1992).

Kress and van Leeuwen (2001) have critiqued the 'geological' metaphor of 'strata', seeking a more dynamic description of the communication process. To do so, they used Goffman's theory of the production of talk (1981). Goffman analyses talk as involving three roles. The 'principal' is responsible for the content, the meaning. It is the person or institution 'whose beliefs are told', 'whose position is established'. The 'author' is the person who 'selects the sentiments to be expressed and the words in which they are encoded'. And the 'animator' is the 'sounding box in use'. Goffman adds that animators "sometimes share this physical function [i.e., of being the 'sounding box'] with a loudspeaker system or telephone". He also adds that these roles may be combined in different ways. In a presidential address, for instance, the president is both 'principal' and 'animator', but the 'author' may be a speechwriter. In a news broadcast, the editor may be the principal, a journalist the author, and a newsreader the animator. In everyday conversation one person may fulfil all three roles.

It is clear that Goffman's roles correspond closely to Halliday's strata of 'meaning' (semantics), 'wording' (lexicogrammar), and 'sounding' (phonology and phonetics), but they are now understood more dynamically, in terms of communicative social practices with divisions of labour. Kress and van Leeuwen have therefore reformulated the 'strata' as (1) *discourse*, defined as 'socially situated forms of knowledge about (aspects of) reality'; (2) *design*, which corresponds to wording, but includes other semiotic modes as well, and which involves designing three things simultaneously—the formulation of a discourse or combination of discourses (the ideational metafunction), a particular form of communicative interaction in which the discourse is embedded (the interpersonal metafunction), and the marshalling of ideational and interpersonal meanings in an integrated and cohesive communicative event, text, or semiotic artefact (the textual metafunction); (3) *production*, which gives material, perceivable form to the design, and which, according to Kress and van Leeuwen, not only executes already designed meanings, but also adds meanings of its own, in the 'parametric' way discussed earlier—the animator's performance, for instance, adds meaning through intonation, voice quality, and rhythm. To these three strata, Kress and van Leeuwen add a fourth, (4) *'distribution'*, which is about the dissemination of the communicative event, text, or semiotic artefact.

Kress and van Leeuwen's view of 'production' reinstated the importance of materiality in social semiotics, which until then had been somewhat neglected. Some accounts of visual communication, such as Kress and van Leeuwen's (2006), deal with patterns of visual design that can be realized as photographs, drawings, paintings, and more, and the same applied to analytical frameworks for other semiotic modes. Others, more recent, have paid more attention to the specific meaning-making potentials of such different media (Johannessen & van Leeuwen, 2017), and also to the meanings that come about when texts and semiotic artefacts are remediated for purposes of recording and/or distribution (Kress & van Leeuwen, 2001).

2.4 Another Look at Mode and Multimodality

In the first section of this chapter, we stated that the concept of mode is somewhat fuzzy. Broadly, it refers to a conventionalized use of resources for meaning-making, but often the term is simply defined through examples (e.g., "image, music and language", Andersen et al., 2015, p. 160). When mode is defined more precisely, the definitions may leave open how modes are semiotically organized, or differ in ways that are ultimately not compatible. Different views also exist in relation to the question of just what multimodality is and how it should be studied. Below we will discuss the main issues.

2.4.1 Mode Revisited

Some of Kress' definitions quite rightly stress the need to include the social into definitions of multimodality but may leave out how modes are semiotically organized. He defines mode as "a socially shaped and culturally given semiotic resource for making meaning" (Kress, 2010, p. 79), and stresses that "[m]ode is that which a community, a group of people who work in similar ways around similar issues, has decided to treat as a mode" (in Andersen et al., 2015, p. 77). For Kress, the concept of mode includes its 'social shaping' as well as its material anchoring: "If a community decides to articulate a particular set of material things, or conceptual things, into a mode, than that is a mode for that community" (in Andersen et al., 2015, p. 77). Jewitt, Bezemer, and O'Halloran also emphasize the materiality of modes:

> Multimodal social semiotic analysis views artefacts as a semiotic material residue of a sign maker's interests mediated through the environment in which the sign was produced. In other words it sets out to examine the social world as it is represented in/through

> artifacts. This analysis may draw on available information about the context of production, or the history of an artefact and its past uses, although this is not always possible and is not a prerequisite for a social semiotic analysis.
>
> (Jewitt, Bezemer, & O'Halloran, 2016, p. 74)

For Bateman (Bateman, Wildfeuer, & Hiippala, 2017), too, materiality is part of what makes a mode a mode. Van Leeuwen on the other hand, defines mode in abstraction from materiality, as an "immaterial semiotic resource, a semiotic resource that is abstract enough to be applicable across different means of expression" (in Andersen et al., 2015, p. 169). Language for instance can be realized in different materialities—the sounds of speech and the graphic traces of writing. These, according to van Leeuwen, are not modes, but *media*, characterized not only by their materiality, but also by the kinds of meaning and the way in which they make them. Whereas modes can realize ideational, interpersonal, and textual meanings, and do so in systemic ways that can be represented as networks of binary choices, media not only realize the meanings made with modes, but also add their own meanings, expressing corporate or personal identities through the styles in which they realize the meanings made by modes, and doing so in the parametric way we described in Chapter 2.3.1. For Bateman et al. (2017), in turn, media are technologies of distribution, such as broadcasting, film, or the Internet. These, to van Leeuwen, would also be media, but 'distribution media' rather than 'production media', which can contribute further meanings through the way they transform what they record and distribute. Abstracting away from materiality makes it possible to map what some or all modes have in common, and yet preserve the specificity of their materialities. Lemke also defines modes in abstraction from materiality, stressing, like Kress, the social dimension: to him, a mode is "a system of meaningful contrasts between forms in a community that has conventions for the interpretation of those forms and contrasts as paradigms and syntagms" (in Andersen et al., 2015, p. 126).

Halliday's metafunctional theory has played a key role in defining modes. According to Kress and van Leeuwen, all semiotic modes can realize all three metafunctions and so function as a full system of communication (Kress & van Leeuwen, 1996; Kress, 2010). More recently, however, the idea that all semiotic modes have the resources for realizing all three metafunctions and that all semiotic modes do so at all times, has been questioned. In an interview, van Leeuwen (in Andersen et al., 2015, p. 106) has pointed out that in visual images, the interpersonal has to 'piggy-back on the ideational':

> Aren't the phenomena we interpreted as interpersonal in images always representations of interpersonal relations rather than that they are directly interpersonal? Doesn't the interpersonal in images

have to piggy-back on the ideational? Close distance to the viewer, for instance, is never actual close distance, only a representation of it.

In sound and music, the opposite occurs, or is at least common. Concepts are communicated by forms of interaction. To return to our earlier example, strict, metronomic tempos, that is, highly regimented interactions between musicians, can signify 'regimentation', and less strictly regimented tempos can signify greater interactional freedom. In short, how musicians *interact* can convey ideational meaning in a context where music is performed for an audience. More generally, "it may be that either the ideational or the interpersonal is more developed in one mode than in another" (van Leeuwen in Andersen et al., 2015, p. 107).

Van Leeuwen has also suggested that not all uses of language are fully trifunctional. In PowerPoint presentations, for instance, the written language on the slides may focus on the ideational, the speech that accompanies it on the interpersonal:

> In studying PowerPoint I found that the written language on the slides is often entirely devoid of interpersonal meanings. There are just nominal groups. No mood structure. . . . We need to be alert about the way in which the metafunctional work is divided among the modes in a multimodal text or communicative event.
> (van Leeuwen in Andersen et al., 2015, p. 107)

These questions have not yet been resolved, and needless to say, without the concept of metafunctions, it would not even be possible to ask them. In this book, we shall restrict the understanding of mode to those collections of resources which are trifunctional, that is, for something to be regarded as a mode, it will need to fulfil the three functions of saying something about the world, being able to describe social relations, and producing entities which are coherent internally and with their environment (see Kress in Andersen et al., 2015).

2.4.2 *Multimodality Revisited*

Our take on multimodality in this book is anchored in social semiotics and in the idea that multimodal communication *integrates* a range of modes and that all modes in principle are of *equal value*. This, however, could be said to constitute a particular phase in the development of multimodality studies, and a particular view on what multimodality is, and how it should be studied.

Pivoting around the pioneering work of scholars such as Hodge, Kress, O'Toole, and van Leeuwen (Hodge & Kress, 1988; Kress & van Leeuwen, 1996, 2001; O'Toole, 1994), the development of multimodal social semiotics can be said to have gone through three basic phases

(Andersen & Boeriis, 2012; Boeriis, 2009). The first is characterized by what Kress and van Leeuwen (2001) call the traditional, monomodal view, known from, and dominant in linguistics. Inspired by Halliday's social semiotic work on verbal language, which he labels 'systemic functional linguistics', visual social semiotics was developed with the intention of describing semiotic modes such as the visual and the aural mode along the lines of Halliday's description of verbal language—as metafunctional—and based on systematic paradigmatic systems. In this phase, different semiotic systems such as visual and verbal language were viewed as separate systems, existing side by side (Kress & van Leeuwen, 1996; O'Toole, 1994) and capable of making meaning independently. The second phase is dominated by a more polymodal view, where there is a growing interest in the interplay between different semiotic modes (Kress & van Leeuwen, 2001; Lim Fei, 2004; Machin, 2007). Different modes are still viewed as more or less separate, but also as affecting each other in complex ways when instantiated as acts of meaning. The third phase, currently under development, is more radically multimodal. The dominant view now is that the various semiotic systems are mere theoretical abstractions, and that meaning-making systems 'unite' in complex combined acts of meaning (Baldry & Thibault, 2006; Jones & Ventola, 2008; Kress, 2010; Lemke, 1998; O'Halloran, 2004). Thus, multimodal theory must seek to understand complex multimodal meaning-making in a consistent way that considers how the modes in the multimodal mix affect each other and transcends the idea of a range of more or less interconnected monomodal descriptions. This has also led to the return of verbal language. In phase one, and especially in phase two, the focus was on modes other than verbal language. Although the approach was inspired by linguistics, modes were considered to be modes in their own right, capable of making meaning independently. As a result, the study of verbal language was overlooked, sometimes even deemed obsolete. Today—and in our view—verbal language is one mode in addition other modes, varying in importance in different practices, but often playing a central role, for instance in many forms of internet communication.

Another more recent development of considerable relevance to organization and management studies centres around the concept of resemiotization, which is influenced by Bernstein's (1990) concept of 'recontextualization' and Latour's (1990) account of the creation of facts in science. Iedema (2001, 2003a, 2003b) describes resemiotization as a process in which changing discursive practices creates organizational change. The discourses that structure organizations, he argues, are first negotiated in face-to-face meetings, then resemiotized as authoritative written documents and finally enshrined in work practices and workplace refurbishments or renovations. Different semiotic modes play a role at different stages of this process and gradually construct the common meanings on which, eventually, the changed social practice will rest. Iedema's concept also includes broad changes in the semiotic landscape, for instance the contemporary move towards visualizing things that were formally done with words. He showed, for example, how Apple, in 1992, provided 'getting started' instructions in the form of a booklet couched in imperative language, with bolded warnings ("**Important!**"), and visuals illustrating the verbal text. By 1999, this had become a fold-out brochure in which the description of the computer was only visual, in which text and image were complementary, not fully understandable without each other, and in which the imperative nature of the writing was downgraded.

Finally, there is the introduction of the concept of social practice in van Leeuwen's work (2008a). Moving away from more abstract descriptions of context, such as Halliday's field-tenor-mode theory, and returning to the Malinowskian inspiration, he first of all describes social practices as involving a set of concrete elements: *actions* in a sequence that may be conventionalized to a greater or lesser degree; *performances* of these actions that must, for example, be more or less formal; *actors*, in certain roles that come with certain *eligibility criteria*, whether it be age or gender or some kind of formal qualification, and with certain conventions of *dress and grooming*; the *times* when the actions are to be performed, which may be regulated to different degrees; the *places* where the practice, or the various parts of it are to take place; and the *resources* that are needed to perform the practice—both places and resources being also subject to *eligibility criteria*. In such a schema, texts become a resource which may play a relatively minor role, for instance a recipe on a kitchen bench while a meal is being prepared, or a major role, as when a book is read to a child before bed, but which are always embedded in the integrated totality of the social practice. The theory is also useful for multimodality studies, because it can relate different aspects of social practices such as place, dress or grooming and resources to different modes and configurations of modes, showing that function and meaning resides, not just in texts, but also in all the other aspects of the social practice in which texts are embedded.

Based on this theory, van Leeuwen offers a perspective on recontextualization. Practices must not only be performed, they must also be taught, regulated, legitimated, and, if need be, critiqued and changed and then newly institutionalized, and it is here that discourse comes in. The discourses which surround social practices (and which are themselves also social practices) not only fulfil interpersonal functions such as teaching, regulating, and so on, but must also represent the practices they teach, regulate, and so on, and provide them with purposes and legitimations (or de-legitimations, critiques). Such recontextualizations will inevitably be selective and transformative. To return to an earlier example, Iedema (2003b) describes how, during the planning of a health facility, written documents recontextualized proposed practices in ways that were different from how they were proposed in earlier face-to-face meetings. Dynamic processes, for instance, (e.g., 'welfare workers working with students') changed into hardened categories ('student welfare workers'), tentative proposals ("Eh, but yes basically we do want it to be kept separately, so that eh the other patients don't get sort of affected by people who were brought in") changed into authoritative and imperative directives ("the patient admission area needs to allow discrete transfer of patients"), and so on, thus gradually bringing about and institutionalizing the proposed practices. Finally, representations of practices can be multimodally realized and must ultimately rest on the values and beliefs of the given cultural context, which, however, will themselves also be subject to constant contestation and change.

2.5 Conclusion

In our overview of social semiotic concepts, we have focused on concepts that can help forge connections between organization and management studies and the social semiotic study of multimodal communication. From the point of view of the discursive turn in organization and management studies, it is important to show how discourse interpersonally enacts and ideationally constructs forms of organization and management, increasingly through multimodal communication. From the point of view of social semiotics, it is important to link semiotic structures and processes to social structures and processes. As corporate forms of organization and management are increasingly dominant in contemporary society, forming a model for many other organizations, they have high relevance for a socially relevant approach to semiotics. The fact that contemporary semiotic structures and processes undergo the influence of corporate genres and styles of communication, in what Fairclough (1992) has called the 'marketization of discourse', lends extra urgency to this. Our selection of aspects of social semiotic theory in this chapter has been informed by these considerations.

The concept of 'context of situation' connects to the practices that make up organizations or fields, and the ways meanings are made in and by these practices. The concept of 'context of culture' resonates with the beliefs and values that underlie organizational cultures or the belief systems present in fields. This is as true of small and informal organizations, such as the family, as it is of global corporations. The semiotic distinction between modes and media, with their different ways of making meaning, aligns with the distinction between functional communication and the communication of identity.

Attention to the concept of context includes focus on the concept of normative discourses—discourses that regulate the conduct of social practices in a variety of ways, some formal, some informal. This in turn points at the importance of the relation between social practices within and between organizations—whether they be the relations between the practices that produce and distribute the resources needed for a given practice, or the relations between specific practices and the communicative practices that teach them, regulate them, legitimate them, critique them, and so on, and this in different ways for different purposes and different audiences.

The metafunctional theory points first of all to the need to keep in mind that communication always both constructs realities and enacts them, however much procedure supersedes content in some contexts (Zijderveld, 1979), and that the two fuse in concrete discursive practices, inextricably intertwining description and prescription. The notion of stratification, as developed in social semiotics, in turn connects structure and process—the structure of semiotic resources and the practice of communication.

Finally, it can be expected that the ongoing debates about the concepts of 'mode' and 'multimodality' themselves will benefit from a dialogue between multimodality studies and organization and management studies, creating a further step towards a theory that can do justice to the many different ways in which contemporary social practices are organized and interlinked, and to the complexity of the contemporary cultural context. In the remainder of this book, and especially in Part III, these connections will be further developed.

Part II

Strategies for Multimodal Scholarly Inquiry

3 Approaches, Methods, and Research Agenda
An Overview

Building on the work by Meyer et al. (2013), we identify five approaches that assign different roles to visual and multimodal artefacts. In what follows, we expand in more detail on archaeological, practice, strategic, dialogical, and documenting approaches. For each, we review central existing studies, discuss methodological issues, suggest appropriate methods, and illustrate our arguments with examples from the literature and, where appropriate, from our own work. Our aim is to develop, for each approach, a promising future research agenda for the field of organization and management studies. A caveat is in order. While we argue that these approaches are distinctive in terms of their focus, the boundaries between them are blurry. Multiple approaches may resemble each other regarding particular aspects (e.g., whether multimodal data are natural or artificial, or whether the researcher or the field actors interpret the data). However, they are clearly distinguishable across their 'configurations' of different characteristics, as Table 3.1 illustrates.

The *archaeological approach* stresses the status of visual and multimodal artefacts as a manifestation of culture whose meaning, relevance, and use are socially constructed by a particular community or society. It focuses on 'pre-existing' artefacts and data which the researcher can collect and interpret to reconstruct underlying meaning structures. The *practice approach*, similar to the archaeological approach, highlights artefacts as manifestations of culture. It differs, however, from it as it aims at analysing the performative effect of multimodality *in situ*, that is, the construction, handling, and use of multimodality in social action and organizational practice. The *strategic approach* focuses on the information processing and subsequent sensemaking of actors in the field. It highlights the impact of visual and multimodal artefacts, both as triggers for individual cognitive processes like perception, remembrance, and evaluation, and as persuasive rhetorical devices working through culturally established codes and symbols. The *dialogical approach* enables researchers to incorporate visual and multimodal artefacts into interview situations to give interviewees a more active voice and get closer to their

Table 3.1 Different Approaches to Multimodal Artefacts

	Archaeological	Practice	Strategic	Dialogical	Documenting
Relevance of multimodal artefacts	Store and transmit social knowledge and allow for the reconstruction of meaning structures	Socially meaningful objects that are created, employed, and manipulated in organizational contexts as part of social practices	Symbolic devices that exert influence and impact on audience perception and evaluation of reality	'Triggers' that elicit multifaceted information from conversation partners; resources to communicate in multimodal languages	A form of supporting theory building, data analysis, and/or presentation of findings in scientific contexts
Nature of data	Natural	Natural	Natural or artificial	Artificial, sometimes natural	Artificial
Producer	Field actors	Field actors	Field actors or researcher	Field actors, sometimes researcher	Researcher
Primary interpreter	Researcher	Field actors	Field actors and/or experimental subjects	Researcher and/or field actors	Researcher
Research focus	Meaning (structures) in multimodal elements of discourse	Use and handling of multimodal artefacts in practice	Impact of multimodal artefacts on audiences	Sensemaking of interview partners	Content and/or meaning of visual artefacts
Challenges of multimodality	Interactions of multiple modes in texts; integrated meanings of modes	Multimodal affordances; interactions between modal affordances	Multimodal stimuli that impact on different aspects of the sensory apparatus	Understanding differentiated literacies; designing appropriate multimodal triggers	Holistic multimodal documentation; information overflow; lack of multimodal conventions

Source: Adapted from Meyer et al., 2013

life-worlds. The *documenting approach* harnesses the power of visuality and multimodality to capture large amounts of information in a limited space to support data collection, data analysis and theory development, or the presentation of findings. In the following chapters, we will discuss the approaches in more detail along the characteristics shown in Table 3.1 and also introduce typical organizational phenomena addressed in the respective approaches, as well as common methodologies used. We will offer exemplary research at the intersection between organization studies and multimodality studies for each approach.

4 The Archaeological Approach

4.1 Core Ideas

Research in an archaeological tradition is primarily concerned with the systematic reconstruction of socially shared meaning based on the analysis of pre-existing (multimodal) artefacts in which such meaning is embodied. Artefacts, or texts, in this regard, serve as a cultural memory—as the 'storage' or 'crystallization' of social knowledge. Whether or not embodied in tangible products, texts are therefore in the first place semantic units (Halliday & Hasan, 1976), meaning(-making) constructs. Actors in the field produce artefacts and other texts to organize and legitimate the social world. Texts, accordingly, constitute traces of such world-building and world-maintenance. In social semiotics, this is reflected in the concept of metafunctions. 'Experientially', texts represent social knowledge. 'Interpersonally', texts enact social communication, including the expression of personalities and personal feelings as well as the (inter)actions that organize the social world. 'Textually', texts structure 'interpersonal' and 'experiential' meanings in such a way that they make sense as plausible messages in a given context. All three are manifested by specific verbal, visual, and other traces in the texts (Halliday, 1978; Kress & van Leeuwen, 2006).

However, texts do not simply represent the social world in one 'true' way. Thus, a central topic for multimodal archaeological research is how exactly texts—and the different modes that they draw on—relate to the social world. For the visual mode, for instance, Preston, Wright, and Young (1996) contend that at least three distinct relationships exist (see also Davison, McLean, & Warren, 2012). First, visuals can be assumed to reflect (i.e., represent) social reality by transmitting unambiguous messages. Looking at visuals from this perspective leads to efforts at reconstructing their intended message(s). Second, accepting that visuals may also mask and/or pervert social reality by transporting ideological messages (Anderson & Imperia, 1992) provides the opportunity to go beyond authorial intent and reconstruct visual meaning on the more fundamental level of "society's deep structures of social classification, institutional forms and relationships" (Preston et al., 1996, p. 113). Third, images may also be perceived as constituting social reality. This makes it possible to challenge the intended message(s) by exploring and constructing alternative realities. Most existing studies in organization research blend notions of representation, construction, and masking of reality. They regard multimodal text as produced, as well as interpreted, in a specific cultural and historical context, thus making use of shared cues and symbols to be comprehensible. A similar 'unmasking' approach is taken in critical multimodal discourse analysis (Djonov & Zhao, 2014; Machin, 2013; Machin & van Leeuwen, 2016), which combines the tradition of critical discourse analysis (Wodak & Meyer, 2016) with social semiotically grounded multimodal analysis.

Accordingly, research drawing on an archaeological approach does not necessarily only claim to reconstruct elements of organizational life, but also acknowledges multiplicities and 'pockets' of meaning, power relations, and the strategic use of text in negotiations over meaning.

4.2 Aspects of Organization

Archaeological research provides opportunities to investigate a vast variety of organizational elements and topics, as long as they leave enduring traces in artefacts and other texts. Whereas some descriptive analyses restrict themselves to identifying and counting such traces, the majority of studies in organization research focuses on their meanings.

A major research area in archaeological research is, accordingly, dedicated to the reconstruction of the prevalent norms, values, rules, and identities in and around organizations, and how they are established, expressed, and transmitted multimodally. Such studies are situated on various levels of analysis, from the whole organization to sub-communities, and to individuals within organizations. Some studies take an even broader lens and reconstruct meaning structures within whole professions or fields. Others apply an archaeological lens to the interfaces between organizations and their environments. Here, traces of the communication between organizations and other relevant actors come to the fore, therefore putting the focus on questions of image, reputation, identity, and/or legitimacy. Especially interesting for multimodal organization research are questions about which norms are expressed primarily through which mode(s), which communities rely on which mode(s), and how modes are combined to create and transmit specific meanings. A variety of empirical studies have employed visual and multimodal data to study identities (Jones & Svejenova, 2018; Schroeder & Zwick, 2004), categories (Croidieu, Soppe, & Powell, 2018; Hardy & Phillips, 1999), or actorhood (Halgin, Glynn, & Rockwell, 2018). Multimodal data enrich such studies by providing aspects of identities that go beyond the purely verbal, and include visual, material, and embodied elements and cues.

Studies with a broader focus take into account whole populations or fields of organizations, and how they interact through multimodal texts. It has, for instance, been suggested that multimodality enhances theories of how novel ideas become institutionalized (Meyer et al., 2018) and facilitates reconstructing the different institutional 'logics' that pervade management discourses (Höllerer et al., 2013). Further, an institutional lens to multimodality has been applied to the legitimation and de-legitimation of field-level issues (Christiansen, 2018; Lefsrud et al., 2018). Multimodal texts have been investigated regarding their potential for blending tradition and modernity (Kamla & Roberts, 2010) and translating generic rational myths into more specific and locally resonating ones (Zilber, 2006). Archaeological research may also look at how meanings transcend and travel through levels of analysis; for instance, how societal level norms and values are instantiated in organizations through multimodal texts. Similar studies have been undertaken by social semioticians, for example studies on the multimodal expression of organizational identity by Aiello and Dickinson (2014) and Maier (2017).

Research from more critical traditions may utilize archaeological approaches to unveil the underlying power structures in the organization of the social—and organizational—world. Prominent questions in this tradition ask who is able to express themselves in particular discourses (i.e., who has 'voice'), and who the benefactors of particular social constructions are. Naturally, power is not only expressed (and resisted) through the verbal mode. Although not all research reconstructing power relations expressly subscribes to the label of critical management research, some multimodal research has been dedicated to such questions, such as Hardy and Phillips' (1999) investigation of stereotypes in media discourse, Davison's (2007) deconstruction of images in the annual reports of an non-governmental organization, and Bell's (2012) investigation into how employees visually resist official discourse on the 'death' of an organization.

What is common to all these topics is that archaeological approaches focus on crystallized traces of meanings that are available over longer periods of time. This, of course, suggests longitudinal studies that look at changes in meaning structures over time. Whereas archaeological approaches are strong with regard to the reconstruction of shared meanings and knowledge, they commonly lack insights on the interactive and situated construction of such meanings, that is, the interactions between actors and artefacts in their construction and reception. The emphasis within social semiotics (e.g., in the 'discourse historical' approach, Reisigl & Wodak, 2016) on combining the analysis of text and context—both the situational and the broader social-cultural and historical context—seeks to fill this gap (van Leeuwen, 2005).

4.3 Methods

Similar to the range of theories, research designs in the archaeological tradition cover a broad area and include both quantitative and qualitative studies. However, systematic quantitative designs are rather rare, with the majority of studies employing qualitative designs. Methods include content analysis, rhetorical analysis, different variants of discourse analysis, framing analysis, semiotics, critical and deconstructive designs, and a variety of hermeneutical approaches. Thus, researchers can draw from a variety of methods that are suitable for data with a certain durability. In contrast, modes that are more ephemeral and difficult to 'freeze' in form of durable texts (e.g., scent) are less conducive to archaeological analysis. Methods that aim at capturing the fleeting character of specific forms of communication (e.g., ethnographic designs) or aim at producing data (e.g., interviews) are more often found in other approaches.

A standard compendium often referred to by archaeological researchers of the visual mode is Rose's (2012) book on visual methodologies. Although it covers more than just the archaeological approach, it is most often referenced within that community. Notably, Rose (2012) distinguishes between different traditions of analysing visual material, namely composition-based interpretation, content analysis, semiological analysis, and discourse analysis. Although the focus of the book is decidedly visual, it discusses some media that also contain additional modes, such as websites, videos, and video games. Rose (2012, p. xviii) is also an excellent choice to inform archaeological research, since she openly rejects any notion that visuals are a 'mirror' of the 'real world': "[M]y own preference—which is itself a theoretical position—is for understanding visual images as embedded in the social world and only comprehensible when that embedding is taken into account". Another comprehensive compendium of visual research methods is Margolis and Pauwels (2011). For multimodal analysis, there are now compendia such as Jewitt (2014) and the 4-volume anthology edited by Norris (2016).

In a recent volume on critical discourse analysis (Wodak & Meyer, 2016), Jancsary, Höllerer, and Meyer (2016) suggest a potential research design for analysing visual and multimodal data critically. Their approach is more concerned with research design than concrete methodical tools but, although originally developed for the analysis of interactions between the verbal and the visual mode, it is, in principle, adaptable to other modes due to the rather general character of their suggestions. In a nutshell, they propose to start from very small units of meaning and a clear division of modes, which allows for acknowledging the specific ways in which different modes accomplish meaning construction.

In subsequent steps, the micro-level meanings identified in the individual modes are abstracted more and more, constantly compared to each other, and finally, embedded in the broader context of the respective text(s).

A different route is taken by Jancsary, Meyer, Höllerer, and Boxenbaum (2018) who aim at a more structural analysis of meanings in a larger set of visual and multimodal texts. Building on systemic functional linguistics (Halliday, 1978; Halliday & Matthiessen, 2013) and a social semiotic perspective on multimodality (Kress, 2010; Kress & van Leeuwen, 2001), they take up the concept of 'metafunctions' as discussed in Chapter 2 and briefly repeated above, as a basis for developing more refined coding procedures that can be adapted for other modes. In their article, they demonstrate the development of such a coding procedure based on how the metafunctions work in visuals. They briefly illustrate this procedure with data on the Austrian CSR discourse. Since their conceptual starting point is relevant for all modes, their methodology can be understood as a 'toolbox' for archaeological research covering a large variety of modes as well as orchestrations of multiple modes.

Greenwood, Jack, and Haylock (2018) outline a methodology for analysing visual rhetoric in corporate reporting. Building on the work of Roland Barthes, they suggest (a) that linguistic theories developed for the study of verbal text are useful, within certain limits, for the study of visual text, (b) that images are reflective and constitutive of social realities, but that the historical and cultural nature of images is vulnerable to being erased in analysis, and (c) that sites of production and consumption of text are vital for meaning-making. Their three-phased approach starts with categorical analysis, that is, counting the number of occurrences of visual elements, as well as size, compositional features, or semiotic elements. Subsequent content analysis involves second-order abduction and both denotative and connotative readings of the material. Phase three, finally, is constituted by rhetorical analysis including photography, non-photographic images, text in relation to image, financial graphics and numbers, as well as typography and layout. These rhetorical elements are interpreted in their interaction and their embeddedness in cultural agreements about rhetorical power.

Methods for the analysis of other modes include van Leeuwen's approach to the analysis of sound and music (1999, 2011), and approaches to the analysis of typography (van Leeuwen, 2006) and colour (van Leeuwen, 2011), as well as approaches to integrating the analysis of different modes (Baldry & Thibault, 2006; van Leeuwen, 2005, 2016).

4.4 Exemplary Studies

For illustrative purposes, we now introduce three empirical studies taking an archaeological approach in some more detail. At the end of this section, we provide a table with further readings.

First, one example of empirical research specifically focusing on the interaction of the verbal and the visual mode is the study of Höllerer, Jancsary, and Grafström (2018) on the multimodal construction of the Global Financial Crisis (GFC) in the financial media. Specifically, their article aims at examining the discursive mechanisms by which a variety of interrelated, but geographically dispersed phenomena become encapsulated in a single event with distinct boundaries. Their study is interesting for multimodal organization research primarily because they focus on how verbal and visual aspects of media articles together achieve such integration and encapsulation. The authors acknowledge that the verbal and the visual both have a distinct rhetorical potential, and that their combination may facilitate processes of sensemaking and sensegiving. Their data encompass news coverage of the GFC in the *Financial Times* between 2008 and 2012. Building on and extending the methodology suggested by Jancsary et al. (2016), they first analyse each mode separately, then capture the respective role of each mode in the construction of the multimodal meaning communicated by each media article, before aggregating these multimodal meanings into higher-level narrative types. In essence, they conclude that specific compositions of verbal and visual meanings (e.g., mutually extending, specifying, or contrasting) enhance both resonance and perceived validity of sensemaking efforts through strengthening theorization and representation of particular aspects of the GFC. In contrast to other research in the archaeological tradition, their study puts the interaction between modes, and the meanings emerging from such interaction, front and centre in their theory development.

Second, Jones et al. (2012) show how materiality can be integrated into research on categories. They focus on the puzzle of how *de novo* categories are created—in their case 'modern architecture'. They criticize that existing research has mostly focused on established categories with discrete boundaries, not yet acknowledging the material aspects of categorization. They set out to examine the formation and theorization of a novel category, focusing particularly on the materials that actors use to create categories. Their study shows that the process of category formation was crucially sponsored by architects and their clientele, and strongly associated with the value spheres of business, state, religion, and family. Furthermore, they outline how the specific mix of clients is mirrored in particular 'artefact codes'—that is, the materials used by these architects for their buildings. For instance, 'modern functional architects' act on the basis of a commercial logic and exhibit a restricted artefact code in their buildings, whereas 'modern organic architects' resist the traditional logic and strongly mix old and new materials in their artefact codes and buildings. Hence the struggle over what constitutes 'modern architecture' has both a discursive and a material dimension, and both are equally crucial in the debate. In the end, the authors find, modern architects resolve the creative tension by integrating aspects of both logics and materials in their buildings, thereby extending the scope of the category. Similar to Höllerer et al. (2013), Jones et al. (2012) aim at addressing the multimodality inherent in their subject matter. Both studies deal with the issue of making modes other than the verbal accessible for empirical research by eventually 'verbalizing' them and plotting them into structural networks.

Third, a study of sonic logos by van Leeuwen (2017) shows how the values of corporate identities can be expressed by sound and music. Analysing the sonic logos of IT companies such as Microsoft, AT&T, and Intel, he shows how logos serve both a 'heraldic' function, announcing a product, service, or organization, and an 'expressive' function, conveying the identity of that product, service, or organization. The heraldic function is expressed by the kind of musical 'fanfare' motifs that have long been associated with power, victory, and triumph (rising melodies, dotted rhythms, etc.). The expressive function is realized by the timbre of the sound, and here the triumphant trumpets of traditional fanfares are now replaced, for instance, by the wind chime-like sounds of Brian Eno's famous startup sound for the Windows 95 operating system. The meanings of timbres can be analysed on the basis of the connotations of recognizable sound effects, instrumental timbres or musical genres, or on the basis of a set of aural attributes such as narrow versus wide pitch ranges, tense versus lax sounds, rough versus smooth sounds, etc. (see Chapter 2, Figure 2.3). Overall, IT logos seek to balance electronic sounds expressing technical perfection with sounds expressing a human touch, whether in the form of those wind chimes or in the form of the nostalgia of old pianos and the sweet retro sound of the Wurlitzer, as in the AT&T logo, which, as described in an account of the making of that logo, combine 'warm and forward thinking' and 'make AT&T more human and expressive' (Kessler, 2014).

4.5 Implications of Different Modes for Archaeological Research

As the aforementioned examples show, one of the main challenges of acknowledging different modes in the archaeological tradition is to do justice to their specific form of meaning construction. All modes need to fulfil the same basic functions, but each of them does so in its particular way (Kress & van Leeuwen, 2006). Research aiming at reconstructing the meaning potential and patterns of meaning from texts encompassing different modes therefore needs to be aware of, and able to capture, these differences.

For instance, Meyer et al. (2018) disentangle what they call the 'constitutive features' of the verbal and visual mode. They suggest that the verbal mode is characterized by primarily conventional forms of signification, a linear, additive, and temporal textual structure, and descriptive perspectives. The visual mode, on the other hand, signifies iconically, indexically, and conventionally; is characterized by a spatial, holistic, and simultaneous structure; and provides embodied perspectives. They further suggest that

Table 4.1 Selection of Further Readings (Archaeological Approach)

Article (in Alphabetical Order)	Brief Description
Cartel, M., Colombero, S., & Boxenbaum, E. (2018). Towards a multimodal model of theorization processes. *Research in the Sociology of Organizations*, 54(A), 153–182.	Based on an archaeological analysis of articles in a French architectural journal, the article explores the role of multimodal rhetoric in the theorization of reinforced concrete as a disruptive innovation. More specifically, the authors argue that a first part of theorization, *dramatization* is heavily multimodal, whereas the second part, *evaluation* relies more exclusively on verbal means.
Christiansen, L. H. (2018). The use of visuals in issue framing: Signifying responsible drinking. *Organization Studies*, 39(5–6), 665–689.	In this article, the author analyses the visual and verbal rhetoric included in a collective organization's campaigns to reconstruct how the organization frames 'responsible drinking' and, at the same time, establishes itself as expert in the field.
Elliott, C., & Stead, V. (2018). Constructing women's leadership representation in the UK press during a time of financial crisis: Gender capitals and dialectical tensions. *Organization Studies*, 39(1), 19–45.	The article examines the gendering of leadership in the popular press during the Global Financial Crisis of 2008–2012. The authors use multimodal discourse analysis to draw attention to the ways in which visual and verbal resources combine to draw attention to tensions and contradictions in leadership discourse.
Halgin, D. S., Glynn, M. A, & Rockwell, D. (2018). Organizational actorhood and the management paradox: A visual analysis. *Organization Studies*, 39(5–6), 645–664.	In this article, the authors study the theorization of organizations as social actors by analysing the visual depiction of organizations on the cover of BusinessWeek magazine. They find that the depiction of actorhood increases over time, and that verbal text highlights paradoxical tensions in the environment, whereas visual text offers interpretations for the management of these tensions.
Maier, C. D., & Andersen, M. A. (2014). Dynamic interplay of visual and textual identification strategies in employees' magazines. *International Journal of Strategic Communication*, 8(4), 250–275.	The authors explore the strategic communication of organizational identity through verbal and visual means in employee's magazines. The study specifically focuses on the interplay between modes in the construction of identity, that is, how modes reinforce, complement, or subvert each other.

the combination of these constitutive features imbues texts building on either mode with particular affordances, with distinct impact on perception and meaning construction. Additional modes can be characterized in similar ways. The aural mode, for instance, shares some features with the verbal, and some with the visual mode, while it is also characterized by a linear and temporal structure (in that sounds have a beginning and an end) and therefore better able to communicate indexically (e.g., by mimicking sounds from particular sources). Kress (2010) stresses both the similarities of the modes developed by a given society and the differences stemming from their different materialities. He also discusses the epistemological consequences of this, in the context of their use in science education. A visual representation of a cell, for instance, requires a different kind of 'epistemological commitment' (Kress, 2010) than a verbal representation—it commits the learner to position the nucleus in a particular spot within the cell, something that is not required in a verbal representation.

What this means is that archaeological research that takes different modes seriously needs to find specific ways of making their distinct meaning-making potentials useful for organizational inquiry. To date, such systematic engagement with the specific characteristics and features of different modes is still in its infancy in organization research. This is one of the areas where a more pronounced engagement with multimodality research could substantially bolster the impact and contribution of multimodal organization studies. At the same time, the field of organization and management research is not one that is commonly engaged with in social semiotic research, which means that this field has the potential to provide for new insights to this theory, for instance, insights into the functioning of modes in different organizational contexts.

In terms of methodology, the acknowledgement of multiple modes of meaning-making also requires more flexibility and innovation in terms of research design. Whereas most of the methods commonly used in organization research are tailored to the verbal mode, such methods are only partially useful for the investigation of other modes. One possibility is the eventual 'verbalization' of information gained from other modes (as in Höllerer et al., 2013 and Jones et al., 2012 presented above). Verbalization has the distinct advantage that it enables the application of a methodological toolbox that has been tested and gradually improved for a long time. Its downside, however, is that researchers risk losing precisely the kind of additional insights into the social and organizational world that motivated their turn towards multimodality in the first place.

4.6 Specific Challenges and Opportunities Regarding Multimodality

In addition to the challenges outlined above, the combination and orchestration of multiple modes within single texts (Kress, 2010) adds an additional layer of complexity. It is necessary not only to assess and capture each mode according to its very own characteristics, but also to find a way to model the interactions of multiple modes (see, for instance, the idea of 'integration' in Baldry & Thibault, 2006).

There is ample potential in organization research to realize the additional insights offered by a multimodal lens, since a substantial number of studies draw on data that are essentially multimodal, however without explicitly addressing the interplay of modes. The study of Zilber (2006) on the translation of rational myths in Israeli high-tech, for instance, draws on newspaper articles as well as ads of Israeli high-tech firms to explore how generic myths (national-religious, secular-humanist-universalistic, and individualistic) become translated into high-tech-specific rational myths (informative, individualistic, nationalistic, and enchantment). While Zilber (2006) acknowledges the existence of visual aspects in her data and also provides examples containing visuals, it would be interesting to see how the visual and the verbal interact in such processes of translation. Similarly, Vaara, Tienari, and Irrmann (2007) study an ad campaign meant to create and communicate a new identity for a Nordic bank after a series of mergers and acquisitions (M&As). They show how multimodal advertisements support the construction of authenticity, distinctiveness, self-esteem, and future orientation. A more systematic engagement with the multimodality of these artefacts could provide additional insights into the 'division of labour' between modes, and the way in which such attributes of organizational identity are created through specific multimodal orchestrations.

Accordingly, to assess the effects of such orchestrations, in which the combined meaning is supposedly greater than the sum of all meanings expressed in each mode, modes need to be made comparable for analysis. A first step in this direction, as has been discussed under 'methods' above, is the idea of metafunctions. When a common analytical scheme is established, research can begin to capture the particular meanings created through the relationality of modes. Van Leeuwen (2005) details four possible approaches to analysing multimodal texts and artefacts: visual composition, which spatially integrates text, image and other graphic elements through the use of layout, colour, and typography; rhythm, which temporally integrates bodily movement and speech, and in audiovisual media, also sound and music and camera work; information linking, which details the semantic relations between different modes such as the visual and the verbal mode; and dialogue, which integrates different 'voices' that might also be expressed through different modes. Van Leeuwen (2016) also explores the common features between graphic form (in typography and decorative graphics), colour, texture, and sound quality.

5 The Practice Approach

5.1 Core Ideas

Whereas scholarly work pursuing an archaeological approach aims at the reconstruction of relevant cultural contexts and meaning structures through the detailed interpretation of multimodal artefacts as types of text, the practice approach enables their study *in situ*. Consequently, visual artefacts are not only seen as carriers of social (or subjective) meaning, but also as objects to be constructed, employed, and manipulated in various processes of organizing. In contrast to the archaeological approach, this approach is therefore not so much interested in the sedimented social meaning(s) and structure(s) that visual artefacts embody as in the processes of inscribing such meaning, the 'careers' that such artefacts have in organizational contexts, and consequently, in the (inter-)actions that they trigger, enable, or prevent—that is, the practice approach is interested in what multimodal artefacts actually 'do'.

Since research in this tradition is more focused on the handling and use of multimodal text, it places more substantial value on the media (Kress & van Leeuwen, 2001) through which multiple modes are disseminated. The distinction between 'mode' and 'medium' that Kress and van Leeuwen establish in *Multimodal Discourse* (2001) is relevant and useful here. 'Modes' are defined as abstract ways of organizing meaning-making which can realize experiential, interpersonal, and textual meanings, and which can do so, in principle, in materially different media. The verbal mode, for instance, can be realized with sound, graphically, or in both media. Thus, verbal language is a mode because it can realize all three metafunctions and do so either in the form of speech or in the form of writing. According to Kress and van Leeuwen (2006), the visual is also a mode because it, too, can realize all three metafunctions and do so in materially different ways—as drawings, photographs, paintings, etc. 'Media' they define as the resources (including bodily articulation through speech, gestures, etc.) that materialize meaning but that themselves can also produce meaning, whether directly, on the basis of a creative use of the affordances of the materials, or, less creatively, on the basis of an unsystematic 'lexicon' of such creative uses that have become clichés. Kress and van Leeuwen further distinguish between production media and distribution media. The latter serve mainly to record or distribute, but the way in which they do so can itself express cultural values, and thus the distinction between production media and distribution media is an analytical one.

The emphasis on media leads to a stronger focus on the materiality of communication. Research on visuality, in this tradition, for instance, understands photographs, plans, and maps as material artefacts that 'travel' through the organization and impact the conduct of human actors in different ways. This is distinctly different from focusing on the content of multimodal communication, and the way in which different sign systems realize this content, as is the case of the archaeological approach (which favours the concept of mode over the concept of medium). A practice approach to multimodality is, accordingly, particularly valuable for studies aiming at understanding how multimodal artefacts are embedded in, and shape, organizational processes and interaction.

5.2 Aspects of Organization

The practice approach to multimodality focuses on what multimodal artefacts 'do' in and to organizations and fields, and to organizational actors (see, for instance, Nicolini, Mengis, & Swan, 2012). It has a particular interest in the material practices which continually make and remake the social and organizational world through the use of tools, discourse, and the body. Multimodality is a natural field of study for practice studies, since tools, discourse, and bodies all express meaning differently, and draw on a variety of modes. Practices require material resources and are expressed through material activity. For instance, how do multimodal technologies such as PowerPoint shape communicative practices in organizations (Kaplan, 2011)? How does the body language of managers influence creative processes (Gylfe et al., 2016)? How do tables and spread sheets in health care facilities govern nursing (Karlsson, 2012)? How do organizations mobilize visual artefacts to communicate category membership (Gehman & Grimes, 2017)? How do decision makers perceive, interpret, and assess the material implications of institutional pressures, and how do they respond to material misalignments between expected and existent material aspects of their organizations (Raaijmakers, Vermeulen, & Meeus, 2018)? Practice approaches may also facilitate a more processual understanding of organizations and organizing in a 'world on the move', which directs attention to the continuous flow of activities and elements (see, for instance, Hernes, 2014). This means that temporality becomes a central focus, and it stresses that retaining stability in a world of flux constitutes hard work.

Practice research that builds on the idea of sociomateriality investigates the role of technology for organizational norms, structures, and capabilities. It claims the 'intrinsic' importance of technology for everyday activities and relationships in organizations and suggests that the material and the social are inherently inseparable (Orlikowski & Scott, 2008). Artefacts, from such perspectives, are enmeshed with human actors in networks of agencies, which means that human agency and material agency cannot be clearly separated. This has become a key theme especially in strategy-as-practice research that seeks to understand strategy as work involving sociomaterial tools (Dameron, Lê, & LeBaron, 2015; Jarzabkowski & Pinch, 2013; Vaara & Whittington, 2012).

In this view, material artefacts 'participate' in organizational processes just as much as organizational actors do, and they substantially shape outcomes. Research inspired by actor-network theory (ANT) stresses the 'agency' of artefacts as participants in interactions. A prominent idea of ANT with regard to artefacts is 'inscription' (Jarzabkowski & Pinch, 2013). Artefacts become inscribed with particular potentials and purposes in their production, and users can either subscribe to such intended chains of activities or attempt to 'repurpose' or 'reinscript' artefacts during usage. The potentials for action and meaning-making thus inscribed in artefacts and texts are often called 'affordances' (see Gibson, 1986; Kress, 2010). They enable and constrain the array of potential forms of usage and are realized relationally among artefacts, producers and recipients. The actual use of multimodal artefacts then becomes a constant negotiation, but not only in the traditional sense (i.e., organizational members negotiating how to understand and use a particular artefact): Since the artefact itself is a carrier of a particular script, it, again, participates in such negotiations as an equal agent.

One lens on the role of multimodal artefacts in organizational practices focuses on their function in coordinating tasks and groups in organizations. Such research has specifically looked at the multimodal construction of boundary objects (Henderson, 1991; Justesen & Mouritsen, 2009), that is, devices that connect disparate communities of meaning and practice through their ability to mean different things in different contexts. Further, multimodal artefacts not only coordinate, but they also mobilize and conscript, that is, they are a means to explain how actors are incentivized to take certain actions, and how they become identified with specific practices and strategies (Vásquez & Cooren, 2012). A third focus of practice research has looked at the role of multimodal artefacts in the creation and transmission of knowledge, particularly knowledges that are hard to verbalize explicitly, because they are based more on aesthetic perception than rational deliberation (Ewenstein & Whyte, 2007, 2009; Stigliani & Ravasi, 2018). Finally, specific artefacts, such as organizational dress, are a crucial feature of identity enactment and identity claims (Dellinger, 2002; Pratt & Rafaeli, 1997).

Practice approaches to multimodality, in summary, focus on interactions—between actors and artefacts, as well as between actors themselves, as mediated through artefacts. This makes them a powerful tool to study the emergence and negotiation of meanings on the micro level, and to see how broader societal meanings are enacted in micro-level interactions.

5.3 Methods

In contrast to archaeological research, practice research does not often draw on methodologies aimed at reconstructing socially constructed meaning from multimodal artefacts, and it instead uses methodologies that enable researchers to capture the use of artefacts *in situ*. The most dominant approach in current literature is, accordingly, the ethnographic case study. Unlike archaeological research, ethnographies of organizations have not neglected modes other than verbal language, since they have always been based on 'thick' descriptions of field observations (Geertz, 1973), although they often have not included other modes explicitly in their analyses. Hence, most standard ethnographical designs are well-suited to capturing the multimodal aspects of organizations and organizing. For instance, Ewenstein and Whyte (2007, p. 693) describe their fieldwork in the following way:

> An interest in local meanings and the in vivo conditions of life and work within a group led to a certain amount of direct involvement. The first author helped to prepare group lunches and went on a field trip with the office to visit existing buildings designed by the firm; he drank tea with the group at 4 pm, and shared photographs taken during the research process back with the practice for their use; he celebrated a leaving do and played pool, was occasionally asked for his opinion on a design issue and even served as a model for a character in a design drawing.

As this quote illustrates, taking a practice approach to multimodal research requires capturing organizational practices and local meaning construction through the collection of artefacts, observation of organizational action, and talk to organizational members. In addition to observation, interviewing is often used in data collection. For instance, Dellinger (2002), in her research on the role of dress and appearance norms for gender and sexual inequality, conducted extensive interviews with staff about the existence and handling of dress codes in both a heterosexual men's pornographic magazine and a feminist magazine.

An increasingly popular method for augmenting and supplementing observational techniques is video ethnography (see, for instance, Hassard et al., 2018, or the recent special issue on video in *Organizational Research Methods*, 2018). Video data are excellently suited for capturing 'elusive' knowledges that resist verbalization (Toraldo et al., 2018). Waller and Kaplan (2018) provide guidance on taking the necessary decisions for 'taming' the vast amount of data that video provides for more quantitative analyses. They suggest that, if designed in a suitable way, video analysis can provide insights that go far beyond what traditional data sources such as surveys enable. In the area of multimodality, Baldry and Thibault (2006), Flewitt, Hampel, Hauck, and Lancaster (2009), Iedema (2001, 2003a), and Norris (2006, 2009) have provided detailed methods for the analysis of video data and occasionally included analyses of organizational processes such as the planning of a new reception area in a mental hospital (Iedema, 2001) and multiparty interaction in an accounting office (Norris, 2006).

5.4 Exemplary Studies

An excellent example for the practice approach to multimodality is Heracleous and Jacobs' (2008) study of strategizing through the creation of embodied metaphors. Their study focuses on the strategic episode of a management retreat, in which senior corporate strategists outlined an ideal strategy development process by actively creating artefacts with toy construction materials. As the authors explain, "a change in mode and medium of the strategy process may influence strategy content" (Heracleous & Jacobs, 2008, p. 313). Their specific interest was how the construction of physical, tangible entities, instead of cognitive maps or semantic metaphors, would influence the strategizing process. Additionally, conversations and negotiations between individual groups about the created objects was encouraged and also observed closely. Their findings suggest that there is an additional benefit to 'concretizing' issues through material manifestations, which triggered additional reflection on the issue. They also point out that such materialization may allow for the inclusion of organizational members other than strategists in the process of strategizing, since it put experts and laymen on more equal footing. Although not explicitly mentioned in their study, the potential meanings inherent in their 'construction material' (e.g., modelling clay, plastic bricks, and so on) triggered different, novel meanings that purely verbal discussions could not. The affordances of different modes and their material manifestations, accordingly, provide additional resources for more creative problem solving.

A study using video data comes from Wenzel and Koch (2018). They examine keynote speeches as a genre of strategic communication. By conducting a video-based multimodal discursive analysis of Apple's top managers' keynote speeches, they identify and elaborate on four discursive practices: referencing, relating, demarcating, and mystifying. Gestures are a key part of these discursive practices. In particular, their analysis demonstrates how levelling and leaping gestures are systematically used in these keynote speeches as part of the discursive practices. Together, these practices play a key role in dealing with both the continuity and novelty of strategies. Thus, their analysis helps to better understand multimodality in micro-level practices through which strategic ideas are 'sold' to larger audiences.

Iedema's work on 'resemiotization' (2001, 2003a) shows how meaning shifted from one materiality to another in the process of planning a new reception area for a mental hospital that would allow a more discrete transfer of patients, and how distinct materialities have different statuses. There were four semiotically distinct stages: face-to-face meetings, written summaries, architectural drawings, and finally the new facility, realized in bricks and mortar (and instituting new work practices). During the face-to-face meetings, architect planners, bureaucrats, and future users negotiated their needs and wants. In the written documents these were 'accepted' and subsequently changed into architectural designs. This created a point of no return, as by this time significant resources had been invested, and so "embedded the project's progress in an increasingly durable and expensive—and therefore *resistant*—materiality", even more so once the new facility was built, reifying "a set of social and discursive relations in the form of a resource-intensive physical construct" (Iedema, 2003a, p. 43).

5.5 Implications of Different Modes for Practice Research

At first sight, a practice approach towards multimodality seems less challenging than an archaeological approach, because the meanings inherent in the different modes of each artefact are primarily interpreted by the actors in the field, and not the researchers themselves. This means that researchers do not need to engage multimodality with pre-made theories of how each mode constructs meaning, as this is, in a sense, a question that needs to be answered empirically. Meaning construction is observed *in vivo*, and in this way, the findings from practice research are of high interest also for scholars in the archaeological tradition, since they provide much needed insights on how interactions between producers, texts, and audiences actually unfold when multiple modes are at play. The vast literature on ethnomethodological conversation analysis (EMCA) (Garfinkel, 1967; Schegloff, 1996) constitutes the foundation of multimodal conversation analysis (Goodwin, 2001). Multimodal conversation analysis is a fine-grained approach to the analysis of people's ordinary everyday practices and incrementally emerging actions for accomplishing everyday tasks in and through face-to-face interaction, including interactions in institutional settings (Arminen, 2005). The resources for constructing these actions for interaction include talk, gaze, bodily movements, and object manipulation (Mondada, 2008), which the co-participants

Table 5.1 Selection of Further Readings (Practice Approach)

Article (in Alphabetical Order)	Brief Description
Arjaliès, D.-L., & Bansal, P. (2018). Beyond numbers: How investment managers accommodate societal issues in financial decisions. *Organization Studies*, 39(5–6), 691–719.	In this article, the authors study how investment managers use calculative devices in their investment decisions. They discover that equity managers used visuals to assess environmental, social, and governance (ESG) criteria, because the dissonance between numbers and visuals produces creative friction.
Islam, G., Endrissat, N., & Noppeney, C. (2016). Beyond 'the eye' of the beholder: scent innovation through analogical reconfiguration. *Organization Studies*, 37(6), 769–795.	Based on a study on innovation in the perfume industry, the authors show how innovation is driven by analogical processes, and how material affordances enable analogical reconfiguration. They claim that in their case, visual and olfactory combinations of modes may be particularly conducive to such reconfiguration.
Kaplan, S. (2011). Strategy and PowerPoint: An inquiry into the epistemic culture and machinery of strategy making. *Organization Science*, 22(2), 320–346.	The study takes a closer look at how PowerPoint is mobilized in strategizing through an ethnographic study of a telecommunications equipment manufacturer. Specifically, the author outlines how the affordances of PowerPoint facilitated mapping and drawing boundaries around the scope of a strategy.
Karlsson, A.-M. (2009). Fixing meaning: On the semiotic and interactional role of written texts in a risk analysis meeting. *Text & Talk* (29–24), 415–438.	The article explores how a group of people at work use spoken and written language as well as material resources to negotiate risks. It demonstrates how low-tech instruments such as pieces of paper, pens, and a whiteboard—because of their semiotic potential—constitute an intricate technology that is fundamental to the achievement of the organization's goals.
Wasserman, V., & Frenkel, M. (2011). Organizational aesthetics: Caught between identity regulation and culture jamming. *Organization Science*, 22(2), 503–521.	Building on Lefebvre's spatial theory, the authors explore how spaces interact with identities. On the basis of the award-winning building of Israel's Ministry of Foreign Affairs, they highlight intentional and unintentional efforts at resisting aesthetic mechanisms of regulation.
Yakura, E. K. (2002). Charting time: Timelines as temporal boundary objects. *Academy of Management Journal*, 45(5), 956–970.	The article studies how timelines as visual artefacts mobilize organization and negotiation in work contexts. The author finds that visualized timelines allow organizational and occupational subgroups to negotiate and manage time. In this way, they are tools for overcoming "pluritemporalism".

coordinate in the process of interaction. Studies within the framework of multimodal conversation analysis have documented how actions, even in institutional settings, are not pre-scripted (Koskela, Arminen, & Palukka, 2013). Instead, co-participants have to organize and systematize groups of actions that incrementally and hierarchically unfold (Streeck, Goodwin, & LeBaron, 2011). However, practice approaches are not without challenges themselves. First and foremost, researchers still need to be sensitized to the different modes at play. Essentially, this means that at the very least they need to be aware of the presence and relevance of multiple modes, and relatively 'literate' in these modes to understand what is going on in the field. At a very basic level, if researchers are not aware of a mode being present, they may not even be able to perceive its effects at all, thereby missing important aspects of what is going on.

Methodologically, researchers need to translate such literacy into specific frameworks for analysis. Whereas ethnographic designs and 'thick descriptions' may be equally relevant for all modes, analysis becomes tricky when these data need to be analysed more systematically and in a more structured way. How exactly can we capture the effect of body language on audience mobilization? What are the analytical tools to assess the effect of different audio cues in spoken conversations? For instance, while Heracleous and Jacobs' (2008) study provides important insights into the outcomes of using embodied metaphors for strategizing retreats, the study becomes somewhat more ambiguous in explaining how exactly materiality and embodiment contributed to these outcomes. It is here that multimodality research can be helpful. Martinec (1998, 2000, 2001), for instance, has created a metafunctionally based framework of analysis for body language, as have Norris and her associates (2009, 2016). In addition, there has been some recent work analysing body language in PowerPoint presentations (Zhao et al., 2014) and live lectures (Hood, 2017).

5.6 Specific Challenges and Opportunities Regarding Multimodality

Compared to archaeologically inspired research, for practice research, it might be even more difficult to tell the effects of multiple modes apart since artefacts may act upon the social world as amalgams, or distinct orchestrations (Kress, 2010). While researchers in the archaeological tradition can potentially analyse the different modes in isolation and theorize on the contribution of each mode to the overall meaning, this is more complicated in the constantly fleeting and momentary world of human interaction. Whether it was the visual, the material, or the verbal part of a photograph that triggered mobilization in a meeting, or whether it was the body language of the person presenting the photograph, is an altogether difficult question to answer. Video analyses which allow for watching particular interactions repeatedly and inferring reactions to specific stimuli help to some degree, but as we have outlined in Chapter 2, it is not at all clear even in theory whether multiple modes are actually separable in practice.

Whereas the interaction of different modes is maybe of less interest if the constructed 'amalgam' is mutually reinforcing (i.e., all modes work together), it becomes less trivial if the modes inscribed in an artefact are internally contradictory. For instance, if the visual aesthetic and the layout of a poster are appealing, but its scent is appalling, how could such interaction be captured? What if, additionally, the poster is very fragile and therefore hard to hang? Which mode will eventually 'win' in terms of the final practical effect? Is the combined effect the sum of all effects, can some modes be isolated, or is it something entirely new?

Within multimodality research, two concepts go some way towards addressing these questions. The first is salience. According to Kress and van Leeuwen (2006), viewers of spatial compositions, such as posters, are intuitively able to judge the 'weight' of the various elements of the composition, and the greater the weight of the element, the greater its salience. This salience is not to be understood as objectively measurable; it results from a complex trading-off relationship between various textual factors, such as size, sharpness of focus, contrast, colour, placement, perspective as well as cultural factors, for instance, the representation of a (known) human figure. Salience is a multimodal concept. It also exists in the realm of sound, where it is expressed by contrasts in pitch, loudness, and duration, and in the realm of body movement, where it is expressed by contrasts of force (Kress & van Leeuwen, 2006). The second concept forms part of rhythm analysis. In complex audiovisual texts such as films, the rhythm of a given mode may act as what van Leeuwen (2005) has called a 'guide rhythm'. The rhythms of other modes are then synchronized with the guide rhythm. This foregrounds one mode over others, speech in dialogue scenes, body movement in action scenes, and so on.

6 The Strategic Approach

6.1 Core Ideas

Work with a strategic take on multimodality is instrumental to the extent that it is interested in the potential of multimodal text to elicit desired responses from audiences. Especially the visual mode is often analysed in comparison to, or in combination with, verbal language. In management studies, its main application has been in the domain of marketing and consumer studies. More recently, the persuasive potential of multimodal text in various instances of claims-making has gained wider attention. One stream of studies in this tradition is primarily interested in the immediate impact of different modes on cognitive processing. Such studies suggest, for instance, that visuals enhance information encoding, storage, and retrieval. Established constructs are attitude, elaboration, belief, liking, recall, and assessment (Heckler & Childers, 1992; Houston et al., 1987). A central objective of this line of research is to assess and understand better the degree to which verbal and visual texts have different—complementary or contradictory—effects.

A more recent stream within the strategic approach argues that visuals are a persuasive rhetorical device—in many cases more powerful than verbal language (Durand, 1983; McQuarrie & Mick, 1999; Scott & Rajeev, 2003). Researchers in marketing and advertising who study visual rhetoric build on earlier work in their domain that explores how visuals are cognitively processed by a target audience; however, they deviate from traditional views by arguing that visual communication is a learned, culture-specific, and purposive activity. Visuals do not automatically trigger cognitive or emotional reactions, but they need to be understood in terms of their incorporated meaning to elicit responses. They are thus part of a system of symbols that is culturally embedded, requires active sensemaking on the part of the audience, and functions as a fully nuanced 'writing system' analogous to verbal language (Scott, 1994; Scott & Vargas, 2007).

6.2 Aspects of Organization

The strategic approach diverges from both the archaeological and the practice approach, first, through its almost exclusive focus on the audience of multimodal communication, which is strongly grounded in psychology and, second, through its heavy use of researcher-controlled multimodal stimuli.

For organization theory, the strategic approach is, consequently, most prominently suited to research the actual impact of multimodal communication in and around organizations. To do so, it probes into the subjective processing of multimodal stimuli and looks for generalizable patterns across individuals. Cognitive psychology underpins large parts of research in this area, focusing on the perception and processing of multimodal information. For organization research, this can be highly interesting, since environmental cues need to first gain attention and be perceived before they can be assigned meaning in the social sphere. Research in cognitive psychology focuses, for instance, on the way in which different modes leave imprints in specific perceptual repositories (Liversedge et al., 2004), or how information from different modes is transferred to the short-term and long-term memory (Atkinson & Shiffrin, 1968). Such theories help explain the speed with which information from multiple modes is perceived and processed, the amount of information that can be gained from text drawing on specific modes, or the way in which such information is stored in the human brain. Consequently, cognitive psychology provides information on the effects of different modes *before* their content is actually assigned social meaning. The potential range of organizational topics that can be investigated with such approach is broad. The effect of multimodal communication and rhetoric is, for instance, central in research on information transmission and processing (Mitchell & Olson, 1981; Smith & Taffler, 1996). Similar designs are also useful for researching emotion, liking, and trust towards different forms of organizational communication (Cho, Phillips, Hageman, & Patten, 2009; Scott & Vargas, 2007).

Studies drawing on semiotics and rhetoric add more social elements by acknowledging that multimodal communication is learned, culture-specific, and purposeful, rather than a simple stimulus-response affair. This adds the central element of 'meaning' on top of the cognitive foundation. Whereas different modes may target specific sensory equipment (eyes, ears, fingertips, etc.) and are therefore subjected to the specific capabilities and constraints of such equipment, they also construct text according to specific rules or grammars, and therefore suggest meanings in different ways. More recent research in the strategic tradition, accordingly, combines cognitive psychological with semiotic explanations (McQuarrie & Mick, 1999) and embeds individual impacts of multimodal communication in a broader cultural context (McQuarrie & Phillips, 2005). In this volume, the study of online shopping (Chapter 13) combines social semiotic analysis of a web shop with insights from marketing literature about the needs and risk management of costumers. Such integration of semiotic and cognitive insights has more recently also been attempted in organizational institutionalism (Meyer et al., 2018). However, these insights are most prominently used in marketing and consumer research. A rather substantial strand of literature in this area of research builds on both cognitive psychological and semiotic theories to explain the impact of visuals in advertising efforts in relation to variables like brand recognition, brand liking, brand recall, and trust.

Although not systematically investigated in organization research to date, strategic approaches to multimodality also have substantial potential for illuminating topics outside of marketing and advertising. For instance, research in the strategic tradition could contribute to the unpacking of multimodal aspects of power, control, and identification. Research that emphasizes the micro-foundations of institutions could benefit from this approach, as could the attention-based view in organization and management studies (Ocasio, 1997). In addition, research on strategy and strategizing could benefit from more psychologically grounded studies on how different modes impact on creativity, comprehension, and persuasion; this is also the case with strategy-as-practice research that has thus far mainly pursued a practice-based approach (see above). Also, whereas organizational reporting has been thoroughly researched from an archaeological perspective, there is little knowledge as to how multimodal text in reports actually impacts on stakeholders' perception of the organization.

6.3 Methods

The strategic approach aims at grounding assumptions about the specific effects of particular modes on individual cognition and meaning constitution in rigorous empirical research. Accordingly, empirical studies in this tradition mostly draw on experimental designs. This is particularly interesting as in organization and management studies, there is a recent resurgence of interest in experimental research designs (Bitektine, Lucas, & Schilke, 2018). The multimodal stimuli used in these experiments are predominantly produced and/or selected by researchers.

The study of Scott and Vargas (2007) is an excellent example of such experimental design in marketing and consumer research. The objective of their study was to investigate whether, and how, visuals impact on the attitudes of consumers towards certain products, and their perceptions of product attributes. To do so, they exposed test subjects to sets of images with the same content (cat, sunset, abstract art) but with varying manifestations of such content (e.g., a photograph of a fluffy cat, a wooden cat toy, and a colourful stylized image of a cat). In a first study, they exposed undergraduate students to random advertisements featuring one of these images. Test subjects had to infer the product attributes from a specific set (soft, strong, absorbent, colourful, and pricy) from the ad. The results broadly confirmed their expectations that specific ascriptions of attributes can be strategically triggered visually.

However, in order to explain a variety of unexpected results, they decided to follow-up their experimental study with a number of interviews of both secretaries and students. These interviews revealed additional cultural norms behind interpretations. For instance, the fact that the fluffy cat was generally interpreted as expensive was due to its perception as "snobbish and as if it belonged in an upper-class home" (Scott & Vargas, 2007, p. 348), an interpretation that could not be inferred purely by any sensory cues in the image itself.

In a third study, finally, the authors tested the effect of verbal text in combination with the images. Again, they conducted an experiment with undergraduate students, exposing them to multimodal (verbal and visual) advertisements with the same visual elements as before. They found that "verbal statements, when set in plain text, are limited in their capability to communicate, as compared to either the images or the more visual presentation of the statements" (Scott & Vargas, 2007, p. 353). They concluded that 'style' is an important characteristic both of visuals and of the lettering of verbal text when communicating product attributes. This is sympathetic to ideas from social semiotics on the meaning inherent in typography (van Leeuwen, 2006).

A common experimental approach to visual research is eye-tracking (see Olk & Kappas, 2011 for a methodological discussion), which is used for psychological research on a range of aspects of the processing of visual stimuli, but has also been applied to the perception of advertising images on newspaper pages (Higgins, Leinenger, & Rayner, 2014; Leckner, 2012). A study by Boeriis and Holsanova (2012), which combines social semiotics with a cognitive approach using eye-tracking, is discussed below. The case study of online shopping in this volume (Chapter 13) also contains an experimental eye-tracking component aimed at investigating how users engage with the visual and verbal elements on online shopping sites.

6.4 Exemplary Studies

A study illustrating the power of the strategic approach excellently is the research of McQuarrie and Phillips (2005) about indirect persuasion in advertisements. The authors set out to investigate how consumers process different types of indirect claims. The initial assumption was that indirect metaphorical claims would make consumers more receptive to positive inferences about the brand. Additionally, the authors wished to find out whether exposure to visual cues would enhance this effect, that is, whether metaphorical claims communicated through pictures would make consumers more likely to generate positive inferences. Empirically, the authors collected a set of ads in popular magazines that contained visual metaphors. They then constructed variations of these ads for fictional brands. In one version, the claim was made directly and verbally (e.g., 'Clears away tough stains'), in the second version, the same claim was made metaphorically and verbally (e.g., 'Bulldozes tough stains'), and in a third version, the claim was made metaphorically and visually (e.g., 'the images of a bulldozer cleaning a dirty piece of tableware'). Their experiment supported the hypothesis that "the use of metaphorical claims in ads appears to make consumers receptive to multiple, distinct, positive inferences about the advertised brand (i.e., weak implicatures), while still conveying the main message of the ad (i.e., the strong implicature)" (McQuarrie & Phillips, 2005, p. 17). The findings also supported the assumption that visual metaphors elicit such multiple inferences more spontaneously. They therefore conclude that indirect visual claims create the fewest constraints on interpretations. The authors also discuss implications for public policy, since their findings confirm the claim of Messaris (1997) that the power of visual persuasion can easily be used for deceptive and manipulative purposes.

Boeriis and Holsanova (2012) combine semiotic analysis with an experimental approach that uses eye-tracking and the recording of simultaneous verbal comments. This allows them to study the relation between 'rank' as defined in social semiotics and the dynamic process of viewers' perception and cognition. The semiotic side of the equation is based on the work of O'Toole (1994) who posited a visual analogue to the segmentation of verbal language in units of decreasing size (morpheme, word, group, clause): component, unit, group, whole. The experiment showed that scenes are viewed in a stepwise process of identification, evaluation, and interpretation that closely relates to the way rank is encoded in the text, but that it is also informed by the viewer's goals, interest, and expectations. Similar results have also been obtained elsewhere. Holsanova, Rahm, and Holmqvist (2006) show that, whereas, for instance, an advertisement may objectively be the most salient element of a newspaper page, this does not necessarily mean it will be the reader's first point of eye fixation. Readers may be primarily interested in the news and, knowing where on the page advertisements tend to occur, avoid the ads. Holsanova et al. (2006) were therefore able to empirically distinguish specific types of readers on the basis of their preferred reading strategies: 'focused readers', who read only one text on each spread, 'editorial readers', who avoid the advertisements, even when they are graphically salient, and 'entry point overviewers', who visit the most important entry points, such as headlines, pictures, and advertisements. Leckner (2012) provides a useful overview of studies of this kind. Bateman (2017) is another influential social semiotician who has advocated that there needs to be more cross-fertilization between insights from recent, experimental cognitive studies of meaning-making and social theories such as social semiotics.

Table 6.1 Selection of Further Readings (Strategic Approach)

Article (in Alphabetical Order)	Brief Description
Cheema, A., & Bagchi, R. (2011). The effect of goal visualization on goal pursuit: Implications for consumers and managers. *Journal of Marketing, 75*(2), 109–123.	The authors show that visualization of a goal through external representations enhances goal pursuit. However, such effect can only be observed when goal achievement is already close. These effects are shown across five experimental studies.
Cho, C. H., Phillips, J. R., Hageman, A. M., & Patten, D. M. (2009). Media richness, user trust, and perceptions of corporate social responsibility. *Accounting, Auditing & Accountability Journal, 22*(6), 933–952.	The study shows that media richness (i.e., multiple cues and responsive feedback) is positively associated with trusting the intentions of an organization, but not with trusting its beliefs. An experimental study tested the effect of presentation medium of corporate social responsibility website disclosures on trust.
Kim, K. J., & Sundar, S. S. (2016). Mobile persuasion: Can screen size and presentation mode make a difference to trust? *Human Communication Research, 42*(1), 45–70.	Differences in presentation mode (video vs. text) are tested with regard to their persuasive effect. The experiment shows that larger screens and video are associated with restricted cognitive effort and easy processing, while small screen and text are associated with comprehensive, analytic processing of information.
Lurie, N.H., & Mason, C.H. (2007). Visual representation: Implications for decision making. *Journal of Marketing, 71*(1), 160–177.	Focusing on the influence of data visualization on the decision-making of managers, the authors suggest that visualizations improve efficiency and offer new insights. However, they may also overly focus attention, increase salience of less diagnostic information, and encourage inaccurate comparisons.
Spangenberg, E. R., Grohmann, B., & Sprott, D. E. (2005). It's beginning to smell (and sound) a lot like Christmas: The interactive effects of ambient scent and music in a retail setting. *Journal of Business Research, 58*(11), 1583–1589.	The article focuses on the combined and interactive effects of olfactory and musical stimuli on individuals' evaluations. Investigating the effects of Christmas scent and Christmas music in a store environment, the study finds that the combined effect is positive, while incongruent effects may even be negative.

6.5 Implications of Different Modes for Strategic Research

The acknowledgement of a variety of modes has substantial potential for research on organizations in the strategic tradition. Existing research clearly shows that modes differ in their specific impact with regard to speed, transmission of information, and memorability. Insights in cognitive psychology substantiate such findings and may be a useful source for theorizing the particular cognitive impact of texts drawing on different modes. However, existing research also shows that, in order to arrive at holistic understandings, the purely cognitive layer of perception and processing of modes needs to be complemented by more semiotic and cultural explanations.

This makes research using a strategic approach a sophisticated endeavour. Essentially, researchers need to generate an understanding of the cognitive aspects of each mode as well as of its culturally shaped potential for meaning construction. Jancsary et al. (2018) suggest the existence of 'modal registers', culturally and institutionally bounded repositories of meaning tied to particular modes. Such registers manifest metafunctions (Halliday & Hasan, 1985; Kress & van Leeuwen, 2006) and, accordingly, also provide specific potentials for addressing audiences. Further work is needed to tease apart the semiotic resources and affordances provided by different modes.

It is equally difficult to disentangle cognitive and cultural elements of audience impact, if such elements can even be understood as separate, that is, if cognition is actually independent from cultural factors. Studies such as the eye-tracking research discussed above suggest a relative independence in which the constraints of the text's design interact with the goals and interest of readers or viewers. Cognition has interrelated with semiotic research in other ways as well, for instance in Forceville's work on metaphors in pictorial advertising (Forceville, 1996), which is based on the cognitive metaphor theory of Lakoff and Johnson (1980). Beyond the visual, Graakjær (2012) has analysed the role of music in Abercrombie & Fitch fashion stores in London and Copenhagen. This study combined musical analysis with a cognitive approach using Fauconnier and Turner's (2002) conceptual blending theory to explain how customers' experience of the various modes in this shop (which also include perfume and dance) are interlinked to form a concept of what Abercrombie & Fitch stands for and have a 'psychobiological' effect of rhythmical attunement to the shopping experience. A metafunctionally based analysis of advertising music can be found in Wingstedt (2017).

6.6 Specific Challenges and Opportunities Regarding Multimodality

In contrast to the practice approach, research in the strategic tradition can build on an advanced set of methods for disentangling the impact of individual modes in a specific orchestration. Strategic research therefore provides a unique opportunity to isolate the effects of individual modes and investigate how their combination changes overall interpretations and impact, and how audiences integrate information from multiple modes cognitively and interpretively. A core challenge, however, remains how to artificially disentangle and isolate modes for the use in such experimental designs. As the study of Scott and Vargas (2007) has shown, even written verbal text has an inherently visual component through typography. Spoken text, on the other hand, combines verbal and aural elements. Disentangling modes, accordingly, is a difficult endeavour that may require sophisticated methodological designs.

It is characteristic of the strategic approach that it focuses on intentional semiotic strategies when it studies the production of multimodal texts and artefacts, and on psychological processes when it studies their reception. This is so in scholarly work as well as in accounts by practitioners. Jackson (2003) describes how his company Sonic Branding (now part of Cutting Edge Commercial), when designing sonic logos, uses an explicit semiotic strategy, starting with the meanings to be expressed and then matching these with musical attributes and intertextual references. In one case, the idea of 'soft technology' was expressed by 'contemporary synthesized drum loops', as familiar from drum and bass music, but played by traditional African drums "to soften things up and add some humanity", and the idea of 'heritage' was expressed by using a string section, referencing the kind of classical music "traditionally used in commercials for banks and insurance companies", but adding synthesized textures to give it an "electronic edge and an unexpected bit of interest" (Jackson, 2003, p. 119). When it comes to reception, psychological terms are introduced. According to Heath (2001) actors rarely use 'active' processing (i.e., actively interpreting stimuli), but rather rely on 'automatic' or 'shallow' forms of processing working at semi-conscious or subconscious levels. The same contrast characterizes scholarly research. Semiotics deals with the conscious meaning-making processes of textual production, and psychology with psychological processes and emotive, rather than rational responses. This ultimately indexes the continuing prevalence of strategic manipulation in contemporary persuasive communication.

7 The Dialogical Approach

7.1 Core Ideas

While in the archaeological and the practice approach it is primarily the researcher who interprets multimodal artefacts that occur 'naturally' (or their handling, respectively), researchers in a dialogical approach use multimodal artefacts to engage in a conversation with actors in the field, that is, artefacts are either brought into or constructed during a research interview to elicit different and richer responses from interviewees, and to gain insights into their life-worlds, experiences, and identities. The conceptual reason for this is the idea that different modes have different potentials for expressing meanings related to particular life-spheres. For instance, aspects of identity that are strongly tied to space and the physical environment can be more precisely communicated through visual than through verbal means (Shortt, 2015; for a more detailed discussion of this study, see further below). Accordingly, by focusing on spoken and written externalizations only, researchers miss large parts of the life-worlds of field actors. Dialogical research utilizing multiple modes, in contrast, allows for communication through multiple senses (Wilhoit, 2017).

The dialogical approach is different from the archaeological approach in that multimodal artefacts are not seen as traces of social meanings, but as 'triggers' for the *in situ* construction of such meaning in interactions between researchers and field actors. As such, the meanings revealed by interviews are more subjective, depending on how interviewees relate images to subjective experiences and understandings. However, by using the same artefacts as cues for larger sets of interviews, shared meaning structures can still be revealed. Similarly to the practice approach, multimodal data in the dialogical approach are often produced by field actors themselves. However, unlike in a practice approach, such production is prompted by researchers, and the use of these artefacts happens in research situations (primarily interviews) instead of everyday organizational life. The dialogical approach is also different from the strategic approach. Although both are interested in how specific multimodal artefacts impact on the meaning constructions of particular individuals, the dialogical approach is more interested in the construction of individual and social meanings, and less in the cognitive impact of artefacts. It is primarily concerned with getting access to deeper levels of consciousness—rather than learning how to best manipulate. Accordingly, interviewees often produce the artefacts that they then talk about themselves. As seen in our discussion of the strategic approach, however, the two traditions can be fruitfully combined to gain more complete insights into the impact of multimodal artefacts.

Especially critical research in a dialogical tradition is primarily concerned with the voice of marginalized groups, and how research can be sure to capture 'silenced' discourses. This is achieved, on the one hand, by paying attention to narratives that are not represented in the (dominant) verbal mode, and on the other, by systematically enabling actors in the field to share their experiences in a multimodal way. This means that multimodal forms of interviewing are often more successful in revealing discourses that otherwise would remain hidden.

7.2 Aspects of Organization

The dialogical approach shares a variety of research interests with the strategic approach. It is also focused on the subjective constitution of social meaning and on the sensemaking of individuals. Sensemaking involves "labeling and categorizing to stabilize the streaming of experience" (Weick, Sutcliffe, & Obstfeld, 2005, p. 411). Cues for sensemaking are provided by the environment, which is itself selectively bracketed and enacted. Multimodal artefacts can both be triggers and results of sensemaking efforts. They are triggers when researchers present field actors with certain photographs and ask them to relate the visual cues to their lived experience. They are results of sensemaking when researchers ask field actors to capture their experiences and identities in multimodal artefacts such as photographs and/or drawings. Accordingly, interviews that allow interviewees to draw on a variety of modes allow for more complex sensemaking and provide better insights into the ways in which interviewees construct meaning.

The dialogical approach also has a pronounced interest in aspects of power. First, power structures are often difficult to explicitly articulate, but they reside in and are materialized in visible elements of organizations (office design, architecture, business attire, etc.). Multimodal interviews provide opportunity to mobilize sign systems other than the verbal to bring sedimented power structures to the fore. Second, verbal literacy is often unevenly distributed among different groups in the organization. Multimodal interviews allow less verbally literate groups to still express their experiences and make them available to analysis (Warren, 2005). Third, some more embodied aspects of the organizational world are hard to verbalize, which often excludes workers on the shop floor from having their experiences acknowledged in research (Slutskaya, Simpson, & Hughes, 2012). Multimodal interviews provide resources for expressing more embodied experiences, thus empowering physical workers. A central interest of dialogical research, accordingly, is to study how marginalized groups in and around organizations may resort to modes other than the verbal to voice their grievances and express themselves. One distinct strength of a dialogical approach for research on organizations is therefore to surface meanings and alternative voices that would be neglected if only verbal text was included in the research data.

A second focus concerns the situatedness of individuals within organizations and institutions. Dialogical approaches to multimodal data are therefore interesting for research studying how institutional and societal meanings are drawn upon, enacted, and adapted by individuals (sometimes called a micro-foundations approach to institutions). Since social structure is instantiated through individual and collective practices, and social meanings are constituted in subjective consciousness, dialogical approaches provide glimpses into the instantiation of institutions and social structure on the individual level. They show, for instance, which multimodal registers (Jancsary et al., 2018) individuals draw upon in talking about their identities and organizational life. Drawings of organizations (Vince & Broussine, 1996) do not only provide insights into psychological aspects, but also about individuals' embeddedness in broader institutional structures. Metaphors, for instance, can be understood as particular invocations of institutions (Powell & Colyvas, 2008). Dialogical approaches are a specifically suitable way to explore in more depth the affective and emotional aspects of institutions (Creed, Hudson, Okhuysen, & Smith-Crowe, 2014; Voronov & Vince, 2012). Dialogical research has found that the use of multimodal artefacts in interview situations can surface additional insights into the identities of organizational members (Bryans & Mavin, 2006; Shortt & Warren, 2012), as well as aspects of disorganization and disidentification (Stiles, 2011). Research acknowledges that organizational members construct their identities *vis-à-vis* their material (e.g., visual and spatial) environment (Shortt, 2015). Such material and spatial aspects of identity work in organizations are often lost in 'pure' talk. They can be revealed, however, by cueing identity discourse through visuals and other multimodal artefacts.

Finally, research in the dialogical tradition also shows that sensemaking and sensegiving in organizations has aesthetic and affective dimensions (Venkatraman & Nelson, 2008). Such affective and aesthetic elements—for instance, regarding organizational change (Vince & Broussine, 1996)—can often be expressed more easily through modes other than the verbal.

7.3 Methods

Different forms of photo elicitation or photo interviews are the most common methods in the toolbox of the dialogical approach. Ray and Smith (2012) provide a systematic overview of photo elicitation techniques. They suggest that a first decision concerns the selection of photographs for discussion during the interview. One option is that the researchers themselves review and select photos and/or images and sometimes organize them into themes or chronologies. This allows researchers greater opportunity for preparation and interviewees greater guidance. The downside is that the selection of researchers may miss photographs that are meaningful to organizational members, which means that some part of their lived experience is left out of the interview. Another option, therefore, is to let participants decide which photographs to discuss. This allows participants to reject photographs they do not want to discuss and more strongly supports structuring the interview according to participants' relevance structures. Accordingly, it is more likely that unexpected understandings emerge. However, it gives researchers less opportunity for preparation, which may hinder their ability to deal with the emerging findings. Additionally, it allows participants to reject photographs that might be crucial for the research project. A third option is to let participants review and discuss photographs before the interview, which means that the interview is about their written notes rather than their immediate reaction to the photographs. The advantage is that it allows for more deliberate and reflective processing of photographs and greater synthesis of interpretations. The main disadvantage is the substantial loss of researcher control, and the ability of participants to 'spin' and tailor their responses rather than respond spontaneously and authentically.

A second decision relates to the participant structure of the interviews. One option is to conduct interviews with one person at a time, which allows for less controlled and potentially more emotional reactions. Alternatively, focus groups can be assembled to discuss photographs among each other and with the researchers. This can provide more depth to the discussion, since individual interpretations and narratives can be challenged and/or further developed by the group. Additionally, group discussions may create additional awareness of each other's lived experiences, which enables a more complex picture of the research phenomenon. However, status differences among group members may inhibit open discussion, and transcriptions of audiotapes becomes more challenging with multiple speakers.

The third decision, finally, concerns the role of the researchers in the process. They can take a guiding role, leading the interview and building on what participants have contributed, which shows interest, lowers perceived power distance, and allows for instant clarification of emerging questions. However, this may influence the results substantially, as participants may interpret what is important to the researchers and adapt their responses accordingly. Alternatively, researchers can also remain mostly inactive, providing photographs and initial instruction, but staying largely silent while the photos are being discussed. This avoids biasing the research, but it prevents probing responses and clarifying open questions.

Whereas most of the existing discussion uses images for elicitation, other artefacts, music, or scent could equally be used in such research designs. The three decisions outlined by Ray and Smith (2012) are of a more generally methodological character and therefore apply to dialogical multimodal research independent of the specific modes used to trigger responses.

7.4 Exemplary Studies

The study of Shortt (2015) on the lived experiences of hairdressers at work centrally draws on the meaning of spaces—and specifically 'liminal' spaces—for their identities. Space, however, is difficult to discuss in verbal interviews, as spaces have a vast variety of characteristics, and involve embodied experiences and relations between actors and objects that are hard to verbalize. Accordingly, the use of visual data was crucial to the study, since visuals are able to provide much more vivid insights into the characteristics of spaces. Specifically, Shortt (2015) employed participant-led-photography for data collection, asking each participant in the study to take 12 images of spaces that they considered meaningful and relevant for their professional identities. Subsequently, these images served as a basis for photo elicitation interviews. Data analysis started with photographer-led meaning attribution, which meant that the researcher categorized images according to the meanings participants assigned to them during the interviews. From this, central themes emerged, which were gradually abstracted further to reveal the meanings structured in the field. Finally, the researcher also conducted an analysis of visual content which enriched insights gained from the interpretations provided by participants. Through the specific resources provided by the photographs, Shortt (2015) was able to identify "privacy and 'being hidden'", "informal staffrooms", and "inspiration" as the most important aspects of space for the lived experiences of hairdressers. This stressed the crucial importance of liminal spaces that are not commonly considered as central for organizations. However, in Shortt's study, these spaces became safe havens, or in the words of the author, "transitory dwelling spaces" that centrally impacted on the identities of employees.

Diem-Wille (2001), researching what determines the ambition of top managers, used narrative interviews to probe their self-image and self-esteem, and their professional career and personality development, but

Table 7.1 Selection of Further Readings (Dialogical Approach)

Article (in Alphabetical Order)	Brief Description
Oliver, D., & Roos, J. (2007). Beyond text: Constructing organizational identity multimodally. *British Journal of Management*, 18(4), 342–358.	The study explores multiple intelligences, emotions, and individual/collective identity representations related to organizational identities. The authors rely on a dialogical design involving structured interventions that allow management teams to construct representations of identities using construction toy materials.
Riach, K., & Warren, S. (2015). Smell organization: Bodies and corporeal porosity in office work. *Human Relations*, 68(5), 789–809.	Exploring the embodied lived experiences of work, the study focuses on bodily integrity in organizational experience. The authors conduct 'smell interviews' that prompt interviewees to talk about their experience of smell at work, combined with the provision of paper strips impregnated with office smells.
Stiles, D. R. (2011). Disorganization, disidentification and ideological fragmentation: Verbal and pictorial evidence from a British business school. *Culture and Organization*, 17(1), 5–30.	The article focuses on processes of disorganization and disidentification on the basis of discourse analysis and social psychology. Asking participants to draw pictures of the organization's 'personality', the author explores ideological tensions between managerial and professional values in a British business school.
Warren, S. (2005). Photography and voice in critical qualitative management research. *Accounting, Auditing & Accountability Journal*, 18(6), 861–882.	The objective of this article is to explore different ways in which photography affords more voice to research participants in management research. The author presents and discusses a variety of photo-centred methodological designs within the dialogical approach.
Wilhoit, E. D. (2017). Photo and video methods in organizational and managerial communication research. *Management Communication Quarterly*, 31(3), 447–466.	The author outlines methods that utilize photo and video to structure the communication between researchers and participants. Videos are especially useful for Participant Viewpoint Ethnography (PVE), as they provide naturalistic data and enable reflexive participant interpretations of their experience.

also asked them to make drawings to dig at deeper, less conscious motivations, and suggesting quite specific topics: "You have described your family situation in words. Could you describe them in a drawing? Imagine that a magician came and bewitched your family. Could you draw what happened then?" (Diem-Wille, 2001, p. 129). She then analysed these drawings in detail and also discussed them with her interviewees. The CEO of a global IT company, for instance, drew himself as a prince on a throne, yet with a pacifier in his mouth, no arms, and his legs in a sack, and with two women dominating him, his mother who had a successful career, and his grandmother who looked after him—his father had left the family. Discussing this drawing brought out the conflict between identification and competition with his mother that had dominated his youth, and the way he had eventually resolved this conflict by moving to another country, thus escaping his mother, while at the same time working in the same profession as she did and fulfilling her wish to be successful in this.

7.5 Implications of Different Modes for Dialogical Research

For dialogical research, modes are resources to be made available to participants to create richer accounts of their experiences and sensemaking, and enable more comprehensive understandings. Most centrally, such an approach builds on the idea that societies are stratified, and different (sub)cultures vary in terms of their modal literacies (Slutskaya et al., 2012; Warren, 2002). While it is common knowledge in social science that participants in interviews need to be addressed in a way that they can understand and relate to, the use of different modes in doing so is still in its infancy. Photo elicitation techniques (Ray & Smith, 2012) have started to find entrance into organization research, but other modes are generally available. There are professions in which smell and scent are as powerful forms of expression as speech (Gümüsay, 2012; Islam et al., 2016), and actors may want to utilize the respective semiotic resources available to them for transmitting their experiences (Riach & Warren, 2015). The same, of course, is true for other modes like sound, or specific modal resources, such as colour, layout, and gesture.

The distinct advantage of dialogical research as compared to archaeological, practice, or strategic approaches is that interpretations are co-produced between researchers and participants. This means that literacy needs to rest, first and foremost, with the participants—although, of course, a certain degree of modal literacy on the part of the researchers is necessary in order for dialogue to unfold. However, such interviews are, most of the time, inherently multimodal, since there is a constant translation between the verbal and other modes during the dialogue. Such translation is primarily facilitated by participants themselves, as they are supposed to be the experts both in the phenomenal area and in the particular mode. Despite the fact that information may become 'lost in translation' when talking about smell, colour, or photography, the physical artefact that serves as trigger and/or product of the interview remains available as a material reference against which interpretations will be constantly evaluated.

7.6 Specific Challenges and Opportunities Regarding Multimodality

Multimodality in dialogical approaches means that a combination of modes is utilized to provide additional resources in conversations with field actors. In contrast to the strategic approach, where the precise impact of different semiotic resources on the audience's cognitive and affective processing is key, the dialogical approach is only interested in triggering and eliciting sensemaking efforts that would not be achieved in purely verbal interviews. Hence teasing apart the concrete effects of individual modes with the at least implicit aim of being able to produce them strategically is here not as important as endowing interview situations with semiotic resources that allow participants to draw on all kinds of meaning-making required to transmit their meaningful experiences in a comprehensive and comprehensible way.

We wish to illustrate the potential power of such multimodal dialogical approaches by briefly discussing a methodology suggested by Becker and Burke (2012) for qualitative data generation and analysis. The authors implicitly acknowledge the power of multimodality when they start their article with a quote from W. E. Holmes (2005):

> You cannot get the full effect of what happened [at the South Canyon Fire] and what it was like until you've walked the ground, felt the steep terrain, seen the vegetation, experienced the heat and had the wind in your face. The whole scenario seemed so different than what I had read.
> (W. E. Holmes, 2005; quoted in Becker & Burke, 2012)

Staff rides for research purposes require either visits at original (historical) sites, or the recreation of such sites and re-enactment of events. Since Becker and Burke (2012) have analyses of historical events in mind when they discuss their methodology, they propose starting with comprehensive research about the characteristics of the site as well as the chronology of events. We suggest that smaller-scale variants of this method can be created, and that it can, in principle, also be used to research ongoing events. Minimally, the principles of the 'staff ride' could simply mean that interviews are conducted at the workplace rather than in a separate office, so that all semiotic resources relevant to the narrative of the participant are readily available, both to elicit experiences and to point them out to researchers.

Becker and Burke's (2012) methodology revolves around three distinct stages. In a first stage, a preliminary study provides a systematic review of all relevant information. This stage is used to familiarize the researcher with the context and form preliminary hypotheses. The second phase is the field visit, in which researchers also include all kinds of other participants, so that the sites and events can be experienced and made sense of together. Researchers then facilitate dialogue with participants selected according to expertise or previous involvement and interest in the event. As the authors outline, "the field visit is rich with respect to the discussion of situated action, with ride participants keenly aware of the varied material landscapes and ecological processes" (Becker & Burke, 2012, p. 321). This is then used to enhance the learning of researchers and to refine and alter interpretations from the preliminary study. Finally, in a third phase, the previous phases are integrated. Again, this can be organized as a form of 'debriefing' through interviews with participants.

We see methodologies drawing on similar principles as 'staff rides' as excellent opportunities to harness the multimodal character of the social world for research purposes. Interviews usually constitute a disruption from the concrete experiences of field actors, and most of the time they prompt participants to reflect on, and therefore abstract from, their concrete embodied experiences. Multimodal interviews would do the exact opposite—they need to maximize the immersion of both participants and researchers in the multimodality of concrete situations and encourage them to draw on visual, olfactory, spatial, and other resources available to them in their physical environment. While it is common in ethnographic research to talk to field actors in spaces relevant to their work and their organizational role, the multimodal aspects of these situations are rarely utilized explicitly and used for sensemaking. We call for a more conscious engagement with multiple modalities and stress their generative potential for eliciting richer accounts and findings.

8 The Documenting Approach

8.1 Core Ideas

The documenting approach is, so far, the least explicitly discussed in organization and management research, but it is nevertheless commonly used in research on organizations and organizing. It also has a long tradition in visual anthropology and ethnography (Collier & Collier, 1986). Much like the dialogical approach, multimodal artefacts are seen not only as data sources to be interpreted, but also as integral tools in the research process itself. More specifically—and in contrast to the dialogical approach—multimodal artefacts are created by researchers to either enrich data from other sources and enable a more sensually complete capturing of organizational life (see also Kunter & Bell, 2006; Ray & Smith, 2012), to support theory building (Swedberg, 2016), to render interpretations more transparent and facilitate the holistic presentation of results (Czarniawska, 2010), or to present findings, for instance, in the form of models (as has become almost 'standard' in articles that develop theory), diagrams (Kvåle, 2016; Ledin & Machin, 2016), photo essays (Jewitt, van Leeuwen, Triggs, & Longford, 2011; Preston & Young, 2000), or non-linear multimedia publications (Goldberg & Hristova, 2007).

What this short overview shows is that multimodality is not only a way of better understanding social and organizational life and its manifold phenomena, but can also help create better science, since modes have specific affordances (see, for instance, Kress, 2010; Meyer et al., 2018). As the documenting approach does not—in contrast to the previous four approaches—provide a specific lens on organizations and organizing, but rather supports the research process, the following sub-section will address three aspects of doing research that may gain from multimodality: (a) data collection, (b) data analysis and theory development, and (c) presentation of findings.

8.2 Aspects of Research

The creation of multimodal artefacts by researchers is already a helpful strategy in the *data collection* stage of empirical research, especially when ethnographic research designs are pursued. Taking visual images of the research sites, for instance, creates more holistic impressions of the phenomenon under scrutiny and helps researchers record their impressions in a more vivid way than purely verbal field notes may achieve. Further, taking visual field notes in this way helps to later enrich ethnographic studies with additional photo elicitation interviews (see the dialogical approach above). Visual field notes are therefore useful tools for 'returning' to the research site in later stages of analysis, and as triggers for conversations with field actors (Buchanan, 1998). Often, it is not easy or even impossible to gain repeated access to certain research sites, and visual notes can remedy this problem. Of course, video ethnography is even richer in its documenting potential. Video provides a richness of information that forces researchers to rigorously select what to focus on during analysis, lest they be overwhelmed by the sheer volume of potential data (Hindmarsh & Llewellyn, 2018; Hassard et al., 2018). Another word of caution is also in order. Although it may seem that photographs and videos from the research site provide neutral, objective, and complete 'souvenirs' for later reuse in the research project, researchers must not forget that these artefacts are always incomplete in that they provide only certain perspectives, frozen in space and time. A photograph always misses more than it shows, and videos are taken from a particular angle, with a focus on particular events. Focusing on what has been recorded during the research visit therefore reifies earlier impressions and may lead to losing information that researchers experienced during the ethnography but did not record on photograph or film. It is therefore advisable to combine field notes using different modes.

Whereas the use of multimodal artefacts in data collection is comparably well documented, and there are some guidelines for good scientific conduct, the use of visual and multimodal 'crutches' for *data analysis and theory development* are much less discussed. Multimodal artefacts, particularly visual and material ones, may support the interpretation of data in that they make preliminary findings tangible and materialize them in a way that facilitates both material permanence and malleability. In the simplest way, drawing research or theory sketches (Swedberg, 2016) to record early ideas helps communicate these ideas to co-authors in a way that is not yet immutable, but has a certain permanence. Collier (2001), in an excellent paper on photo elicitation, advocates the use of 'photomaps', mounting a large number of photos of, for instance, an urban neighbourhood, on a board in systematic ways, so as to discover patterns, both through 'rapid open viewing' and through structured analysis. He also advocates team analysis which allows for "comparing views and linking them to identifiable phenomena in the visual records" (Collier, 2001, p. 54). Visual text is also much better able to capture spatial properties of ideas, which helps to communicate and materialize relational properties of different parts of data, or of different elements of an emerging theory. Simple ways of materializing data (e.g., printing preliminary categories and cutting them into rearrangeable bits) help to constantly 'play around' with different avenues of clustering and interpreting findings (see also Ravasi, 2017). Of course, the digitalization of data opens up vast potential, too. Mind-mapping techniques can be used digitally as well as analogically and are quite frequently used in actual research practice. A rather novel way of using visuals in ethnographic research is suggested by Stowell and Warren (2018), who utilize their visual field notes to conduct photo interviews with the researcher conducting the participative ethnography. This allows for auto-ethnographic theming, which is then used to sensitize the researchers towards the embodied experiences of field actors.

Finally, multimodality is also an excellent resource for improving the *presentation of findings* to audiences. Different graphs and diagrams as ways of stressing the conceptual and analytical aspects of data (Kress & van Leeuwen, 2006, see also the chapter on diagrams in this volume, Chapter 11) are commonly used throughout the sciences. Lately, some researchers have utilized photography to provide audiences with more direct and holistic access to their data (see, for instance, Czarniawska, 2010). Some academic journals (most notably the *Academy of Management Discoveries*) are experimenting with novel ways of writing research articles, including the option to include video. The use of multimodal artefacts to communicate research findings and interpretation procedures is an excellent way to make analyses and findings more transparent to audiences, which increases the quality and impact of research. However, some challenges need to be considered. First, privacy regulations and copyright laws may be a serious hindrance to making visual data available (Bell & Davison, 2013; Meyer et al., 2013). Researchers are well advised to clarify early on which opportunities exist to print and publish visual material from their study. Second, the same limitations as regarding the use of multimodal artefacts for data collection also apply to data presentation. Whereas visuals and video are seemingly more 'objective' than verbal descriptions of researchers, such impression is misleading. Visuals also afford rhetorical usage to stress aspects of the data that fit the desired narrative. Transparency regarding the process according to which visuals were selected to illustrate findings is therefore paramount from an ethical perspective.

8.3 Exemplary Studies

There is a relative paucity of research in organization and management studies that openly accounts for the use of multimodal artefacts to document research. An often referred to example for research in this tradition is the study of Buchanan (1998). In this study, the author reconstructs the patient trail in a hospital, beginning with the referral to a specialist and continuing through the stages of admission, treatment, and discharge. The aim of the study is to achieve a systematic process mapping of what is happening on this patient trail. To do so, Buchanan (1998) applies a multi-method ethnography, which combines document analysis with prolonged periods of intensive observation, 'mystery shopping', as well as open-ended interviews. The study is of particular interest for illustrating the documenting approach, since the author collected a variety of verbal as well as visual data. Visual data consisted primarily of approximately 150 photographs that document different stages in the whole process. Apart from using these photographs as visual field notes, Buchanan (1998) also later employed them in photo elicitation sessions, which meant that various staff groups were confronted with researcher-taken photographs in the open-ended interviews. As a complement to his empirical article, Buchanan (2001) provides a methodological manuscript in which he elaborates and reflects extensively on the use of visual methods. He suggests that the use of visual artefacts enabled richer conversations with field actors (which relates to work in the dialogical tradition), but also allowed for deeper insights into organizational processes, as the photographs taken during the study helped capture richer details of the research setting than verbal field notes would have afforded. He also contends that these photographs revealed insights that did not emerge from the oral interviews, and therefore allowed for confronting field actors with aspects of organizational processes that they themselves were not personally involved in. In addition to capturing and preserving information for the researcher, the photo material, accordingly, was also employed to create additional transparency about the processes for the participants in the study.

Researcher-taken photographs play a slightly different role in Czarniawska's (2010) study of an urban recovery program. Here, the author aims at following the 'chains of translations' from a political decision to their actual unfolding in the city, which she finds to be difficult due to different factors making accounts less transparent. To do so, Czarniawska (2010, p. 420) conceptualizes city management as an "action net"—that is, "a set of actions accomplished within a seamless web of inter-organizational networks, wherein city authorities constitute just one point of entry and by no means provide a map of the whole terrain". Of particular interest for the documenting approach is her decision to present a narrative in form of a photo-reportage alongside her analysis and findings. This photo-reportage, in essence, constitutes a parallel narrative that illustrates parts of the study in vivid imagery, for instance, a board explaining proper behaviour on a bicycle–pedestrian track that has been vandalized by multiple layers of graffiti, or a photograph of a specific part of this track where fences preventing reeds from overgrowing were supposed to be placed. In her discussion, Czarniawska (2010) explains that she sees visual accounts such as her own photo-reportage as one possible way in which researchers can act as 'translators'. She calls for the research community to become multilingual and abandon their specialized discourse, which she sees as a prerequisite for making multiple communities speak to each other.

Unlike photography, video not only allows the visual recording of real-time processes, but it also records sound. In his studies of the passing on of information about patients during shift changes in the emergency departments of large hospitals, Iedema (2015) uses a 'video-reflexive' method in which the research problem is first collaboratively determined by the researcher and the participating clinicians. The clinicians' work practices are then recorded on video, and the researcher asks the participants for 'hot feedback' immediately after the recording. Next, the videos are analysed, and the analysis is presented to the participants in the form of clips of up to 4 minutes, showing, for instance, moments of vagueness or omission. These clips are then discussed with the participants who often develop proposals for change during these discussions. Video is therefore used at different stages of the process, for data collection as well as for presenting the analysis to the participants. This, Iedema stresses, makes the analysis more vivid and accessible than is the case with the way researchers usually frame and present their data, and results in a "less predictable and more exciting research process" that "opens research up for different views and expectations" (Iedema, 2015, p. 196).

8.4 Implications of Different Modes for Documenting Research

The potentials for different modes in the documenting approach are closely tied to their different ways of meaning-making and meaning representation (Kress, 2010; Kress & van Leeuwen, 2001). Meyer et al. (2018) disentangle such potential of the verbal and visual mode by suggesting that texts drawing from the two modes provide distinct affordances in the sense of potentials for meaning construction that need to be realized between producers and consumers of texts in particular social situations. The core of such a perspective is that different problems require the use of different modes, depending on the potentials the modes offer. We wish to illustrate the power of the visual mode for both data analysis and the presentation of findings on the basis of a recent research project that one of the authors was personally involved in (Jancsary, 2013).

In this study, the author was interested in the latent understandings of 'leadership' as manifested in written leadership principles of companies. Whereas the study analysed purely verbal text, multimodality nevertheless featured heavily during data analysis and presentation of findings. Methodologically, the author was interested in the implicit (and often incomplete) arguments behind specific statements about leader–employee relationships. As an intermediary step, leader and employee roles were reconstructed based on the actions that leaders and employees were supposed to perform. To support the classification of actions into roles and further connect typical actions into specific forms of leader-employee relationships, the author created print-outs of subject–verb–object relations on pieces of paper that he could physically rearrange (see Figure 8.1a). This facilitated the interpretation and discussion of the data in a team (two

Table 8.1 Selection of Further Readings (Documenting Approach)

Article (in Alphabetical Order)	Brief Description
Powell, W. W., Oberg, A., Korff, V., Oelberger, K., & Kloos, K. (2017). Institutional analysis in a digital era: Mechanisms and methods to understand emerging fields. In: G. Krücken, C. Mazza, R. Meyer, & P. Walgenbach (Eds.). *New themes in institutional analysis* (pp. 305–344). Cheltenham, UK & Northampton, MA, Edward Elgar.	The article is a good example of how visualization can offer richer and novel ways of presenting complex data and findings. The authors suggest circular network graphs to visualize mechanisms of field emergence based on relational features of the world wide web.
Ravasi, D. (2017). Visualizing our way through theory building. *Journal of Management Inquiry*, 26(2), 240–243.	This essay offers a pointed reflection on the potential of visualization techniques in doing research, especially on how visualization can strengthen the analysis of qualitative data.
Rowley-Jolivet, E. (2004). Different visions, different visuals: A social semiotic analysis of field-specific visual composition in scientific conference presentations. *Visual communication*, 3(2), 145–175.	Based on an analysis of conference presentations, the study inquires how visual resources create cohesion, logical relations, discourse structure and rhetorical claims. The author shows that different disciplines exploit such resources in distinct ways.
Swedberg, R. (2016). Can you visualize theory? On the use of visual thinking in theory pictures, theorizing diagrams, and visual sketches. *Sociological Theory*, 34(3), 250–275.	Although not directly related to organization research, this article provides interesting insights into how visualizations like theory pictures, diagrams, and sketches may improve theory crafting through visual thinking. The author suggests that this may require the development of new visual conventions.
Toraldo, M. L., Islam, G., & Mangia, G. (2018). Modes of knowing: Video research and the problem of elusive knowledges. *Organizational Research Methods*, 21(2), 438–465.	Starting from the main argument that video-based methodologies offer unique potential for multimodal organization research, the authors discuss how video may be able to capture and translate embodied, tacit and aesthetic knowledge (what they call 'elusive' knowledges) into discursive and textual forms.

people not involved in the research project joined for interpretation). The material properties of the print-outs allowed for shifting them back and forth according to emerging conceptual explanations, and photographs were taken whenever critical decisions were made, to enable a return to previous stages if needed. Photographs were then imported into an image-editing software, where the emerging interpretations were extended, and overlaps between types could be visualized in the style of Venn diagrams (see Figure 8.1b). Eventually, topoi and relationship types were plotted into a network-like diagram in PowerPoint and used to 'map' the different elements in relationship to each other (for the first draft of the map, see Figure 8.1c). The final plot was both a tool for data analysis as well as the presentation of findings, since the visualization of the network afforded a spatial representation of the data structure that facilitated the communication of the central findings to the readers. It was the specific affordance of the visual mode to present information in a spatial and relational way (Kress & van Leeuwen, 2006; Meyer et al., 2018) that made it attractive as a resource for this specific research project.

The distinct advantages of presenting research findings multimodally are discussed by Jakubowicz and van Leeuwen (2010) through a comparison between a traditional article and a non-linear online publication on the same issue (Hurricane Katrina) by the same author (David Theo Goldberg, an American sociologist). The multimodality afforded by online publishing not only adds an affective dimension, but also strengthens the presentation and analysis of the data. To start with the affective dimension, as Katrina is introduced, readers/viewers hear the sound of violently whooshing water and see a dramatic darkening of the screen. Later, African-American music underscores the plight of the black population of New Orleans. But digital publication can also combine incisive argument with much more extensive and detailed archival and documentary evidence than can be included in traditional linear texts, which often have to argue their point on the basis of much more selective and restrictive sets of examples. It can simultaneously provide a foreground and a background, for instance to ensure that a given argument is read against the background of a specific historical, political or social context. And it can make use of typography to provide elements of a text with specific textual identities, such as 'main argument' or 'supplementary material', and mark the modality of textual elements as, for instance, a piece of political activism (through typography reminiscent of handset activist leaflets) or as piece of historical evidence (sepia).

8.5 Specific Challenges and Opportunities Regarding Multimodality

Video is arguably the most clearly multimodal artefact that can facilitate and support research in a documenting approach, at least in terms of data collection and partially also data presentation, provided the format of publication supports it. Lately, there has been a renewed interest in the use

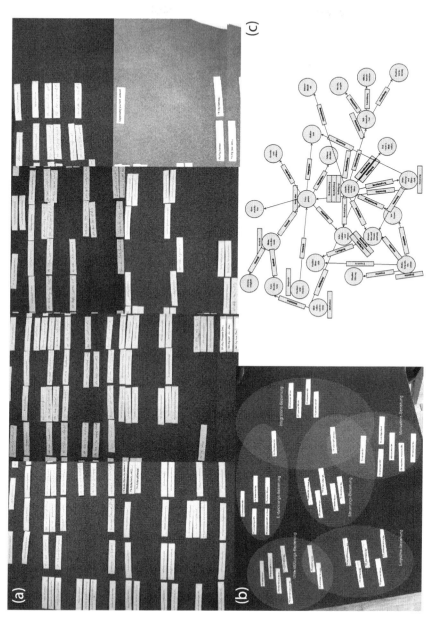

Figure 8.1 Illustration of Multimodal Support in the Research Process: (a) Arranging Print-Outs on the Floor; (b) Enhancing Photographs Through Software; (c) Creating a Conceptual Map

and potential of video and video analysis in organization research (see, for instance, the recent special issue on video in *Organizational Research Methods* in 2018). Christianson (2018) provides a literature review of articles published in top-tier organizational journals focused on publications where video was central to the research design. He finds a strong upward trend in the use of video over the years, including the following categories: video as detailed and permanent record, video as a way for examining non-verbal behaviours, video as a way for studying the temporal aspects of interaction, and video as a way of studying multimodality. All of these topics pertain to the documenting approach as outlined here.

The advantages of video for capturing organizational reality are manifold. Toraldo et al. (2018), for instance, outline that video allows for integrating what they call 'elusive knowledges', that is, tacit, aesthetic, and embodied aspects of organizational life. Iedema (2015) makes a similar point when he says that video reveals "facets of practice of which practitioners and patients themselves were not necessarily aware, or no longer consciously aware" (Iedema, 2015, p. 198). Hindmarsh and Llewellyn (2018) add that video recordings capture a 'bewildering' amount of detail. Congdon, Novack, and Goldin-Meadow (2018) particularly stress the ability of video documentation to capture small gestures, information that is often ignored in experimental research. In essence, this means that video documentation would also be a helpful complement to research in the strategic tradition (see above). However, there are also some voices arguing caution. Mengis, Nicolini, and Gorli (2018) show how video recording practices construct their subject matter in a particular way and are therefore far from being neutral ways of capturing reality. They illustrate how different views and angles in the recording of video privilege different understandings of space by directing the viewers' gaze. Additionally, Whiting, Symon, Roby, and Chamakiotis (2018) remind us that video research implies particular subject positions for researchers and participants and that these often involve tension and paradox.

However, even video cannot capture the complete multimodal experience of 'being in' a certain place at a certain time. As Becker and Burke (2012) remind us, researchers in the field are exposed to a plethora of sensory impressions, not all of which are consciously perceived. Scent, for instance, is a particularly subtle and ephemeral mode, and researchers could strive to find ways of preserving the smell of particular field locations. Materiality, as well, is only incompletely retained in video data: Only its visual aspects are captured, but not the feel of texture, or, for instance, the weight and stability of artefacts—all of which may play important roles in the field. Additionally, insights on the role of sound need to be extended, encompassing both a closer focus on ambient noise in the field (as there is never truly a complete absence of sound anywhere) and the potential of sound and music as facilitators of data interpretation and theory generation. So far, we have barely scratched the surface of how multimodality can support researchers in their work.

9 Summary: Towards Multi-Approach Studies in Multimodal Organization Research

We have discussed the different approaches to multimodal organization research separately, but it is clear that they need to be, and often are, combined. We have already seen several examples: for instance, the way in which Boeriis and Holsanova (2012) combine semiotic analysis and experimental research to empirically test semiotic constructs, or the way in which Iedema (2015) embeds the documentary approach (analysis presented in the form of video clips) in a dialogic approach (using these clips to elicit discussion). Shortt and Warren (2017), in a recent contribution to visual methodologies, combine the archaeological and the dialogical approaches in a method they call 'grounded visual pattern analysis'. Their intention is to integrate the strengths of the two approaches, namely a 'dialogic' commitment to the importance of meaning assignment by field actors and an 'archaeological' recognition that photographs are 'of' something, that is, that they contain sedimented social meaning. Their approach is sequential, meaning that the dialogical analysis comes first and is followed by archaeological analysis.

The key is to understand the limitations of each approach and the ways in which other approaches can be used to overcome these limitations. A project about PowerPoint presentations (Zhao et al., 2014) also used different approaches in a sequential method. First, PowerPoint itself was analysed, using the archaeological approach to ascertain its multimodal affordances and constraints. This established what you *can* (and cannot) do with PowerPoint, thus studying PowerPoint as a resource for multimodal meaning-making. Next, PowerPoint presentations were video recorded in corporate and educational settings, and these were analysed for the way in which they used the multimodal resources, again using the archaeological approach. Then the presenters were asked *why* they used the medium the way they did, and how they learned to use it in that way—questions which need the practice approach. In other words, the archaeological approach here set the stage for the practice approach, generating questions which it could not answer itself. Finally, analysis of historical sources was used to investigate strategic questions, questions of why PowerPoint was designed the way it is. This way of combining textual analysis, ethnography, and archival approaches is also explained in the first chapter of van Leeuwen (2005).

But it is equally possible to go the other way around. In a study of teddy bears, Caldas-Coulthard and van Leeuwen (2003) began with the practice approach, eliciting narratives of people's everyday experiences with their teddy bears. They then became curious about the similarities between these stories. A new question arose: What are the 'normative discourses' behind these stories? They then conducted an archaeological analysis of children's books with teddy bear characters and found these to have a limited number of plots, and as it turned out, these were more or less the same plots that were also enacted in the lives of the participants in their ethnographic research. So here the practice approach raised questions that could, in part, be answered by archaeological research, linking personal experiences to their cultural context. In short, in research designs of this kind, each approach, although yielding some findings itself, also generates further questions, which can only be answered by another approach. The lesson is that research should indeed be 'searching', an open-minded journey working with a wide set of methodological resources, rather than a mono-disciplinary approach in which research questions and data are determined before the journey has even begun. This approach is demonstrated by our case studies in Part III, which do not follow a standard method, but each uses the methodological resources we have described in this part of the book in specific flexible ways, adapting them to the topics and research questions which the various studies address.

We close Part II of this book with a general remark about the status of multimodal research in organization and management studies. Although the literature review across the five approaches is far from exhaustive, a clear tendency emerges. Despite a distinct widening of the research agenda, the visual and verbal modes are clearly dominant in the field. Other modes, like materiality and, increasingly, scent, are gaining ground, but are still confined to either specific approaches or specific research areas. Materiality research, for instance, is strongest in the practice approach, and scent is most elaborately theorized in marketing and consumer research. Moreover, studies relating to multiple modes simultaneously are still the exception rather than the rule. When multiple modes are studied in a single research project, designs are mostly comparative rather than integrative; it is most often the differences, rather than the synergies between modes that are stressed. In the terminology of Chapter 2, we can see that organization and management research has contributed strongly to the monomodal and polymodal research agenda, while more radically multimodal designs are still the exception. This is not to say that radical multimodality is inherently more valuable than polymodal approaches, but we do wish to encourage future research to address this gap. Across the five approaches, we have sketched the potentials and challenges of such a radically multi-disciplinary and multimodal understanding of organizations and organizing, and we hope to see more of it in the future.

Part III
Application

10 Introduction to Four Case Studies

In Part II, we have provided a detailed overview of fruitful intersections between organization studies and multimodality research. Furthermore, we have discussed in some detail the challenges and potential of in-depth multimodal research on organizations and organizing. Whereas Part II has been conceptualized as an overview that introduced a plethora of different studies from a 'bird's eye' point of view, Part III is meant to get into the 'nitty-gritty' of actually doing multimodal research on organizational issues and topics. In the following four chapters, we will introduce four cases that 'span' the space of both multimodality and organizations.

10.1 Case Selection

It has been our intention for Part III to illustrate multimodal research while covering as much ground as possible. The sampling of cases, accordingly, is meant to ensure that several types of communicative relations in and across organizations, organizational phenomena, as well as semiotic modes and media were covered. Additionally, we want to show that multimodal research on organizations can take many different forms, so we intentionally made the template for the individual cases rather loose and flexible. Some cases focus more on the specific role and relevance of multimodality, going into much depth regarding the ways in which semiotic modes construct meaning, and the ways in which researchers can analytically reconstruct meaning structures. Other cases expand more on the organizational context and organizational questions, using multimodality to shed new light on the specific organizational phenomenon at hand. All of them, however, combine these two elements to demonstrate the potential for cross-fertilization between the two areas of research.

Our first case focuses on the role of diagrams and charts in representing—and constructing—organizational structure and processes. After clarifying the crucial relevance of charts and diagrams for organizations, we delve into a detailed discussion of the characteristics of diagrammatic communication and outline a 'grammar' of diagrams. We then exemplify the social semiotic analysis of two diagrams in particular. Finally, we discuss resources for producing diagrams in and about organizations, before we draw a number of conclusions about diagrammatic communication in organizations.

The second case explores multimodal organizational logos and their relevance for organizational identity. In contrast to the first, this second case builds upon a single empirical example, namely that of the merger of several Finnish universities into what is now known as Aalto University. Accordingly, we briefly touch upon the challenges of identity-building during mergers and acquisitions (M&As) and, specifically, the role of logos in identity-building. After providing some information about the context of the Aalto merger, the visual identity of Aalto is described and analysed in a detailed manner. We close the case with a brief discussion of reactions to the new visual identity and an account of its further development.

Case three takes digital 'resemiotization' (Iedema, 2001, 2003a) as its starting point and discusses how multimodal meaning is constructed in the context of online shopping. Online shopping moves the organization–customer interface away from face-to-face communication and into the digital realm. Accordingly, it is important to understand how multimodal websites create relationships. Using Zalando's online shop as an example, this case study discusses the different registers on the website, explores how meaning is made multimodally on the web, delineates the practice of online shopping, and touches on the topic of customer motivation, before concluding with implications for organization and management studies.

Our final case revolves around the multimodal construction of the role of organizations in broader society. On the basis of two previous studies about the visual and multimodal construction of corporate social responsibility (CSR) in the coordinated market economy of Austria, we discuss how multimodality can be a resource for organizations to legitimate themselves in the face of growing institutional and societal pressures. After introducing the central concepts, we illustrate the analytical procedures in detail. We then summarize the central insights and conclude with a discussion of the implications of multimodality for legitimacy research. Throughout, we illustrate analysis and findings with typical imagery.

10.2 Case Presentation

To keep the case studies broadly comparable, we made sure that each of them addresses a number of guiding questions. First, each case relates to different *communicative relations* in and around organizations. Such relations can be intra-organizational, inter-organizational, or concern the relationships between the organization and its customers. The most extensive relationships are constituted by the embeddedness of organizations in broader society. Second, each case introduces a specific *organizational phenomenon*, that is, an area of activity within or around organizations.

The examples we have selected here are hierarchy, M&As, point-of-sale, and CSR. Third, each case introduces an *organizational issue*, a typical and timely topic that organization theory is concerned with. Here we have chosen control, power, identity, and legitimation. On the social semiotic side, the cases include a variety of different *texts and media*, such as websites, diagrams, logos, and corporate reports, and a number of *semiotic modes*, such as pictures, words, spatial layout, graphic shape, colour, materiality, and the logic of diagrammatic resources. Table 10.1 provides an overview of the four cases and how these parameters cluster around them.

In addition to these aspects, each case study includes two further components. First, we aim to show, for each case, *how multimodal analysis can actually be conducted*. While it is, of course, not possible to present each analytical step in its entirety, we want to convey a certain hands-on attitude by making the analytical methods selected for each case as explicit as possible. Second, we utilize each case to reflect on the question of *what multimodality can contribute to central concepts* in organization and management theory, and how organization and management theory can strengthen the social grounding of multimodal theory and analysis, in short, how the two disciplines can learn from each other and contribute to each other's research objectives.

Table 10.1 Illustrative Cases Described Along a Variety of Parameters

	Case 1	Case 3	Case 3	Case 4
Communicative Relations	Intra-organization	Inter-organization	Organization–customer/stakeholder	Organization–environment
Phenomena	Hierarchy	Mergers	Point-of-sale	CSR
Issues	Power	Identity	Control	Legitimation
Texts	Diagrams	Space, logos	Online shopping	Reports, websites
Semiotic Modes	Logic of diagrammatic resources	Spatial layout, graphic shape, colour, materiality	Verbal (written words) and visual (pictures) modes	Verbal (written words) and visual (pictures) modes

11 The Power of Diagrams

Diagrams play an increasingly important role in organization and management practices. Flowcharts represent and manage work processes and procedures, including decision-making processes, organization charts represent and enact organizational structures and lines of command, and mission statements and strategies may take the form of 'balanced scorecards' and 'strategy maps' (Ledin & Machin, 2016). Timelines organize and integrate understandings of temporality (Yakura, 2002). Such diagrams not only represent structures, processes, strategies and visions, but they also institutionalize and regulate them. They create a specific 'layer' of organizational reality that becomes performative and impacts perception, thinking, and practice. How organizations are represented in diagrams, charts, and sketches may have very concrete implications for how organizational members understand the organization, and how they act. In terms of the metafunctions discussed earlier in this book, then, diagrams realize both the ideational and the interpersonal metafunction, and they do so through their own, specific textual resources. Accordingly, the discussion of how to best represent organizations has been a staple in more applied organization research (see, for instance, Mintzberg & van der Heyden, 1999).

Historically, diagrams have often been invented for limited scientific or technological purposes, but subsequently used in many other fields, and this continues to be the case today (see Lima, 2011). The cybernetic model, for instance, originated in the 1920s as a blueprint for electronic control systems, but it was soon applied to psychology, sociology, neurology, philosophy, as well as in organizational and management practices, resulting, among other things, in the ubiquity of 'feedback' practices. Networks were first developed by American sociologists in the 1920s as a quantitative model for understanding social relations based on studies of who interacts with whom and how often in schools and workplaces, but they were soon applied to other scientific and practical domains, including city planning, the classification of information, and, of course, the Internet. In all these applications, specific types of diagram became powerful new ways of understanding the world and blueprints for (re)shaping social life and its institutions.

Despite this, semioticians and multimodal analysts have largely neglected diagrams, with the exception of Kress and van Leeuwen (2006). Design theorists have mostly focused on information graphics, maps, and charts (Bertin, 1983; Lima, 2011, 2013; Tufte, 1983, 1990, 1997), and they rarely touched on the use of diagrams for purposes of management and organization. However, Lima's (2013) excellent book on tree diagrams does pay some attention to the history of organization charts, as well as to some of the new developments made possible by contemporary information technology. In general, however, the focus has overwhelmingly been on images rather than diagrams, and the key handbooks of visual analysis pay little or no attention to the role of diagrams in organizational life. Some scholars have introduced new types of diagrams or new ways of using existing diagrams, for instance, in the field of human-computer interaction. In addition, Shneiderman's (1997) has conducted research on using tree diagrams to represent the structure of websites and data bases; and in management studies, Kaplan and Norton (2004) have worked on strategy maps. But the analytical and critical discussion of 'communication models' which flourished in 1970s media and communication studies (see, for instance, McQuail & Windahl, 1982) appears to have faded out. This is all the more surprising since semioticians, social scientists, and others have increasingly begun to themselves use diagrammatic representation in their work. In this chapter, we discuss diagrams from a social semiotic point of view, focusing specifically on flowcharts and organization charts. We will highlight some of the general characteristics of diagrams as a specific mode of visual communication, introduce some tools for analysing diagrams, and demonstrate the rich potential of diagram analysis for organization and management studies with a range of examples.

11.1 Some Characteristics of Diagrammatic Communication

The table in Figure 11.1 (represented only in part, for purposes of legibility), illustrates some key characteristics of diagrammatic representation. It is taken from a document prepared by the Pro Vice Chancellor (Research) of an Australian University to explain the criteria for setting Faculty research grant income KPIs and, at the same time, for imposing these KPIs on Faculty Deans, with the aim of improving the University's research income from Government grants and other sources.

Visual syntax. Although most diagrams contain many words, linguistic syntax no longer plays a role. The role of verbal language is by and large only lexical, realized by nouns and nominal groups rather than clauses. Syntax has become visual, realized by spatial relations, as will be discussed in more detail in Chapter 11.3. In Figure 11.1, it is the spatial structure of the table which creates meaningful links between the information in the boxes, classifying it along the vertical axis and specifying these classes in

		SAMPLE "BUSINESS AS USUAL" FACULTY TARGETS - BUSINESS FACULTY						(NOTE FINAL TARG
SUMMARY REPORT		**PERFORMANCE DOMAIN: RESEARCH**						
		UTS HISTORICAL PERFORMANCE					UTS FUTURE PERFORMANCE	
KPI REF NO.	KPI TITLE	KPI METRIC	SPONSOR	PREVIOUS RESULT (usually 2003)	BASELINE RESULT (usually 2004)	TARGET TYPE T=Threshold I=Improvement	2005 TARGET	2006 TARGET (TENTATIVE)
R1	Grant application success	% of national competitive grants received by agency and scheme	PVC (Research)	ARC DISCOVERY: 1.44% (2004) ARC LINKAGE: 3.89% (2004)	ARC DISCOVERY: 2.01% (2005) ARC LINKAGE: 4.00% (2005)	T	ARC DISCOVERY: 2.00% (ACTUAL) ARC LINKAGE: 4.00% (ACTUAL)	ARC DISCOVERY: 2.00% ARC LINKAGE: 4.00%
		% of Category 1 Income from non-ARC funds		34%	35% (TARGET)	I	37% (21% NHMRC, 16% OTHER)	39% (22% NHMRC, 17% OTHER)
R2	Research commercialisation outcomes	No. of IP disclosures made & provisional patents filed	PVC (Research)	IP DISCLOSURES: 7 PROVISIONAL PATENTS: 1	IP DISCLOSURES: 28 PROVISIONAL PATENTS: 7	(beyond 2005) I	IP DISCLOSURES: 10 PROVISIONAL PATENTS: 10 STRETCH	IP DISCLOSURES: 11 PROVISIONAL PATENTS: 5
		$ commercial income (trade sales, start up dividends, royalties, licence fees, IP assignments, licensing and sales) - 3 yr moving average		n/a	$75,879	I	$91,055	$109,266

Figure 11.1 Research KPIs in an Australian University

terms of various attributes along the horizontal axis. The horizontal axis in fact fuses attribution with a timeline, as the table is horizontally divided in a 'historical performance' and a 'future performance' section.

De-personalization. The absence of visual syntax means that there are no verbs, and therefore no 'mood' and 'modality'. This causes language to lose most of its interpersonal dimension. It is the 'mood' element which necessitates a choice between declarative, interrogative, and imperative and thereby makes every clause into a speech act; and it is the 'modality' element, expressed by modal auxiliaries such as 'may', 'will', and 'should', which necessitates every declarative clause to express a degree of probability, or more generally, truth value, and every imperative clause to express a degree of permission or obligation. Together with the direct address created by the first and second person personal pronouns, it is mood and modality which make language, in Halliday's words (1985a, p. 70): "something that can be argued about—something that can be affirmed or denied, and also doubted, contradicted, insisted on, accepted with reservation, qualified, tempered, regretted, and so on". Without mood, modality, and direct address, information becomes a *fait accompli* that cannot be argued about. Yet documents such as the one partially reproduced in Figure 11.1 may still have interpersonal power. There may not be a visual equivalent for the imperative or the obligatory modal 'should' in it, yet the document is authoritative, signed off by an authority, the Pro Vice Chancellor. In Iedema's words (2003b, p. 175), it is "writing order to structure work", aimed at "an organizationally productive outcome" (Iedema, 2003b, p. 145).

Objectification. The table in Figure 11.1 also lacks the logical connectives, which, in language, play a fundamental role in *explaining* things. A (partial) 'translation' of Figure 11.1 in linear prose might read something like this:

> The Key Performance Indicator 'Grant Application Success' is the responsibility of the PVC (Research). Success is measured as the percentage of national competitive grants received by a particular agency or scheme. *To* set a target, historical performance should be taken into account, and the previous year's result taken as a baseline. *If*, say, the percentage of ARC Discovery Grants was 1.44 and the percentage of ARC Linkage grants 3.89 in 2004, and *if* the percentages were 2.01 and 4.00 in 2005, *then* the 2006 threshold targets could be 2.0 and 4.00.

As shown by the italics, conjunctions like '(in order) to', 'if . . . then' create logical connections between the items of information displayed in the table. Tables have no resources for expressing this kind of connection. They objectify the information, creating a kind of filing cabinet which organizes the information in a neat classification system.

Context-dependency. As a result of de-personalization and objectification, the same diagram can be interpreted in different ways. Kress and van Leeuwen (2006), for instance, describe how different authors provide different glosses of the famous 'communication model' of Shannon and Weaver (see Figure 11.5) differently. However precise diagrams may seem, their meaning is context-dependent, in need of complementation by spoken discourse, to re-personalize it and de-objectify it—in the case of Figure 11.1, a meeting between the University's senior management and Faculty Deans. This kind of context-dependency is characteristic of what elsewhere has been called 'the new writing' (van Leeuwen, 2008b). It also characterizes PowerPoint slides, for instance, where the dot points often just list items of information and lack mood, modality, and direct address. It is then up to the presenter to supply the explanations and the interpersonal element and to attune the slides to the specifics of the occasion where and the audience to which they are presented.

De-professionalization. Whereas the writings of Tufte, Lima, and others almost exclusively deal with professionally designed information graphics, the table in Figure 11.1 was designed by the Pro Vice Chancellor herself. Multimodal literacy, the ability to produce multimodal printed or electronic documents, including diagrams, is now a requirement for employees in a wide range of industries and sectors. But it is not taught in school and often acquired on the job, not always with much support from management in the form of training, feedback, and so on. The same applies to scholars creating diagrammatic representations of their data or of aspects of their theories. It is here that Microsoft comes to the rescue, with easy to use software (an early version of Excel, in the case of Figure 11.1) and an abundance of ready-for-use templates, and 'help' resources:

> *SmartDraw offers a complete set of tools to help organizations of any size develop a successful strategic plan. These include SWOT diagrams, strategy maps, balanced scorecards, value chain analyses and many more.*
>
> *Download our free white paper to learn more. Buy SmartDraw Today For The Lowest Price.*

Abstraction and comprehensiveness. Diagrams can provide comprehensive maps of what they represent, overviews of complex issues that can be taken in at a glance. Diagrams can also enforce comprehensiveness in ways that linear text cannot. In teaching the use of diagrams for purposes of designing websites (Martinec & van Leeuwen, 2009), the students were asked to convert the information in a booklet on Greek vases published by the British Museum into tabular form. The selectivity of the information in the booklet was immediately obvious. If for one period the booklet mentioned how the pots were fired, it did not do so for another period. If for one period it mentioned the colours of the vases, for another it did not. Each period was described in terms of a different selection of attributes. Linear prose does not require such attributes to be integrated into a single system. To be able to fill all the boxes, our students had to do additional research.

Symbolization and aestheticization. The spatial arrangement of diagram elements may not only provide 'syntactic' meaning, as in the case of Figure 11.1, but also symbolic meaning. Figure 11.2 differs from many other organization charts by placing the CEO in the centre rather than at the top of a tree (although radial organization charts have existed since at least the 1920s, see, for instance, Lima, 2013). Kress and van Leeuwen (2006, p. 196) explain the meaning potential of Centre–Margin structures as follows:

> For something to be presented as Centre means that it is presented as the nucleus of the information to which all the other elements are in some sense subservient. The Margins are then these ancillary, dependent elements.

A common kind of Centre–Margin diagram is the mind map or concept map, with a central idea or concept as its Centre, and a range of associated ideas as its Margins. Alternatively, we can interpret Figure 11.2 symbolically as an apple with Steve Jobs as its core.

In their account of spatial composition, Kress and van Leeuwen also stress salience, the way the elements of a diagram can "attract the viewer's attention to different degrees, as realized by such factors as placement in the foreground or background, relative size, contrasts in tonal value (or colour), differences in sharpness, etc." (Kress & van Leeuwen, 2006, p. 177). In Figure 11.2, the central circle stands out because of its size and because the black and white form the strongest tonal contrast of the diagram. The other elements then decrease in size, and hence in importance, the further they are removed from the Centre, as in the medieval maps of cities, in which the city itself is drawn large and in the Centre, whereas the representation of the surrounding countryside diminishes in scale and detail as distance from the city increases.

Finally, shape and colour also carry meaning. Kress and van Leeuwen (2006) discuss the meaning potential of basic shapes such as rectangles, circles, and triangles, asking why different versions of the 'communication model' use differently shaped elements, and concluding that, in many cases, rectangles make the diagram seem more technical, and circles more human and organic. In Figure 11.2, only the members of the executive team are represented by rectangles, surrounding the CEO like a wall of solid bricks. The meaning of colours may be fixed by a legend, as in Figure 11.2, where blue represents vice-presidents (circles in the outer ring), orange the executive team (rectangles in the inner ring), and grey

110   *Application*

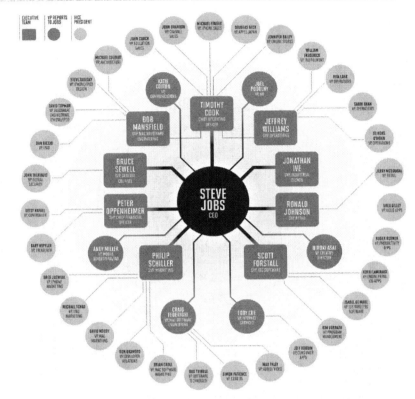

Figure 11.2 (Reconstructed) Apple Organization Chart
Source: Fortune Magazine, 2011

vice-presidents reporting to the CEO (circles in the inner ring).[1] But they may also have symbolic meaning. In Figure 11.2, the central circle has a white aura, which shades into an intense yellow that desaturates as it gets closer to the outer ring, perhaps representing the radiance of Steve Jobs' charisma. The lines that connect Jobs to his reports gradually shade from the black of his central circle to the orange of the executive team and the grey of the vice-presidents. The colours also lend an aesthetic element to diagrams, which formerly might have been more austere and black and white. Today, documents must not only be functional, but also look good (van Leeuwen, 2015), and company structures must not only be understood but also loved.

As Kress (2005) has argued, in studying semiotic change we need to consider both gains and losses. It may be a good thing for diagrams and other forms of 'new writing' to be flexible, able to be used in different contexts, and for different purposes, but social order also needs stable meanings, for instance rules that mean the same thing in different places and at different times. De-professionalization, too, may be a good thing, heralding an increase in multimodal literacy that will empower more people, provided it will not cause all invention and innovation to be outsourced to Microsoft. Maps are a powerful form of representation, providing an omniscient, Gods-eye view. For instance, a map produced by Macrofocus GmbH shows two thousand companies as polygons whose size represents the companies' market values and whose colours (red and green) represent their profits and losses (Lima, 2013). But quantification may cause detail to be sacrificed. We learn little about these two thousand companies and about the reasons for their market values and their profitability or lack thereof. The design follows the principle of the Google map—the greater the area surveyed, the more holistic the representation, but the greater the loss of detail; the smaller the area surveyed, the greater the detail, but the more the whole disappears from view.

The crucial point is that diagrams enable a new way of thinking, a new, spatial logic, on the one hand open to interpretation, on the other hand authoritative; on the one hand comprehensive and systematic, on the other hand abstract and lacking concrete detail; on the one hand open to all, on the other hand increasingly monopolized by Microsoft; on the one hand factual and precise, on the other hand symbolic and aesthetic. For all these reasons, we need tools for their critical analysis. Some of these will be introduced in the next section.

11.2 Aspects of the Grammar of Diagrams

Some diagrams are dynamic, modelling actions and events. Others are static, modelling structures in which depicted elements are understood as parts in a part-whole structure or categories in a classification, or as modelling identities by means of visual attributes. This distinction was developed in the study of images (Kress & van Leeuwen, 2006), but it also applies to diagrams. In dynamic ('narrative') visuals, Kress and van Leeuwen argue, a vector will emanate from one of the elements (the Actor, the element, or 'participant' who or which does the deed) and lead to another participant (the Goal, the participant to whom or which the deed is done). A vector is a line with a sense of directionality, for instance an arrow. Kress and van Leeuwen's key example is shown in Figure 11.3.

112 *Application*

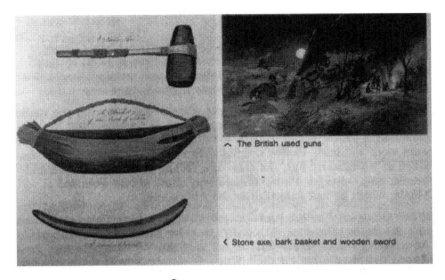

Figure 11.3 'The British Used Guns'

Source: Early-nineteenth-century engraving; see Oakley, 1985; see also Kress & van Leeuwen, 2006, p. 45

It was taken from an Australian primary school social studies textbook titled *Our Society and Others* (Oakley, 1985), and, within that book, from a section of a chapter on Australia's Indigenous peoples which dealt with their technology. It shows the 'British', as they are called in the caption, aiming their guns at an Aboriginal group seated around a fire. Their outstretched arms and the guns form the vector that connects them to the Aboriginal group. However, Aboriginal peoples vigorously defended themselves against the invaders, but this is not shown. Note also that the caption says 'The British used guns' (i.e., not 'the Australians') and makes no mention of who they used those guns against.

The engraving on the left of Figure 11.3 depicts Aboriginal technology. Whereas 'British' technology is shown dynamically, Aboriginal technology is shown in a static way, in what looks like an old-fashioned museum display. It is what Kress and van Leeuwen call a 'conceptual' image, purporting to show, not an action or event, but the more or less permanent structure, constitution, or identity of what it depicts. Here the connection between the participants is not realized by a vector, but by the way the participants are arranged in the picture—symmetrically, equal in size, at equal distance from each other, and so on. It is a classificatory image. The arrangement suggests that the three participants are to be interpreted as belonging to the same category. Precisely which category this is, is never made explicit. The caption just says 'Stone axe, bark basket and wooden sword'. Clearly, it would also have been possible to show a static exhibit of early nineteenth-century guns and a narrative image in which Aboriginal spears form the dynamic element. Images can construe different interpretations of the same history.

Narrative diagrams. Figure 11.4 is a likeness of a narrative diagram from the website of a Norwegian engineering company, Kongsberg Maritime, which has a 'Cybernetics R&D Group' to "contribute to the cutting edge of research-based and market-oriented innovation" (Kongsberg Maritime, 2017). It represents an action, or rather, a sequence of actions. A Controller acts to 'input' something into a System, telling it to behave in a certain way. The System then provides feedback about its actual behaviour to the Controller, who adjusts the Input accordingly, for example by making the message more persuasive or insistent or reassessing strategy. A neatly closed loop. But there is also an arrow that comes from nowhere, the (green) arrow on the left. Kress and van Leeuwen call this an 'Event'. There is a process, represented by a vector, and there is a Goal, an affected party, the Controller. But there is no Actor. Who decides what is to be desired? What might cause undesirable behaviour? This is not represented—and therefore not necessarily included in research or management processes based on this model.

The most common narrative diagrams are linear processes, cycles, and flowcharts. We have already mentioned one of the most well-known examples of a linear process, Shannon and Weaver's communication model, of which Figure 11.5 shows one version—googling 'communication model' will show a myriad of others. There are five participants in this diagram. An Information Source 'does something to' a Transmitter, which in turn 'does something to' a Channel, which in turn 'does something to' a Receiver, which in turn 'does something to' the Destination. But what is it that they do? Here the meaning of the arrows is not labelled, although we can deduce what processes are involved from the

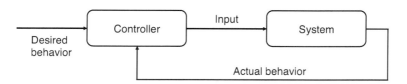

Figure 11.4 A Likeness of a Cybernetic Diagram
Source: Reproduced with permission from Kongsberg Maritime, Norway

114 *Application*

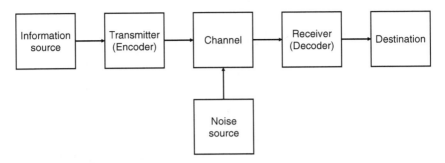

Figure 11.5 Shannon and Weaver's Communication Model

nominalizations in the boxes ('transmitting', 'channelling', and so on). And what is it that is being 'transmitted', 'decoded', and so on? This, too, is not represented in the diagram. And while this may not matter in terms of the original technical purposes of the diagram (accurate transmission of signals), it does matter when the diagram is used to model human communication, as it frequently has been.

The cybernetic diagram in Figure 11.4 is an example of a cycle. Here each participant is Actor in one process and Goal in another. In a food web, similarly, plants may provide food to animals, animals to bacteria, whereas bacteria may be broken down by plants. But, as we have already discussed, such 'closed loop' diagrams cannot take account of external factors that may impinge on the represented processes, in the way that 'noise', in Figure 11.5, impinges on the accurate transmission of signals.

In flowcharts, the link between participants is sequential. Here the arrows realize temporal ('and then'), alternative ('or'), and conditional ('if . . . then') connections, rather than processes. Clearly arrows, which play such an important role in many diagrams, are vague and open to many interpretations (Boeriis & van Leeuwen, 2016). They can represent actions (such as 'The Controller inputs into the System') as well as temporal, causal, and conditional relations between such propositions (e.g., 'if the problem is getting worse—refer the patient to a specialist'). This, as we have already mentioned, is part of the power of diagrams. It allows them to function as templates that can be applied to many different domains. But it also opens them up to different interpretations.

Like other types of narrative diagrams, flowcharts can represent technological processes (e.g., automated production processes), as well as social practices (e.g., medical consultations), and they can represent them as well as regulate them. Ventola (1987), for instance, uses flowcharts to describe the way service encounters unfold. The chart in Figure 11.6, on the other hand, is a likeness of a chart designed by an Australian public health professional (who, however, had no previous experience

The Power of Diagrams 115

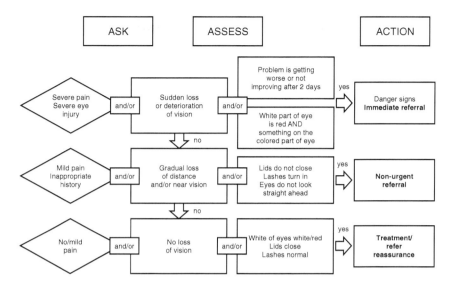

Figure 11.6 A Likeness of a Flowchart for Medical Consultation

in drawing diagrams of this kind) for nurses in African clinics, where a shortage of ophthalmologists necessitated 'task shifting'—training nurses to conduct medical consultations. A close reading of this diagram reveals a range of issues. Why are there no arrows between 'ask', 'assess', and 'action'? Why are there no downwards 'no' arrows between 'severe pain', 'mild pain', and 'no pain'? More generally, does this diagram foresee all the possible situations the nurses could be confronted with? And how can 'refer' be the outcome of so many of the consultations given the scarcity of qualified eye doctors? Such questions become even more important when flowcharts become the algorithms of the digital programs that regulate so many of the things we do, whether in organizations or as private citizens, requiring us to conform to pre-envisaged options in ways that are often entirely non-negotiable.

Conceptual diagrams. The most common forms of conceptual diagram are analytical diagrams, classification diagrams, tables, networks, and mind maps. Analytical diagrams show the parts of a whole and how they fit together to form that whole, linking participants on the basis of metonymy, part–whole relations. Maps are a clear example, but so are diagrams that represent more abstract things as part–whole structures. The pie chart in Figure 11.7, for instance, depicts the outcome of a staff survey, showing the company in question as consisting of three groups of employees—'can do' employees who welcome innovation and say things like 'we need to work together with management', 'maybe . . .

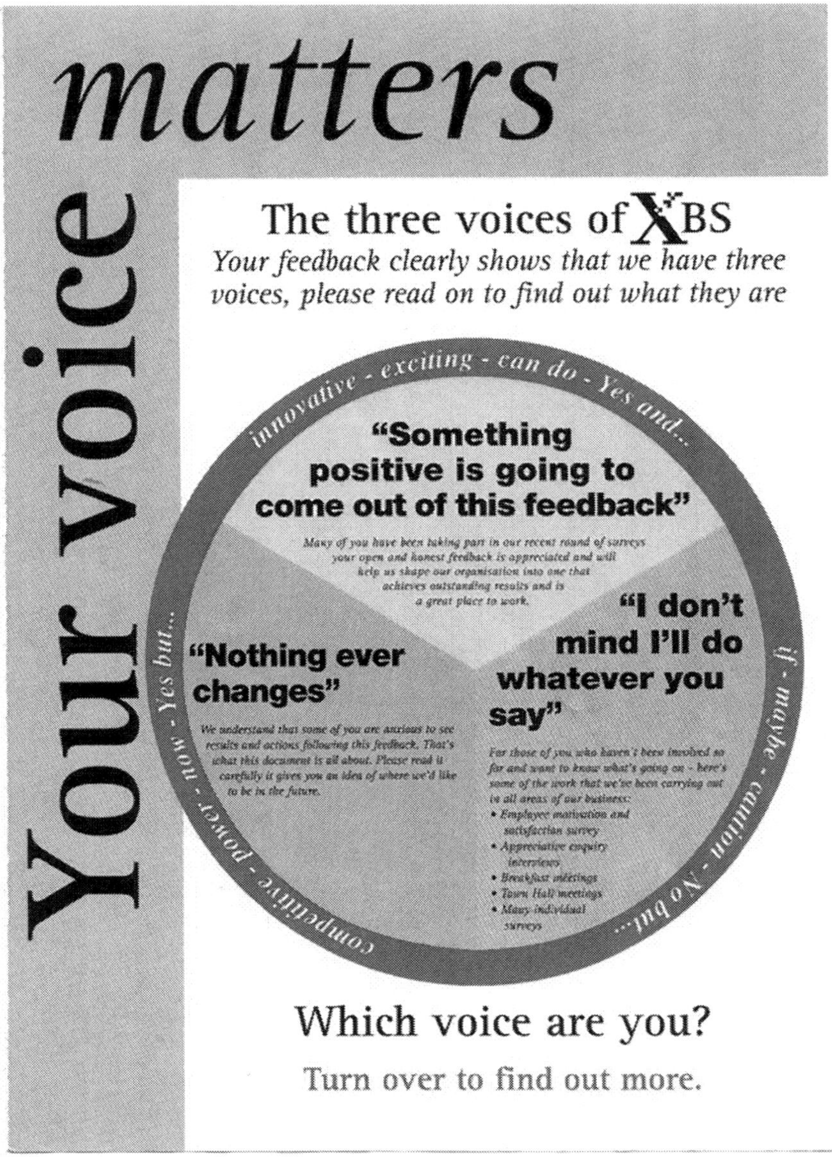

116   *Application*

matters

The three voices of XBS
Your feedback clearly shows that we have three voices, please read on to find out what they are

innovative - exciting - can do - Yes and...

"Something positive is going to come out of this feedback"

Many of you have been taking part in our recent round of surveys your open and honest feedback is appreciated and will help us shape our organisation into one that achieves outstanding results and is a great place to work.

"Nothing ever changes"

We understand that some of you are anxious to see results and actions following this feedback. That's what this document is all about. Please read it carefully it gives you an idea of where we'd like to be in the future.

"I don't mind I'll do whatever you say"

For those of you who haven't been involved so far and want to know what's going on - here's some of the work that we've been carrying out in all areas of our business:
• Employee motivation and satisfaction survey
• Appreciative enquiry interviews
• Breakfast meetings
• Town Hall meetings
• Many individual surveys

Your voice
now - Yes but...
competitive - power
No but...
caution - if - maybe

Which voice are you?
Turn over to find out more.

Figure 11.7 The Three Voices of XBS
Source: Rank Xerox, 1997; reproduced with permission from Xerox Limited

if' employees who worry about change and say things like 'so and so tried and look what happened to him', and competitive 'yes but' employees, who say things like 'why should I help when I am not going to win'. Analytical diagrams can be topographical, drawn to scale, or topological, in which case they are not drawn to scale, but accurately show the connections between, and the relative location of, the participants. Such locations are sometimes symbolic. In Figure 11.7, the 'can do' people are on top, in bright, sunny yellow. Needless to say, the same 'whole', for instance the same company, can be analysed into 'parts' in many different ways.

Analytical diagrams are often embedded in other diagrams. If, for instance, the participants in narrative diagrams are depicted in enough detail to distinguish their various parts, they can themselves be interpreted as analytical diagrams. To give an example, diagrams of tectonic activity may use arrows to show erupting volcanoes and rising magma while also depicting how the earth's crust consists of different layers.

Figure 11.1 showed how a symmetric arrangement of participants can realize classification. The words or phrases in lists, with or without bullet points, are also symmetrically arranged in this way, and also position their participants as belonging to the same category, for instance in the menus of computer interfaces. Tree diagrams also realize classification, with overarching categories branching out into subcategories that are of the same kind and belong to the same order or rank. For instance, in zoology, orders such as mammals branch out into families such as bears, which branch out again into genera such as black bear and brown bear, and into species such as Asiatic black bears. But branching can also be used to signify hierarchy, for instance in organization charts that map the 'reporting' lines in organizations, or to signify origin, as in family trees. Like arrows, branching can mean different things in different contexts.

As already mentioned, tables combine the analytical and the classificational, analysing along one axis, and classifying along the other. In Figure 11.1, the classification is vertical and the analysis horizontal, but the opposite also occurs. However verbal the content of the boxes, the structure of tables is again visual—even the words can, in principle, be replaced by visuals, provided suitable icons are available.

As mentioned, social network diagrams originated in studies of social relations focused on metrics rather than meaning and replaced specific forms of association such as kinship, class, and workplace relations with mere association (see Freeman, 2004). The diagram in Figure 11.8 is an early example. This principle was later also applied to information, where the frequency of the links between items of information became more important than their semantic relations. But networks are also used to reshape social practices, including the work of academics, through sites like ResearchGate, which replaces peer review with popularity (ranking in terms of number of 'followers'), and publishing with posting and networking, and which includes everyone with a University address on an equal basis ("11+ million researchers"), ignoring the hierarchical managerial systems in which academics work. Arrangements of this kind are then legitimized by keywords

118 *Application*

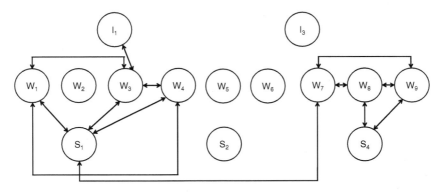

Figure 11.8 After 'Friendships in a Bank Wiring Observation Room'
Source: Adapted from Warner & Lunt, 1941

such as 'community', 'collaboration', 'self-organization', 'flexibility', 'diversity', multiplicity', and 'democratization' (Djonov & van Leeuwen, 2018).

'Mind maps', finally (originally called 'idea maps'), were developed in advertising in the late 1940s as a brainstorming technique. They can be seen as combining the analytical model with a Centre–Margin structure which has the 'whole' in the middle, and the parts around it, connected to the Centre by lines. They are often topographical in an abstract way, depicting different participants as closer or further away from the Centre

The examples in this section showed that a close reading of diagrams cannot always lead to firm conclusions. As likely as not, it will raise questions, questions which can only be answered by studying, not only the diagrams themselves, but also the situated practices in which they are embedded and the broader historical, social, and cultural contexts of which these practices form part, in other words, by creating specific combinations of what, in Part II we have called the archaeological approach, the practice approach, and the strategic approach. We will address this in the next section, using examples of the background of which one of the authors has first-hand knowledge.

11.3 Analysing Diagrams

The diagram in Figure 11.9 shows a likeness of the funding model of an Australian University, where one of the authors worked as a Faculty Dean at the time. The leftmost column ('Step 1', 'Step 2', etc.) suggests the diagram should be read from top to bottom, as a linear narrative process, the process of allocating funding to the University's Faculties, administrative divisions, and independent research institutes. To the right of each 'step' box are other boxes in different arrangements and combinations. These specify the nature of the steps so that the relation between the 'step

The Power of Diagrams 119

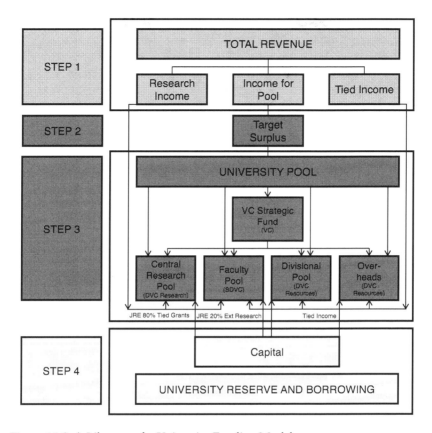

Figure 11.9 A Likeness of a University Funding Model

boxes' and the boxes on their right is one of identity: 'Step 1' consists of specifying the total revenue received by the University, 'Step 2', of deducting the 'target surplus', and so on.

Embedded in the 'total revenue' box is a tree, hence a classification. There are three kinds of income it shows: research income, which must necessarily be allocated to the projects for which it is intended; income for pool, which the University can distribute as it sees fit (this combines Government funding per student with fee income), and other 'tied income'. The branches of the tree, however, are extremely faint, so that, at first sight, the Step 1 boxes could be mistaken for what Kress and van Leeuwen (2006) call an 'unstructured' analytical diagram, a diagram that shows the parts of a whole, but not the way they fit together to make up that whole. The arrow that connects the 'total revenue' box to the 'target surplus' box is equally faint, and between the 'steps' there are no arrows at all. As a result, the narrative nature of the diagram, its nature as action, is backgrounded, making the funding model look like an objectified structure, rather than a process. Note also that the Actors of the funding distributions are included inside the boxes in small print. It is, for example, the SDVC, the Senior Deputy Vice-Chancellor, who determines the target surplus and subtracts it from the operating funds.

Step 3 is the crucial one for those who have to run Faculties and administrative divisions. The Vice-Chancellor's discretionary fund is on the one hand one of these pools, but on the other hand it is prioritized, literally and figuratively elevated above it, and provides further funding to Faculties and administrative divisions, for which they often have to compete (but that is not represented in the diagram). Again, the arrows are extremely faint, so that the diagram is on the one hand narrative, because of the arrows (the operating funds *go to* the five pools below it), but on the other hand *looks* like a classification, as if it says 'there are five kinds of pool'. The size of these pools is visually equal, even though in reality they differ in size. The only exception here is the funding the University receives from the Government for research, of which 20 percent goes directly to the Faculties, and the remainder to the Deputy Vice-Chancellor Research. What is finally allocated to Faculties and Divisions is then determined by the Deputy Vice-Chancellors whose titles are indicated in the boxes, between brackets, and in small print. The criteria in allocating funding are of course also not part of the diagram. Step 4, finally, consists of a further allocation, this time from the University's capital—faint arrows connect this box to the different pools.

Two other things can be noted. The colour of the 'Step 2' and 'Step 3' boxes is an alarming red (dark grey in Figure 11.9), and hence particularly salient, while the Step 4 boxes are of a reassuring pale blue (light grey in Figure 11.9), a colour often used for business, especially conservative business such as accounting, insurance, and banking (van Leeuwen, 2011). The 'Step 1' boxes, which represent the University's income, are a light violet, hence a mixture of red and blue (medium grey Figure 11.9).

The diagram therefore recontextualizes the funding process in ways which, perhaps, make it less than transparent—by omitting things, by making things less salient, by representing things that differ in size as being equal in size. Above all, it objectifies management processes, making them look like hardened structures rather than processes which specific managers are responsible for, or, in terms of the terminology introduced earlier, making them look analytical rather than narrative, and like a map rather than a like flowchart.

The organization chart in Figure 11.10 was produced, with the help of SmartArt, by the Faculty Manager of the Arts and Social Sciences Faculty of a university, as part of a restructure following the merger of three former Faculties, the Faculty of Humanities and Social Sciences, the Faculty of Education, and the Faculty of International Studies. The Dean of the Faculty wanted to create a matrix structure in which staff members would belong to three different units, one representing their

The Power of Diagrams 121

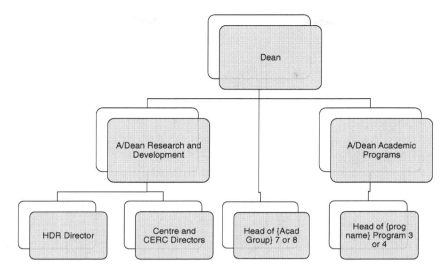

Figure 11.10 Organization Chart of a University Faculty

academic discipline, another their teaching area, and a third their research group. To give an example, the three merging Faculties all employed linguists, yet the Faculty did not offer degrees in linguistics—linguists were employed in International Studies to teach modern languages, in Education to teach teachers of English, English as a Second Language, and Academic English, and in Humanities and Social Sciences to teach units on discourse analysis and various forms of writing. The same applied to other academic disciplines. The new structure would allow academics to form part of a larger academic group representing their discipline, which was thought to help foster academic excellence and staff satisfaction. At the same time, staff were encouraged to take part in interdisciplinary research groups, so as to take advantage of the academic diversity of the new Faculty. However, staff would continue to teach in the areas they had taught in before.

The Faculty Manager however, objected. She foresaw difficulties in financial management and in the re-organization of the professional support staff. At one point in the negotiations she came up with the organization chart in Figure 11.10, offering it as a compromise. The Faculty would have Academic Groups, but they would report directly to the Dean and be quite separate from the bi-partite structure of Research and Development and Academic Programs, and hence not funded or supported by professional staff (but that was not shown in the chart). An archaeological analysis of this diagram would undoubtedly raise the question of why there is no Associate Dean heading the Academic Groups. But without background knowledge it would be impossible to answer this question.

122 *Application*

11.4 Resources for Producing Diagrams: Microsoft SmartArt

Kress and van Leeuwen's framework for analysing diagrams has two basic types of narrative diagram and three types of conceptual diagram, each with two to five subtypes. These types can of course be combined in different ways, for instance by embedding analytical diagrams in narrative diagrams, or by backgrounding vectors to make flow diagrams look like analytical diagrams, or in many other ways. More or less at the same time as Kress and van Leeuwen developed their visual grammar, Microsoft had begun to develop SmartArt, which has eight major diagram types, each with up to forty subtypes—a total of 233 types of diagram, thus providing a comprehensive visual syntax, the boxes and circles of which could be filled with many different kinds of textual information (but more rarely with images—only two of the diagrams are said to "also work well with no text"). Today SmartArt is widely used, in academic as well as in corporate presentations and publications.

Here are SmartArt's eight basic categories, together with glosses of their meaning potential, as formulated by Microsoft:

Lists	"use to show non-sequential or grouped blocks of information"
Process	"use to show progression or sequential steps in a task, process or workflow"
Cycle	"use to show a continuous sequence of stages tasks, events, in circular flow"
Hierarchy	"use to show hierarchical information or reporting relationships"
Relationship	"use to compare or show the relationship between two ideas"
Matrix	"use to show the relationship of components to a whole"
Pyramid	"use to show proportional, interconnected or hierarchical ideas with the largest component at the bottom and narrowing up"
Picture	"use to show a series of pictures"

Office.com, finally, includes a selection from the above types.

These descriptions clearly overlap. 'Hierarchies', for instance, are said to convey "hierarchical information", but 'Pyramids' also convey "hierarchical ideas". 'Processes' are said to show "sequential steps in a task, process or workflow", but 'Cycles' also show "continuous sequence of stages, tasks, events in a circular flow". Looking at the subtypes confirms this. 'Cycles', for instance, includes pie charts and Venn diagrams which are "used to show how individual parts form a whole", but the 'Matrix' (which has only four subtypes) also shows "the relationships

The Power of Diagrams 123

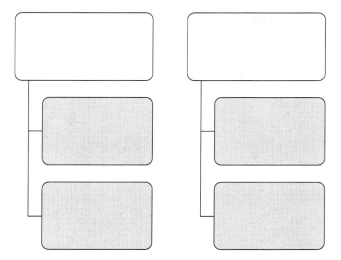

Figure 11.11 SmartArt 'Hierarchy List' Template

of components to a whole". Many of the subtypes combine major categories, for example, the 'List' and the 'Hierarchy', or the 'List' and the 'Process'. The template in Figure 11.11, for instance, is to be used "to show hierarchical relationships progressing across groups" but "can also be used to group or list information". In other words, it can be read as a tree turned on its side, because of its use of branching, or as a list because of its vertical symmetry—or both.

Our earlier examples showed that this form of blending also occurs in diagrams that are not created with SmartArt, and it usually has ideological reasons, such as representing actions as immutable and agentless structures. Clearly many of SmartArt's templates present ample opportunity for creating such ideologically tinted meanings.

SmartArt also provides some diagram types that are not included in the framework we presented earlier in this chapter. There is, for example, the category of relations, where "related or contrasting concepts" are placed inside large arrows which spatially relate to each other in different ways ('convergence', 'divergence', and 'opposition')—a spatial version of lexical relations such as synonymy and antonymy. The template in Figure 11.12, for instance, is to be used "to show two opposing ideas, or ideas that diverge from a central point".

Many of the SmartArt templates represent the formation of 'goals' and 'ideas'. The template in Figure 11.13, for instance, represents such a brainstorming process. It is to be used, says Microsoft, "to show, through a series of steps, how several chaotic ideas can result in a unified goal or idea".

124 *Application*

Figure 11.12 SmartArt 'Opposing Arrows' Template

Figure 11.13 SmartArt 'Random to Result' Template

Many SmartArt diagram templates have symbolic meaning potential, expressing, for instance, ideas such as 'creativity' and 'innovation'. The glosses provided for these templates do not necessarily verbalize this aspect of their meaning. The 'Funnel Process' template, for instance, is to be used "to show how parts merge into a whole", but the selectivity, the narrowing down implied by the idea of a 'funnel', is not included in the description.

Overall, Microsoft SmartArt appears to have six broad functions: grouping, sequencing, hierarchizing, showing the components of a whole, comparing, and brainstorming. These can combine in many different ways, and other strategies, too, can create subtypes:

Directional variation. The arrow in Figure 11.14, for instance, "shows a progression or steps that trend upwards in a task, process or workflow", and therefore allows users to convey ideas such as 'progress' or 'growth' ("works best with minimal text", Microsoft suggests).

Framing variations. Organization charts, for instance, may provide separate boxes for the picture and the name and/or title of a given staff member, so as "to show hierarchical information or reporting relationships in an organization, with corresponding pictures".

Graphic shapes. Text boxes may vary in shape, even if the overall visual syntax remains the same. Thus, the text boxes in a tree diagram may take the form of closed rectangles, closed circles, open circles, chevrons, etc. As mentioned earlier, shapes of this kind also have symbolic meaning potentials, whether in typography or graphic design generally (van Leeuwen, 2006). Literal openness, as in Figure 11.15, for instance, can come to express the idea of 'openness' or 'transparency'. But this aspect of the meaning potential of diagrams is usually not stated explicitly. In the case of Figure 11.15, for instance, the gloss simply says that the diagram is to be used "to show hierarchical information or reporting relationships in an organization".

Backgrounds. Diagrams may also have background elements such as arrows or pyramids—or images. These elements, again, have metaphoric potential. The background arrow in Figure 11.16, for instance, may not only serve to suggest "progression or sequential steps", but also to suggest the idea of 'progress', 'growth', and 'sense of direction'.

Aesthetic embellishment. Aesthetic embellishments such as relief or colour emphasize the importance of aesthetics and affect in contemporary communication (van Leeuwen, 2015). It is not for nothing that Microsoft uses the term 'art' in the branding of text production resources such as SmartArt

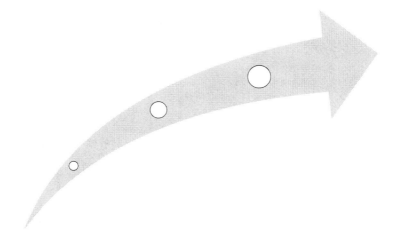

Figure 11.14 SmartArt 'Upward Arrow' Template

126 *Application*

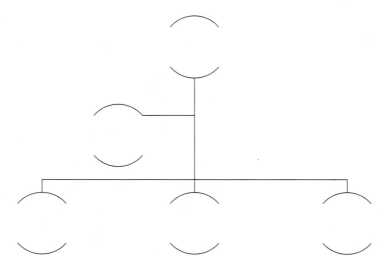

Figure 11.15 SmartArt 'Half-Circle Organization Chart' Template

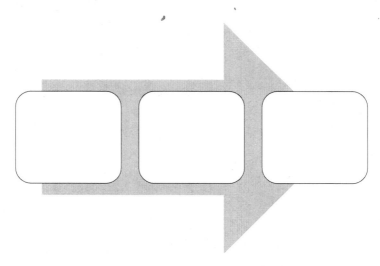

Figure 11.16 SmartArt 'Continuous Block Process' Template

and ClipArt (Kvåle, 2016). Kvåle has described how Microsoft originally supplied only organizational charts and, in their manuals, explicitly referred to them as such. As their diagrams began to be used beyond their original purposes, for instance in education, they broadened the range to 'relationship diagrams' and finally to SmartArt in its current form. But the organization chart remained a dominant model. She concluded that, today

[t]he most effective visual style of organizational charts is infused into all social practices including education—not explicitly, by verbal instruction, but by being buried in the templatized formats for multimodal representation.

(Kvåle, 2016, p. 269)

11.5 Conclusions

We have identified three important aspects of the multimodality of diagrams. First, diagrams realize their function of conceptualizing and regulating processes and structures by connecting words and longer stretches of text through a *visual* syntax. Second, they do so in ways that enable the visual realization of the value-laden concepts that play such a key role in today's organizational mission statements and strategies, such as goal orientation, unity, progress, growth, creativity, innovation, etc. Third, they increasingly seek to do so in an aesthetically attractive way, so that people will not only understand them, or comply with them, but also like them.

Diagrams have often moved from relatively limited, specialized uses to become models for understanding and regulating a much wider variety of practices and social and natural phenomena, whether or not through technological mediation, thus creating close links between dominant organizational practices and our understanding of the world at large, and playing a key role in institutionalizing and legitimating the practices they are based on. Given the importance of diagrams, and the authority they exercise, we need analytical tools that can bring to light just how they represent what they represent—what they omit, and what they transform, and how. This is not only of interest for academics. Practitioners in organizations, as well, need to better understand what their charts and diagrams 'do' to the organization and to its members. As some of the examples provided in this case have shown, the people who create diagrams and force them on others are rarely experts in this area. The organizational realities created through charting structures, processes, and other static and dynamic aspects of organizations are often neither projected nor assessed after the fact. A better understanding of how diagrams work is therefore crucial for better organization. The analytical methods developed for verbal language in critical discourse analysis (see, for instance, Fairclough, 2003; van Leeuwen, 2008a), such as the role of nominalization in deleting agency and objectifying practices, can and should have their counterparts in the critical analysis of diagrams, and we hope that this chapter has demonstrated that this is possible. Archaeological' analysis, however, needs complementation by 'practice' analysis and 'strategic' analysis if an integrated study of the way diagrams construct social reality is to be achieved.

Finally, close analysis of diagrams can also reveal how diagrams might be improved. We have, for instance, pointed at the vagueness of key diagrammatic resources such as branching and arrows. In the age of Enlightenment many new conjunctions were invented where previously people used only 'and' and 'but' (Milic, 1970). This was necessary, as John Locke argued at the time, because

> The words whereby the mind signifies what connexion it gives to several affirmations and negations that it unites in one continued reasoning and narration are generally called particles; and it is in the right use of these that more particularly consists the clearness and beauty of a good style. . . . To express methodical and rational thoughts, a man must have words to show what connexion, restriction, distinction, opposition, emphasis, etc., he gives to each respective part of his discourse.
>
> (Locke, 1972 [1706], p. 21)

Given that diagrams have become such a powerful form of discourse, it is perhaps time to invent more arrows and diagrams to improve 'methodical and rational' visual thought. And as John Locke so nicely said, clarity does not need to exclude beauty.

Note

1. A version of this organizational chart in colour can be found, for instance, on http://fortune.com/2011/08/25/apples-core-who-does-what.

12 The Use of Logos in Post-Merger Identity Construction at Aalto University

Multimodality in general and visuality in particular play a central role in inter-organizational communication. In this chapter, we will exemplify the role of visuality in post-merger identity-building. We will focus on the role of logos, that is, emblems or symbols used by organizations to promote specific identities or images of themselves. The case in point is the recent university merger that led to the creation of Aalto University in Helsinki, Finland. Based on this case analysis, we elucidate the use of visual logos in internal and external identity-building and specifically argue that such identity deals with authenticity, distinctiveness, self-esteem, enabling/constraining future orientation, and power relations. What follows is based on a compilation of material from a larger research project following the creation of Aalto University, including participant observation by several researchers, interviews, and gathering of documentary material, and we especially make use of the analyses conducted by Aula in her dissertation and articles with colleagues (Aspara, Aula, Tienari, & Tikkanen, 2014; Aula, 2016; Aula & Tienari, 2011; Aula, Tienari, & Wæraas, 2015).

12.1 Identity-Building in Mergers and Acquisitions

Mergers and acquisitions (M&As) represent significant challenges for the actors involved (Graebner, Heimeriks, Huy, & Vaara, 2017), and this is especially the case with identity-building (Clark, Gioia, Ketchen, & Thomas, 2010; Drori, Wrzesniewski, & Ellis, 2013; Tienari & Vaara, 2016; Vaara et al., 2007; Vaara & Tienari, 2011). Organizational identity is a multifaceted and dynamic phenomenon, the essence of which is the sense of organizational members of what 'we are as an organization' (Gioia et al., 2013; Pratt, Schultz, Ashforth, & Ravasi, 2016). When the focus is on actors external to the organization, one can also talk about the external identity or image of the organization.

In this chapter, we will follow the trajectory of work that conceptualizes identity construction in M&As as a discursive process where discursive resources are mobilized to construct, transform, and at times destruct senses of organizational identity (Tienari & Vaara, 2016). While prior research has typically focused on more abstract discursive resources such as stereotypes, tropes (e.g., metaphors and metonymies), or narratives, we follow the emergent stream of work that seeks to highlight the concrete visual or multimodal elements in this process.

In particular, we draw from the example of Vaara et al. (2007) who focus on the role of advertisements in the identity and image-building in post-merger integration. Their analysis concentrates on the pan-Nordic financial services sector that led to the creation of the Nordea group. In particular, their study uncovers how the visual images in advertisements serve identity-building along the following dimensions: authenticity, distinctiveness, self-esteem, enabling/constraining future orientation, and power relations. Such an approach can serve as a general framework as a constructed post-merger identity should ideally be authentic ('we' share something that is 'real' and meaningful for the actors), distinctive ('we' are unique and different from others), promote self-esteem ('we' are capable and 'strong' together), create an enabling future orientation ('we' can achieve positive things together), and help to deal with power struggles ('we' can work together even if tensions exist) (see also Tienari & Vaara, 2016). Nevertheless, often identity-building is complex, controversial, and ambiguous, which means that actors struggle with the new organizational identity—and interpret for instance visual messages in different ways.

12.2 Logos in Identity-Building

Logos may play an important role in identity-building in organizations. Nevertheless, research on logos has been limited to date. In an early exception, Floch (2000) examined the role of logos as key means of visual identity construction. The analysis focuses on IBM's and Apple's logos, which are seen as exemplifications of 'logocentricism' in visual communication (Chapter 2). Central in this analysis is the tension between continuity and change and what that means in terms of the narratives that can be constructed with the logos. Hodge (2003) has studied logos by taking McLuhan's (1963) famous argument 'the medium is the message' as the starting point. By analysing the logo of America Online (AOL), he demonstrates how 'messages' are encoded in new visual forms associated with the new electronic media. On this basis, he argues that logos are key part of new spaces that can be linked with the 'unconscious dimensions of media'. Thurlow and Aiello (2007) have examined airline tailfin design from a visual genre perspective. Although not focusing on logos alone, their analysis highlights how the designs are used both to construct international brands and to maintain or promote national identity (as 'national carriers'). This is achieved by balancing cultural symbolism and iconicity, and different airlines have distinctive solutions to cater for these needs. Interestingly, their analysis highlights aspects such as a sense of movement that are rarely scrutinized in more conventional analyses.

More recently, Johannessen (2017) has argued for a focus on logos as key elements in organizational identity-building: "Corporate logos are an extremely important species of discourse in processes of globalization and in the post-industrial social order" (Johannessen, 2017, p. 2). He analyses the meaning potential in Topaz Energy (an energy group having gas stations in Ireland) and highlights the multiple ways in which the meaning potential of the logo makes a difference in identity and image construction around this group. In particular, he develops an approach that distinguishes between the 'graphetic' and 'graphemic' elements:

> In order to fully come to terms with the meaning potential of logos, we must look beyond our preference for understanding meaning 'from above' and instead take a 'from below' look at graphetic (like phonetics interested in all material detail of the graphic expression such as bodily movements, qualities of tools and materials) and graphemic (like phonemics only interested in distinctive features of graphic form such as shape, colour, orientation) qualities of graphics.
> (Johannessen, 2017, p. 2)

In this section, we will mostly focus on the graphemic elements, but maintain that a deeper analysis should also consider the graphetic aspects in future research. What we do draw from Johannessen (2017) is the view that logos—although simple in structure and visual affordances—can play a key part among other things in corporate identity-building in general and in post-merger identity-building in particular.

There are also other types of logos, and van Leeuwen (2017) has recently focused attention on 'sonic' logos. By using the case of the Australian ABC news signature tune, Eno's Windows tune, AT&T's tune, and INTEL's sonic logo as examples, he elaborates on how these sonic logos combine a practical function with the expression of identity. In what follows, we shall not focus on this aspect of multimodality, but maintain that it is likely to be a very important part of organizational logos in the future.

While organization scholars have rarely examined logos, an interesting and useful exception can be found in the work of Drori, Delmestri, and Oberg (2016). They studied the role of emblems and logos as iconographic narratives of university identity. In a recent chapter (Oberg, Drori, & Delmestri, 2018), they identified five processes central to the creation of the visual identities of organizations: imprinting (enactment of the contemporary script), imprinting-cum-inertia (persistent enactment of epochal scripts), renewal (enactment of an up-to-date epochal script), historization (enactment of a recovered older epochal script), and multiplicity (simultaneous enactment of multiple epochal scripts). Interestingly, their analysis also includes the Aalto merger, although only as one of the examples. In particular, they point out that the Aalto case exemplifies 'imprinting' in the sense that that the themes of multiplicity and choice reflect current-day cultural norms of individuality and expressivity.

12.3 The Aalto Merger: Key Events

Aalto University was born from the idea to create an innovative, world-class university by merging science and technology, design and art, and business and economics. The Rector of the University of Art and Design at the time, Yrjö Sotamaa, first presented the idea in his opening speech for the academic year in 2005. A year and a half later the idea turned into a more concrete plan as the government's Permanent Secretary Raimo Sailas presented it in the memorandum of the working group in February 2007. Soon after that, the preparations began after the new government had included the establishment of a new university into its program as part of the larger university sector reform. The merger was a priority project in a broader Finnish higher education reform, intended to create a multidisciplinary community fostering innovation in education and research.

In July 2007, preparations were made by 500 members from the three Schools that were to merge—Helsinki School of Economics (established 1911), Helsinki University of Technology (established 1849), and the University of Art and Design Helsinki (established 1871). The project had various working names at first, such as *Innovaatioyliopisto* (Innovation University) and *Huippuyliopisto* (Top University). The name *Aalto-yliopisto* (Aalto University) was selected in May 2009 as the result of a name competition that received 1600 entries.

Aalto as such means a wave in Finnish, and it thus signifies dynamism as a key characteristic of the new university. In addition, the name honours the nationally and internationally renowned Finnish architect Alvar Aalto (1989–1976), famous for his architectural, design, and related entrepreneurial accomplishments. Aalto was also the main planner of the Helsinki University of Technology park campus that was built in Otaniemi in the 1950s and today forms Aalto University main campus. Not least because of this architectural heritage, the Otaniemi campus has been chosen as one of the most innovative areas in Europe twice, and it has received the EU Award of Excellence. The use of Aalto's name for the university was accepted by the Aalto foundation and Aalto family.

In June 2008, the Minister of Education formally approved the merger by signing the Aalto University charter in the presence of representatives from Finnish industries and organizations, and in December of the same year, Professor Tuula Teeri was selected as the first President of Aalto University. Aalto University was officially formed and started operating on January 1st, 2010 when Helsinki School of Economics, Helsinki University of Technology, and the University of Art and Design Helsinki merged into a single university.

12.4 Aalto University's Visual Identity

In spring 2009, as part of the preparations, a design contest was organized for a new logo and visual identity for the new university. An entry called 'Invitation', designed by graphic designer Rasmus Snabb, was chosen as the winner. After the contest, Snabb continued working on the design and on refining the university's final visual identity which was then revealed in fall 2009. It is stated in Aalto University Visual Design Guidelines that Aalto University visual identity "reflects the essence of Aalto University" and "aims at the creation of a living, yet consistent whole". The guidelines include a set of general principles and specific instructions, intended to help in creating a visual identity that is uniform in spirit yet flexible in the use of different visual elements. Particularly the following characteristics are central to the Aalto visual identity: fit for purpose (functional, well thought-out, practical), distinguished (uncomplicated, simplified, stylish), clear (fresh, colourful, strong, graphic), influential (sympathetic, narrative, informative, genuine, warm, honest), natural and easy (light, lively, unaffected, spontaneous, relaxed).

In the centre of Aalto University's visual identity is its logo, the basic version of which is a capital A with a question mark. In addition to the basic form, the official logo has two variations where the capital A is followed by an exclamation mark and a quotation mark. Interestingly, these three versions are used randomly and appear equally often in Aalto visuals. The question mark in the basic version carries the central symbolism of Aalto University: It seeks not to predefine Aalto's identity, but rather asks the viewer to form their own idea of it and participate in the identity creation. It is also noteworthy that the typographic character of the letter A and the punctuation marks that follow it are bold and expansive, which underscores the central role of A and Aalto in the university's visual identity in a way that invites questioning and taking a stance. Aalto's values such as being open for discussion, criticism and change are thus represented in the logo. Figure 12.1 below provides an illustration of these variants.

In addition to the form of the logo, colours are central to Aalto University visual identity. The primary colours blue, red, and yellow are used in the logo with the letter 'A' always written in black.[1] This symbolizes the core idea of Aalto University as a combination of three basic elements and the vast potential this combination unlocks. In addition to the primary colours, Aalto uses six additional colours that have been selected from the traditional colour wheel with even difference in tone, and one neutral grey. The six additional colours are now used as the signature colours of the schools, even though the Aalto scheme originally had no school-specific colours. Like the logo, the broadness of the colour scheme symbolizes the values of Aalto University: being open, tolerant, and diverse. Figure 12.2 below offers a summary of the colours used.

Figure 12.1 Aalto University's Official Logo in Nine Variants
Source: Reproduced with permission from Aalto University

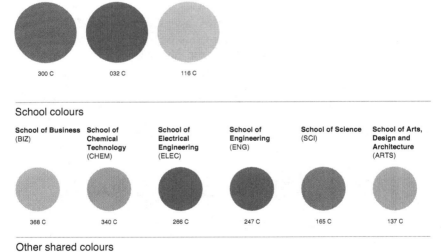

Figure 12.2 Colours Used in Aalto University's Official Logo
Source: Reproduced with permission from Aalto University

The Use of Logos 135

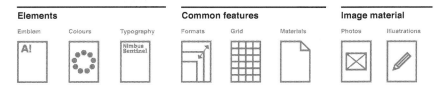

Figure 12.3 Guidelines for the Use of Aalto University's Official Logo
Source: Reproduced with permission from Aalto University

These central visual elements are supported by guidelines for typography, formats, layout styles, materials, and imagery in line with the uniform visual spirit and its characteristics, 'a neutral style and universal, basic visual elements', as Snabb described the sustaining principles of Aalto University visual identity. Figure 12.3 above provides a summary of these guidelines.

12.5 Use of the Logo in Intentional Identity Construction in Internal and External Arenas

The intentional use of the logo was linked with other activities of identity construction to the extent that the logo itself became a key—although not the only—symbol through which issues related to identity were dealt with. Based on the information available, and especially the research by Aula and colleagues (Aspara et al., 2014; Aula & Tienari, 2011; Aula et al., 2015), we can develop an understanding of the ways in which the logo supported intentional identity-building along the dimensions discussed above: authenticity, distinctiveness, self-esteem, future orientation, and power aspects.

Authenticity. The new logo is in a way similar to those of other new (or merged) universities that intend to develop a new start with symbolism of the new era of globalization, where branding is a key tool to manage one's identity and image. Thus, for instance Oberg et al. (2018) see Aalto's visual identity-building primarily in terms of 'imprinting' linked with this era and as a 'new start'. Such efforts, however, often run a risk in terms of authenticity as a constructed visual imagery that does not use elements of the past may appear as an artificial construction. This is also the case with Aalto's logo as the decision was to deliberately break away from the past in terms of not using any of the elements in the emblems or logos of the three previously separate universities. Indeed, the new logo does not have anything in common with the old ones (see Figure 12.4 below).

However, there is an important element that does bring authenticity in terms of a connection to what the university is based on and stands for. The essential point is the letter A which refers to Aalto as the name of the university as well as to the famous architect-designer-entrepreneur

136 *Application*

Figure 12.4 Logos of the Three Merger Partners
Source: Reproduced with permission from Aalto University

(Alvar) Aalto, whose career and success are used to exemplify and personify what Aalto stands for. This connection is almost self-evident for most Finns, but not for all stakeholders of Aalto, which limits the logo's meaning potential. Thus, this case—as many others—shows that the meaning potential of a logo may be different for different stakeholders.

Distinctiveness. In several ways, the logo provides a distinctive identity for the new university. Making the university 'distinguished' or 'distinctive' was one of the initial objectives set for the new logo. The double meaning of the letter 'A' (wave and reference to Alvar Aalto) makes the logo distinctively different from others. In addition, aspects such as the randomly changing exclamation and question marks and the colours are quite unique features in university logos and thus provide a distinctive basis for Aalto's identity and image. This is also supported by the colour scheme: not only are the colours differentiated, but they are also highly saturated, unmodulated, and bright (van Leeuwen, 2011). Indeed, in comparison with many other universities or business schools, Aalto's visual identity comes across as quite distinctive—and one that can clearly be linked with openness, creativity, and innovativeness as explained above.

Self-esteem. In terms of the self-esteem, these same aspects (reference to Alvar Aalto and imagery supporting openness, creativity, and innovativeness) can be seen as very positive features for most of Aalto's stakeholders. In particular, they offer a meaning potential for a construction of 'world class' university that focuses on innovation. Interestingly, this positivity can be linked with both the national heritage (Alvar Aalto) and the open global outlook that the simplistic corporate type of logo signifies—analogous to the case of national airline logos mentioned above (Thurlow & Aiello, 2007). This meaning potential is also reinforced by specific characteristics of the logo. For instance, the typographic character of the A and the following punctuation marks are bold and expansive (van Leeuwen, 2006), which supports the positive self-esteem that can be derived from visual design. The fact that the letter A is the first letter of the alphabet and can be associated with excellence (grade or category) further emphasizes this self-esteem.

Future orientation. These very elements also offer an enabling future orientation. What may be lost in terms of breaking away from the emblems and logos of the past, may be seen as enabling in terms of the future. This is shown in all elements of the logo, and especially the typography and the use of colour are characteristically novel and move away from those traditionally used in university or even corporate logos. The new visual imagery is clearly internationally or globally oriented when compared to those of the merging universities (focused on Helsinki). Nevertheless, because of the linkage with Alvar Aalto, the logo for the new university also combines nationalism with that of a global orientation. In this regard, the logo works in a manner that is somewhat similar to the case of Nordea mentioned above (Vaara et al., 2007; Vaara & Tienari, 2011).

Power aspects. One of the key issues in post-merger integration is the potential confrontation between the merger partners. As in many other cases, a break from the past may help to provide a basis that helps to go beyond 'us versus them' confrontation which could be more apparent with names or logos that would explicitly link with the previous ones. Also, as one of the merger partners (Helsinki University of Technology) was significantly bigger than the others, there has been a concern for domination among the others. Thus, rather than retaining names or visual images of the past linked with Helsinki University of Technology, the new name and logo imply a new fresh start based on equality and balance of power. In this respect, the visual identity strategy resembles that reported in other studies—for instance in the case of Nordea (Vaara et al., 2007; Vaara & Tienari, 2011) that sought to alleviate the risks of confrontation. The breakaway from the previous logos and the use of the changing colours and punctuation marks in Aalto's case can be seen as helpful choices in this regard. Furthermore, the fact that Alvar Aalto can be associated with each of the three merger partners underscores the idea of cross-disciplinary collaboration in the merged university.

12.6 Reactions and Use of the Logo

This new visual and multimodal basis offered by the logo became a key part of the discussions about the new university (Aula, 2016; Tomperi, 2009). Without going into detail, three different kinds of reactions and uses of the logo can be distinguished. First, those behind and supporting the merger appeared by and large satisfied and enthusiastic about the new identity and image as crystallized in the logo. While key people could differ in terms of their orientation and could perceive specific issues in different ways, the new logo and the visual identity around it were seen as a useful tool for the construction of the new university. This included a new, more international orientation summarized in the term 'world

138 *Application*

class' (Aula & Tienari, 2011). Also, the fact that the new logo was a clear break-away from the past was seen as beneficial in terms of easing the tensions between the merger partners.

However, many people voiced concerns, especially in the schools, where a loss of independence was feared. In particular, many people in the former Helsinki School of Economics had come to value its heritage as symbolized by its logo, with its distinctive dark green colour, and by the architecture of its main building (not designed by Alvar Aalto, see Karhunen, Jyrämä, & Knuutinen, 2012). Aula's (Aula et al., 2015; Aula & Tienari, 2011) research shows that these reactions were often linked to the transformation of the school in terms of the establishment of an Anglo-American tenure track system implying very limited career prospects for those not selected to be part of it. Often the new logo and the visual imagery became targets of criticism and resistance along these lines.

Finally, there were also reactions that were more ideological in terms of criticizing or resisting the new university reform in Finland *per se*. Aalto became the key symbol of this general transformation that many feared would lead to a decrease of public funding, establishment of fees for students, elitism, and/or a gradual privatization of the sector. In this connection, the logo—or versions of it—were used to criticize Aalto University and the university reform it was linked with. In particular, critics developed their own ironic representations as a form of resistance (Tomperi, 2009). Figure 12.5 below offers an example of such representations.

The issue of reception and reaction to the new logo is one in which previous archaeological studies of the Aalto logo could usefully be complemented with other approaches, particularly from a practice and strategic perspective. Practice approaches would look in more detail into the way in which the logos are (ab)used and manipulated in actual organizational practice. The ironic representations as shown in Figure 12.5 are a good example of what can happen to a multimodal artefact if audiences do not

Figure 12.5 Use of Aalto's Logo in Criticism and Resistance

Source: Tomperi, 2009, p. 14; left: reproduced with permission from Miika Salo and Sami Syrjämäki; right: reproduced with permission from Voima Magazine

agree with its intended meanings. Other interesting aspects could include when and how the logo is shown and by whom, to what degree the official guidelines are complied with, and how the logo is combined with other multimodal resources in public appearances of university members. Strategic approaches, on the other hand, might provide insights into how newcomers react to the logo, and how they respond cognitively and affectively. It would be interesting to examine, for instance, whether the use of specific punctuation marks and colours—and their combination—changes audience reactions when they first encounter the logo.

12.7 Conclusions

While it is difficult to provide a comprehensive overview of what has happened over time, some conclusions may be drawn. As is usually the case with post-merger integration, issues of identity and identification may be long-lasting. In Aalto's case, even more so than initially planned, the logo has been extensively used in university branding, communication in international and external arenas, and in all kinds of design decisions ranging from internal processes to architecture in the main campus.

Nevertheless, several years after the initial merger the role of the logo seems to have changed. On the one hand, it has—for better or worse depending on the perspective—become an established part of the university alongside other aspects of its identity. Thus, the logo is no longer seen as a novel element that pushes the university's identity to a new direction or provokes critical reactions. Rather, it seems to have stabilized as part of the university that has already become established both in Finland and internationally. On the other hand, the visual imagery still works as a tool with specific meaning potential. Interestingly, the logo and other elements of the visual identity are continuously and systematically used, and they are also playing a key role in the new architectonic and design decisions throughout the main campus.

Note

1. The complete Aalto University Visual Design Guidelines, which also contain the figures in colour, is available on http://materialbank.aalto.fi/BetterDownloader.ashx?rid=0207338b-a1c5-48af-8017-a1be012d05f6.

13 Multimodal Meaning-Making in Online Shopping

Increasingly many everyday practices and interactions are digitally 'resemiotized' (Iedema, 2001, 2003a), that is, adapted and transformed to suit online modes of communication. So all-encompassing is this tendency in contemporary society, and so fundamental is the change for humans in this digital age that the term 'the digital turn' has been coined (Westera, 2013). Digital systems and algorithms now structure and regulate many of the things we do, whether in organizations or as private citizens. They do so in new and non-negotiable ways, pre-determining what actions we can perform and how, and in the process creating a permanent record of everything we do, which can then be used to control the online practices in accordance with the interests of their providers.

In this chapter, we investigate what happens when everyday face-to-face interaction moves online. We will focus on online shopping, a rapidly growing phenomenon which is not only transforming the high streets of our villages and towns, but also the way buyers and sellers interact, the way sellers present goods and services to buyers, the way buyers can examine goods, and the perceived and real risks customers as well as sellers are exposed to. What was, in face-to-face shopping, an embodied and situated interaction, now comes to resemble a text, as goods that could be physically displayed, touched, and handled in markets and brick-and-mortar shops must now be presented, inspected, and selected by means of words and images.

Shopping is a crucial case here, since the fierce competition among online retailers constantly pushes semiotic innovation, making it a rich case for studying the use of a range of semiotic resources. Furthermore, it can be argued that all online practices are ultimately modelled on the principles of the market, which positions us as consumers rather than as citizens (or students or patients), and in which consumer choice and consumer satisfaction are the central concerns, while at the same time cost must be minimized and profits maximized (Davies, 2016).

More generally, studying online shopping allows us to study how digitalization remediates and transforms the communicative relations between organizations and stakeholders. We focus on the issue of control: how the algorithms of the technology constrain and enact the relationship between organizations (i.e., retailers) and stakeholders (i.e., customers) when this relationship is resemiotized, mediated by pictures, words, typography, colour, layout, and icons. We therefore need to closely analyse the digital texts that act as the interface between customers and retailers, and thereby regulate their interaction.

Our investigation will move from micro to macro, so to speak, that is, from text to context. We will answer three interrelated questions in the following order: (a) What is in the text? (b) How do people interact with the text? and (c) Why do people interact with the text the way they do? To answer these questions, we will start by analysing the semiotic modes at stake in an online shopping universe, focusing on the way the website of the online fashion retailer Zalando uses a range of semiotic resources to enable its functionality, hereunder to try to control the customer's journey, and to make the meanings it seeks to make. Secondly, we will outline the results of a number of eye-tracking experiments and follow-up interviews conducted with customers shopping in Zalando's online store. Thus, we describe the 'text in use' and ask why it is used the way it is. The latter part of this question, the 'why', builds a bridge to the final part of our investigation, where we explain some motives for the way customers engage with online retailers.

13.1 Multimodal Meaning-Making in Zalando's Online Shop[1]

Halliday and Hasan (1976) define a text as a semantic unit, although at the same time maintaining that it is an indeterminate concept, that is, "not something that has a beginning and an ending" (Halliday, 1977, p. 47), since it is intertextually related to surrounding texts. Furthermore, "the essential feature of text . . . is that it is interaction" (Halliday, 1977, p. 51). Websites are fundamentally organized as hypertexts, linking text elements to other text elements (Barnet, 2014). By clicking and linking, users construe their own total text (experience) from these text elements. This constitutive element of interaction in the construal of any web text makes a website appear more 'indeterminate' and less self-contained as a semantic unit than, say, an e-mail or a TV commercial. However, since the meaning-making resources used on the Zalando website (e.g., its colour scheme and general layout), together with its menus and internal linking to other parts of the website, demarcates it from all other sites on the world wide web, we can still understand Zalando's website as a semantic unit, that is, as a text. As such, it combines not only a large number of actual text elements (pictures of clothing, descriptions of clothing, size charts, etc.), but also, on a more general level, a number of distinct text types—or registers. In social semiotics, the term register is used for 'text type' (Halliday & Matthiessen, 2013). In multimodal terms, a register "is an integration of resources (both semantic and lexicogrammatical resources) typically associated with a certain text type" (Andersen & Boeriis, 2015; see also Halliday, 1978). This understanding of register is closely related to Firth's notion of 'restricted languages', which he uses for (functional) varieties of text that have their "own grammar and dictionary" (Firth, 1957, p. 87) and are typical of certain 'fields of experience and action' (Firth, 1957, 1968). As such, the concept of register resembles what some sociolinguists call 'style', e.g., Holmes, who mentions the following examples of styles:

> Journalese, baby-talk, legalese, the language of auctioneers, race-callers, and sports commentators, the language of airline pilots, criminals, financiers, politicians and disc jockeys, the language of the court room and the classroom.
> (Holmes, 1992, p. 276)

13.1.1 An Overview of zalando.co.uk

Zalando's online shop is an elaborate website consisting of a large number of webpages for customers to glance at and read through as they engage with the website. Emphasizing the connectivity between the various types of pages, the sitemap in Figure 13.1 presents a (somewhat simplified) overview of the website.

13.1.2 Register Variation at zalando.co.uk

A multimodal social semiotic text analysis of the website reveals that Zalando employs five distinct registers in their online universe:

(a) A 'catalogue' register, on dedicated catalogue pages.
(b) A 'product sheet' register, used on pages dedicated to a single product.
(c) A 'retail' register, primarily found on the title page, on the catalogue pages, and on the check-out pages.
(d) An 'advertising' register, mostly found in the general descriptions of the various categories of products sold in Zalando's online shop, for example, on the dedicated catalogue pages, and also on the title page.
(e) A 'fashion magazine' register, which is salient on the catalogue pages and on various pages that are designed like spreads from fashion magazines. This register is also instantiated in the global menu for the website.

Of the abovementioned registers, the first three are most central, since they are necessary for the website to fulfil its commercial purpose. We will now describe how these registers deploy multimodal semiotic resources to realize their communicative functions.

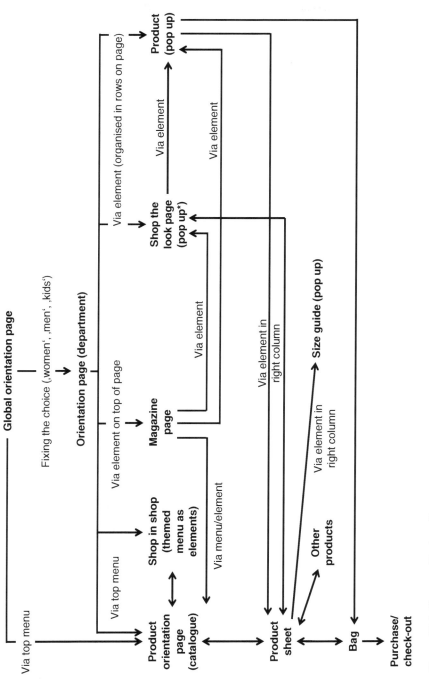

Figure 13.1 Sitemap (Reduced)

144 *Application*

13.1.3 The Catalogue

Shopping will always involve customers selecting and inspecting their purchases, but this will be done differently on the street market, in the corner shop, in the supermarket, or online. On the Zalando website, it is the catalogues which allow customers to select and inspect the products available in specific categories, while at the same time stressing the abundance of products on offer: Each catalogue contains hundreds of pictures, displayed in identical fashion, and arranged in tight symmetrical rows of three photos with similar captions, without foregrounding any product over others. Not only the pictures, that is, the items in the catalogue, are organized in a tight grid structure with fixed positions, but also the menus, the submenus (at the top and to the left on the webpage), and the search field.

Catalogue photos either show the product in Full Shot and frontally photographed against a blank background, or a model wearing the product, framed in such a way that the entire item of clothing is displayed (but as much as possible only that item, so that not all of the model may be shown). This decontextualized way of showing the clothes (and the models) contrasts with fashion photos, which typically show models in Medium Long Shot and 'on location'. Catalogue photos are therefore 'analytical' images (Kress & van Leeuwen, 2006), images that are designed to show all the parts of a whole, in as much detail as possible. The analytical function of these images is enhanced by moving the cursor over them, which produces further images, showing, for instance, the back of the product, or details such as pockets, special stitching, buttons, or the texture of the fabric. The function of these pictures is therefore primarily representational. But when the face of the models is included, an 'interactive' element (Kress & van Leeuwen, 2006) may intrude, as the model may smile at the viewer or, if not looking at them, entice them (in the women's section) with a slight pout or a half open mouth and a wistful stare. The captions, finally, simply list the brand (e.g., 'Lauren | Ralph Lauren | Woman'), the name of the garment (e.g., 'BENNY'), the type of garment (e.g., 'blouse'), its colour (e.g., 'black'), and its price.

Each catalogue page also includes, usually in its leftmost column, a purely verbal introduction to the category of product it displays. Although less salient than the pictures (see, for instance, Kress & van Leeuwen, 1996, 2006), it is nevertheless interesting in the way it mixes different registers: the retail register, because it is directly related to the catalogue display; the fashion magazine register, because it presents information about the type of product displayed; and the advertising register, because it also seeks to persuade the reader to buy.

13.1.4 The Product Sheet

The product sheet provides the buyer with further information about products selected from the catalogue. As the buyer has already selected

Figure 13.2 Screen Shot of Catalogue Page

the product, it does not appraise or evaluate the product, although it will try to persuade the buyer to purchase additional products. Its main purpose, however, is to provide a pictorial rendition of a product and a concise overview of its specifications together with a recommended retail price (RRP).

Like the catalogue, the product sheet is characterized by a grid structure which organizes every element in a fixed position on the page. Most salient is the picture of the decontextualized product in the centre (Kress & van Leeuwen, 1996, 2006). Below this there are additional pictures of the product, presenting it from different viewpoints. To the left, there is a repetition of the caption from the catalogue, together with some practicalities regarding delivery and the right to return. On the right, customers are shown the price, given the opportunity to choose colour and size, and to click the 'ADD TO BAG' link, or add the product to their wish list. Here they are also urged to buy additional, matching items via 'Shop the look' which displays the product as part of a whole outfit. At the bottom, finally, there are details of shape, measurement, and fabric and washing instructions, as well, as, yet again, suggestions for the purchase of further, similar products ('you might also like').

146 *Application*

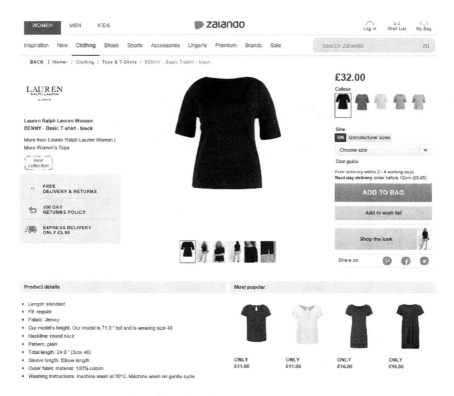

Figure 13.3 Screen Shot of Product Sheet

13.1.5 Retail Register

The retail register is characterized by

(a) A dialogic style, with opening and closing greetings (Halliday & Hasan, 1985) and much use of first and second person personal pronouns.
(b) Transactional talk expressing motives and actions at the point of sale: The seller offers something (to the costumer), and the costumer prefers, chooses, looks for, needs, or tries the various items of clothing.
(c) An emphasis on the price of the goods.
(d) Details about payment, delivering, and return options.
(e) Size, which plays a crucial role when shopping for fashion.

We will now discuss and exemplify these characteristics. Dialogic style already comes in play at the entry to Zalando's website, where we are met with the greeting 'WHO ARE YOU SHOPPING FOR TODAY?', in salient capitals. This greeting not only welcomes the customers but also

Multimodal Meaning-Making in Online Shopping 147

Figure 13.4 Screen Shot of the Catalogue Page for 'Women's Blouses and Tunics'

leads them to the relevant department of the store ('Women', 'Men', or 'Kids'). When the purchase is completed, the transaction is closed with 'Thank you for shopping with us! Your order has been received'. The use of personal pronouns, transactional talk, and pricing can be illustrated with the catalogue page for 'Women's blouses and tunics':

Here we find abundant use of personal pronouns (e.g., 'you' in the following examples) and transactional talk (see the underlined verbs below):

- '*Women's tunics on the other hand offer you a more relaxed style*'
- '*whether you prefer plain, muted colours such as navy or white, or are looking for a more fun and funky style, tunics and blouses can be found to suit every style*'.

The price of the goods is saliently displayed—below any picture to the right, as a kind of caption, and on the product sheet pages, where it uses the largest font size on the entire page.

Payment, delivery, and return options are fundamental in the 'checkout' phase, as illustrated in Figure 13.5, which shows the result of an eye-tracking experiment dealing with online shopping behaviour in Zalando's web universe. Clearly 'Billing address', 'Delivery address', 'Delivery options', and 'Estimated time of delivery' are closely scrutinized by the customer.

148 *Application*

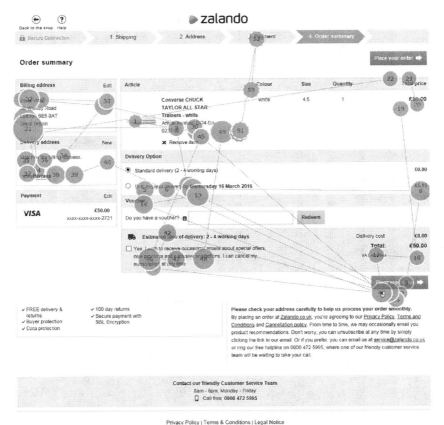

Figure 13.5 Eye-Tracking in Check-Out Phase

But information about payment, delivery, and return options can also be found elsewhere—on pages specially designated to describe how easy it is to shop online in Zalando's store or to return an item.

Choosing the correct size, finally, also plays a significant part in the retail register. The product sheet pages, for instance, contain descriptions of size and measurements, for example, in the 'product details' for the T-shirt shown in Figure 13.3: 'Length: standard', 'Our model's height: Our model is 71.0″ tall and is wearing size 48′, 'Total length: 24.0″ (size 48)'. The Zalando website contains no less than nine different size guides (for different product categories such as suits, shoes, and blouses), and from every single product sheet the relevant size guide is only a click away.

All this shows two key characteristics of the retail register. First, it is dispersed through the entire site. Wherever you are, and whatever you are doing, browsing, reading information, or leafing through a fashion magazine, the signs that lead to the check-out are never far away, like the signs that lead from minor roads back to the highway. And second, as much as websites are multimodal, verbal language plays a key role here, and visual communication is mainly used to make the key signposts and buttons salient. This focus on verbal language may have its drawbacks, despite efforts to reduce processes to easy-to-handle steps; for instance, when complex size guides have to be negotiated, or when choices have to be made from drop down menus of fabrics or types of collar which not even English speakers may be familiar with.

13.1.6 Advertising Register

Like the retail register, the advertising register relies primarily on verbal language. Although it makes some use of colour and display typography, the glamorous imagery and elaborate visual rhetoric described in classic accounts of advertising photography such as Berger (1972), Dyer (1982), and Williamson (1979) is largely absent here.

Here are some of the register's characteristic verbal features (see Andersen, 2007; Machin & van Leeuwen, 2007):

(a) Direct address, that is, reader-involving speech functions (Andersen & Holsting, 2015), especially suggestive commands, often in the form of imperative clauses.
(b) A dialogic style making much use of the first and second person personal pronouns.
(c) Frequent and salient mention of the name of brands and/or stores/retailers.
(d) Appraisal of the products and the values associated with them, often realized by adjectives.
(e) The use of poetic language (see, for instance, Jakobson, 1960b) in the form of stylistic devices such as alliteration and rhyme.

These characteristics can be illustrated with examples from the verbal product introduction of the 'Women's blouses and tunics' catalogue. Examples of suggestive commands include: 'Try a leopard print or sheer black blouse with some skinny jeans and platform heels for a glamorous daytime look, or a floral tunic top with some shorts and sandals for an easy summer style', and in 'Get your fashion fix with **women's blouses and tunics** from Zalando.co.uk!'. These examples also illustrate the use of first and second person pronouns, the naming of a retailer ('Zalando.co.uk'), and the use of poetic language in the alliteration 'fashion fix' and the rhyme 'fix'—'tunics'. Another alliteration is 'fun and funky' in "whether you prefer plain, muted colours such as navy or white, or are looking for a more fun and funky style,

150 *Application*

tunics and blouses can be found to suit every style", which also exemplifies the positive appraisal of a style.

13.1.7 Fashion Magazine Register

The fashion magazine register makes more extensive use of images. Zalando's fashion pictures differ from their catalogue pictures in two ways—the model is seen from a frontal angle, in Medium Long Shot, hence displaying a whole outfit rather than a single product, and in a location that attributes fashion meaning to this outfit, for instance the canopied entrance to an expensive hotel, or a tennis court. Fashion pictures may also show only a product or range of products, without a model. These will be carefully arranged, often together with additional elements, for instance flowers to signify the fashion season. The difference between catalogue and fashion pictures is illustrated in Figure 13.6.

However, verbal language also plays a key role in the fashion magazine register, as brilliantly explored in Barthes' *The Language of Fashion* (2013 [1960]) and, more recently, in Moeran's (2013) anthropological study of fashion 'glossies'. Both insist on the normative role of language in fashion magazines: "It is language that defines what fashion is, or is not" (Moeran, 2013, p. 132; see also Barthes, 2013, p. 109). Moeran then further characterizes fashion language as follows:

> [W]ritten-clothing consists of two inter-related classes of utterance. One includes all the vestimentary features (forms, fabrics, colours, and so on) that signify different kinds of clothes; the other all evaluative ('discreet', 'amusing', and so on) and circumstantial ('evening',

Figure 13.6 Catalogue Pictures and Fashion Pictures

'weekend', shopping', 'party', and so forth) features that signify the kinds of lives we lead in the world.

(Moeran, 2013, p. 132)

Moeran's evaluative category should, we believe, be further divided into aesthetic evaluation (e.g., 'amusing') and functional evaluation (e.g., 'summer skirt'). In short, verbally the fashion magazine register combines:

(a) Descriptions of vestimentary features (material/fabrics, shape, colour), that is, categorizations of the clothing according to its type; such categorizations do not appraise or evaluate the clothing.
(b) Appraisals of the clothing according to an aesthetic norm, that is, evaluations according to taste.
(c) Circumstantial descriptions (Halliday & Matthiessen, 2013) that point to the situation where it would be appropriate to wear the clothing.
(d) Resultative descriptions of the effect of the clothing on the perception of the users' body.

We can illustrate these four registerial features with a text from the webpage for 'Women's heels' that functions as an introduction to that product category:

> A wardrobe staple for every woman, the right high heels can elongate your leg, create an instant slimming effect and bring a touch of elegance to any outfit. Also, with so many different styles, colours and heel heights to choose from in this curated selection of women's heels, you're sure to find a striking pair to update your seasonal look. With court shoes and Mary Janes perfect for the office or a dinner date, to wedges and stilettos you can wear from day-to-night in the city, you can easily channel this season's latest women's heels trends. A popular footwear option for centuries, classic women's heels are a must for modern, fashion-conscious women looking to transform their everyday look.
>
> - Update every outfit with an exquisite pair of women's heels.
> - Inject confidence into your wardrobe this season by creating a bold and exciting city style. Slip on a stunning pair of stiletto high heels in a sumptuous hue for cocktail parties or a wedding reception, and wear with a fitted little black dress or structured jumpsuit. Black lace-up or tan block heels are perfect for making a fashion statement in the office. Team these strong women's heels with a sharp pencil skirt or tapered trousers, completing the look with an on-trend pussy bow blouse. Classic kitten heels are great for everyday wear as they offer a little extra comfort, so wear a feminine Mary Jane style pair with a retro midi bell skirt

Figure 13.7 Screen Shot of Catalogue Page for 'Women's Heels'

and a bejewelled top. Wedge heels look great worn with denim shorts and a vest top, or even with jeans and an exotic print kimono jacket.

This text contains examples of all four of Moeran's categories: descriptions of vestimentary features such as 'With *court shoes* and *Mary Janes* perfect for the office or a dinner date, to *wedges* and *stilettos*' or '*Black lace-up* or *tan block heels*'; appraisals of the clothing according to some aesthetic norm, for example, 'a *striking* pair', 'an *exquisite* pair of women's heels', 'a *bold and exciting* city style'; circumstantial descriptions, such as '*for cocktail parties* or a *wedding reception*' or 'Classic kitten heels are great *for everyday wear*', and one resultative description: 'the right heels can *elongate your leg*', creating 'an instant *slimming effect*'.

Note also that the text does not make use of any verbal markers for modality (e.g., modal verbs such as *can* or *may* and modal auxiliaries such as *maybe, to some extent*, or *typically*), that is, the information is presented as something that is not to be negotiated (Halliday & Matthiessen, 2013); instead, the information is presented with great certainty, as in 'Black lace-up or tan block heels are perfect for making a fashion statement in the office'. This illustrates a fifth feature of the fashion magazine register, namely "*the authoritative wording* of someone who knows everything that is behind the confused, or incomplete appearance of the

Multimodal Meaning-Making in Online Shopping 153

visible forms" (Barthes, 2013, pp. 108–109 [emphasis in the original]; see also Machin & van Leeuwen, 2007).

A sixth and seventh feature of the fashion magazine register is lexis referring to the fundamental visual nature of fashion (expressions such as 'the look' and 'the style'), such as 'fashion-conscious women looking to transform their everyday look' or 'with so many different *styles*', and to the transient nature of fashion trends (e.g. '*this season's latest* women's heels *trends*'). In the navigation menu in Figure 13.8, this type of lexis plays a significant role.

The fashion magazine register is also instantiated on dedicated 'lifestyle web pages' that style themselves after printed fashion magazines. The purpose of these webpages is to create attention to a particular, overarching theme, for instance by profiling role models such as personal trainer and blogger Carly Rowena (see Figure 13.9).

The feature about Carly Rowena contains many pictures, showing her engaged in activities such as exercising, cooking healthy food, etc., all in the same nuances of olive brown, white, and grey. While fashion pictures show models from a frontal angle, these shots are mostly taken from a more oblique angle, as records of Carly's activity, rather than as posed fashion shots. What matters here is the display of trendy lifestyles

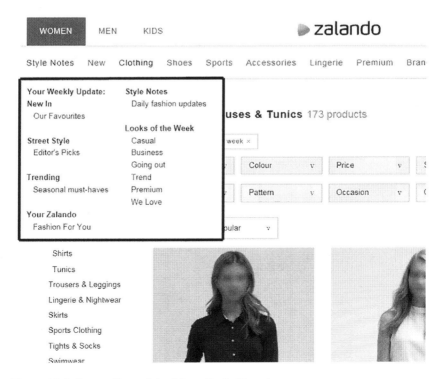

Figure 13.8 Screen Shot of the Menu 'Style Notes'

154 *Application*

Figure 13.9 Screen Shot of Feature About Carly Rowena

(Chaney, 1996) that can be related to trendy fashions—the commercial purpose of these features is of course to inspire the customer to purchase one or more of the items Carly is wearing—for example, trainers, sports shirts, tracksuits, etc., and there are immediate links to mini-catalogues of these items and to a special catalogue page with the heading 'Carly's workout picks 290 products'.

13.1.8 Meaning-Making at zalando.co.uk—In a Nutshell

In our analysis we have focused on (written) language and pictures, that is, on the verbal and the visual mode. This is because meaning-making on Zalando's website must be done with words and pictures, not, for instance, with sound or smell or tactility, modes that play an important role in brick-and-mortar fashion shops. This leads us to the observation that online shopping is less multimodal than shopping in brick-and-mortar shops.

In Zalando's online shop, it is first and foremost the visual structures that organize meaning. The website is structured on the basis of visual compositional principles (see, for instance, Kress & van Leeuwen, 1996, 2006), especially those of salience, 'framing', and 'Centre–Margin', whereas the idea of 'Given-New' also plays a role with the movement from the menus to the left ('Given') towards the preferred action (e.g., 'Add to bag') on the right ('New'). Language nevertheless plays a very significant role on the Zalando website, first of all because it must express what, in face-to-face shopping episodes, would have been apprehended by touch—by feeling the fabric and fitting the clothes, for instance—and second, because verbal language plays a fundamental and authoritative role in defining what fashion is and what specific fashions mean. The Zalando site thus requires a command of relatively specialist vocabularies (e.g., in drop down menus with the names of different fabrics), as well as skills such as taking one's measurements, neither of which all customers may have.

We have also observed how the registers are instantiated in a spatial rather than a linear structure. Although some elements may be more salient than others, for example the bright 'ADD TO BAG' option, essentially there is no pre-designed step-by-step process leading to a final stage that realizes the (communicative) goal of the website as a whole. The deployment of text elements adhering to different registers allows for different reading paths to realize different communicative goals. The only exception is in the check-out phase, which follows a highly controlled, non-negotiable sequence that includes the obligatory disclosure of personal data, something which in traditional shops was not required.

Like other online shops, the Zalando website mixes shopping with registers which formerly were (and to some degree still are) found in separate media such as fashion magazines, lifestyle magazines, and lifestyle newspaper supplements. In doing so, hybrid text types such as the 'advertorial', the 'friendvertorial', the sponsored social media conversation, etc., are taken a step further—all fashion advertising and all fashion information now leads directly to the check-out.

13.2 The Practice of Shopping on www.zalando.co.uk

In this section, we will describe how shoppers interact with Zalando's online universe by outlining the results of some eye-tracking experiments and follow-up interviews conducted with customers shopping online with Zalando. In doing so, we engage in what Björkvall has labelled social semiotic ethnography ("sociosemiotiska etnografin", see Björkvall, 2012), making use of eye-tracking, "the process of recording the gaze of a person and the movement of the eyes from one point to another" (Saldanha & O'Brien, 2013, p. 136).

156 *Application*

The map in Figure 13.1 showed, in a slightly simplified way, the various webpages in Zalando's online shopping universe and the connectivity between them. Although there is only one entrance to the shop, from there on many different trajectories are possible, not all of them leading to the check-out. Of course, if customers do buy something, there will be a number of obligatory elements—they will have to make at least one selection, they will have to inspect that selection, even if only cursorily, they will have to choose a size and colour, confirm the order and pay, but a purchase does not necessarily need to be made. A user can also leaf through the fashion magazine or walk into the shop to inspect what is on offer without buying anything—even though this will be noticed by Zalando and followed up with advertisements that will pop up on other sites frequented by the user, for example, on online newspapers, Facebook, or YouTube.

In short, the pathway through the shop is constructed by the users on the basis of their own plans and goals. But it is also closely watched by Zalando, which will follow users every step along the road, and even outside the shop. In the case of our eye-tracking experiments, those plans and goals were chosen for the shoppers[2] with the result that all subjects took more or less the same path through the Zalando labyrinth, as shown in Figure 13.10. Because we asked them to buy, they did not linger to read about Carly Rowena or Yoga outfits.

Even though the customers in the experiment followed the same general trajectory, there were individual nuances. We will describe two behavioural patterns to illustrate this (see Figure 13.11).

Customer A hardly looked around on the website. Using the menu on the top of the webpage, she headed straight to her preferred product category (in this case 'Men's Jewellery'), and on that page spent quite some time scrolling and moving the mouse over the displayed products, so as to be able to examine the products in detail from various angles. In the end, she added only one product to her bag, and then proceeded to buy it. She did not interact with the verbal text elements but was solely oriented towards the pictures.

Customer B headed directly to the 'Women's Polo Shirts' catalogue, and then meticulously examined a number of products by moving backwards and forwards between the catalogue and the product sheets for each single product. On the product sheets, she carefully examined the pictures, moving the cursor over them to zoom in on details. She also paid attention to the verbal text, reading about the functionalities of each product in the bullet-pointed product details (see Figure 13.3). Each time a product interested her, she added it to her bag. Once she had bagged a number of products, she changed her behavioural pattern: Instead of moving between catalogue and product sheets, she now moved between her basket and the product sheets, using the basket as a wish list, or as a sub-selection from among the many options in the catalogue. From this list she then went back to once more examine each product, discarding them one by one, until she was left with the one product she chose to buy.

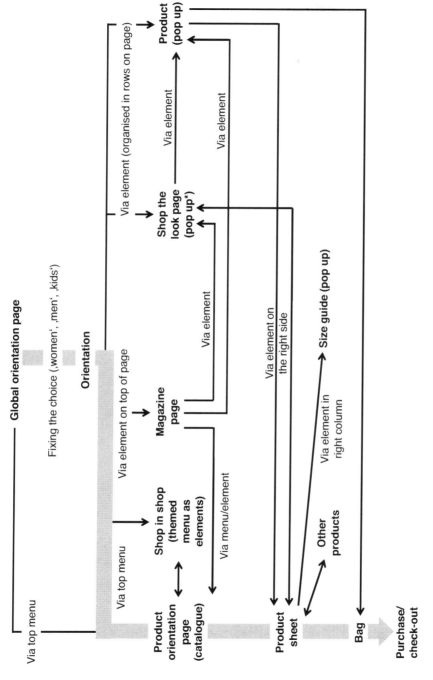

Figure 13.10 Trajectory of Experimental Subjects Making Zalando Purchases

13.3 Customer Motivation

In the beginning of this chapter, we emphasized that the practice of online shopping entails an effort by the shop to control its customers and their journey, ultimately in order to avoid so-called shopping cart abandonment (Huang, Korfiatis, & Chang, 2018; Kukar-Kinney & Close, 2010). In this section, we flip the coin and take a look at how customers in an online shop try to reduce—and as much as possible to control—the perceived risk of online shopping. The impossibility of physically examining products is the single largest barrier in online shopping (Blazquez, 2014). Kim and Forsythe (2009) and Schramm-Klein, Swoboda, and Morschett (2007) have shown that this risk factor is especially high for clothing and apparel shopping, partially—and more generally—because customers do not experience any personal contact with the retailer, which would be the case in a brick-and-mortar shop, and partially because many of the characteristics of apparel that are important to consumer decision-making, such as fit, fabric quality, and colour, are difficult to present on the screen, whereas standard descriptors of a product are often insufficient for product evaluation (Kim & Forsythe, 2009).

To reduce the perceived risk, many customers apparently order the same item in different sizes rather than struggling with the size guides, and then return those that do not fit, something which of course comes at a cost for the company (Dusto, 2012). This might help explain why Zalando puts so much semiotic effort in its many size guides and extensive list of measurements and fitting descriptions.

Marketing studies have further shown that two factors are decisive in deselecting particular online retailers (see Melander, 2016): (a) reviews and comments from dissatisfied (former) customers (e.g., on Trustpilot or Facebook), and (b) bad pictures and missing contact information. Endo, Yang, and Park (2012) and Aghekyan-Simonian, Forsythe, Kwon, and Chattaraman (2012) point to the first of these factors in their investigations of online shopping, but a recent report shows that a lack of product descriptions and bad product pictures is the largest barrier. If a website is flawed in this regard, 81 percent of customers opt out altogether. This finding can help explain the plethora of product images, precise captions, and 'Product detail' lists we found in our textual analysis of Zalando's website. Clearly Zalando's many detailed and clear product pictures impact on customers' purchase intentions indirectly by decreasing risk perception (see Aghekyan-Simonian et al., 2012).

Aghekyan-Simonian et al. (2012) divide perceived risk into three types: (a) 'product performance risk', (b) 'financial risk', and (c) 'time risk'. Product performance risk is about the customer's expectation of the quality of a product, and it is therefore easier to sell products from well-known brands than no-name products (see also Blazquez, 2014). For this reason, brands are very salient on Zalando's website, both as logos on the

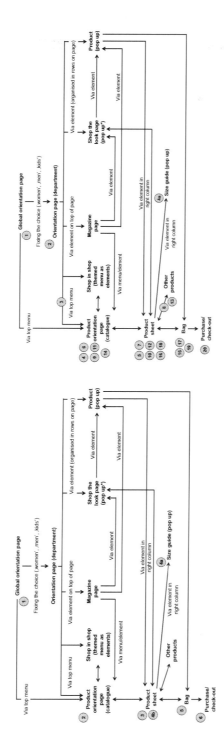

Figure 13.11 Trajectory of Customer A and B; Each Number Represents an (Inter)action Sequence on a Particular Part of the Website

product sheet pages and in the captions accompanying the pictures on the catalogue pages. In the latter case, the brand name is highlighted with bold and placed on the top line of the caption. Financial risks and time risks relate to payment, delivery, and returning, and for this reason Zalando presents the process of returning an item as consisting of just a few very simple steps, thereby again decreasing the customer's perception of risk. In this context, it could be noted that each of the steps in the description of how to return an item is depicted by an icon. This use of icons seeks to make the process even more easy-to-handle (Morrow, Hier, Menard, and Leirer's psychological study, which suggests that icons can improve comprehension by reducing the need to draw inferences, and that icons reduce the time it takes to decode a message [1998]). The very simple and transparent process of shopping (and returning) is furthermore emphasized in e-mail notifications sent to the customers while they await their goods. Such 'post-purchase customer service' is found to be pivotal in establishing a good reputation as an online retailer (Azar, Khan, & Shavaid, 2015; Endo et al., 2012).

Both Blazquez (2014) and Kim and Forsythe (2009) distinguish 'hedonistic motives' from 'utilitarian motives' for shopping behaviour (see also Miller, 1998). From a social semiotic point of view, hedonistic motives are interpersonal, whereas utilitarian motives belong to the experiential realm. In our eye-tracking experiment, where the subjects were given a concrete task, utilitarian motives dominated, especially in the behaviour of customer B, who scrutinized all the products she was interested in twice before selecting one for purchase. The hedonistic motive was seen in the behaviour of only one of our subjects: Her fixations in the eye-tracking experiment, and her answers in the follow-up interview, revealed that she generally was more interested in looking at the faces of the "beautiful models in the pictures" than at the clothes they were modelling or the captions accompanying the pictures. In other words, she was guided by an aesthetic motivation.

Benn, Webb, Chang, and Rediy (2015) point out that pictures are more important than verbal language for online shoppers, and that verbal descriptions only become relevant when products visually appear alike but are in fact different. This resonates with customer B's behaviour: She was looking at seemingly similar products (polo shirts) and reading extensively about the different products to make a choice from seemingly identical options.

13.4 Conclusions

So far, we have contextualized our social semiotic text analysis with insights from marketing literature, and this has given us an understanding of the motivations behind online shopping behaviour, and the ways in which retailers try to reduce and control the perception of risk.

Furthermore, we can point out that our combination of text analysis, eye-tracking experiment, follow-up interviews, and review of relevant literature show some of the strengths of combining the more qualitative approach of semiotic text analysis with the more quantitative approach of the behavioural sciences. On the one hand, behavioural studies can explain text analytical findings, and on the other hand, text analysis can show in detail how retailers respond to the challenges identified in the marketing literature.

Within the field of multimodality, the analysis demonstrates the renewed importance of verbal language (see also Chapter 2) in online communication, as many actions which do not need verbalization in face-to-face shopping, must be verbalized online. Buying clothes online involves drop-down menus verbally specifying a range of fabric and other options, and verbal language also plays a key role in the elaborate instructions for taking measurements. All this requires a good command, not only of written English, but also of specialist vocabularies.

Within the field of organization and management studies, our case study shows a combination of the archaeological approach and the practice approach, together with a modicum of the dialogical approach. Using an archaeological lens, we explored the meaning (potential) of the many text elements in Zalando's online universe; using the practice approach lens we treated Zalando's website as a textual artefact and employed eye-tracking to show how the text is engaged with in a concrete shopping situation; and our use of interviews, finally, added an element of the dialogical approach to the study.

Notes

1. It should be noted that our analysis represents the setup of www.zalando.co.uk in March–June 2016.
2. In the experiment, we asked six shoppers to buy two items on Zalando: (a) "Something you decide beforehand to buy for yourself but which you have not bought online before", and (b) "a present for someone you know". The shoppers performed one purchase at the time, so the experiments gave 12 instances of online shopping and in total more than 3 hours of eye-tracking recordings. Afterwards, the subjects were interviewed about their experience and asked to explain their behaviour. The experiment provided rich data, but also showed that we had made two false assumptions. Several of the subjects noted that they would not normally look only at one website, but 'shop around', just as they would on high streets or in shopping malls with many smaller fashion shops. Evidently, we had biased our experiment (a) by assuming that visiting a fashion site would always lead to one or more purchases, when a site may in fact also be visited for other purposes, and (b) by not taking into account that shopping sites are connected to a range of other sites.

14 Multimodal Legitimation and Corporate Social Responsibility (CSR)

Legitimacy—the general assumption that an organization and its conduct are appropriate within a specific institutional and cultural context (Deephouse, Bundy, Tost, & Suchman, 2017)—is a central precondition for organizational success and survival. During the past decades, CSR has emerged as a guiding idea with regard to the changing role of business in society (Crane, McWilliams, Matten, Moon, & Siegel, 2008), and has diffused globally, with a broad variety of local adaptations and translations. In this section, we analyse how companies' communication in CSR reports manifests their discursive legitimation strategies (van Leeuwen & Wodak, 1999). These legitimation strategies extensively combine verbal and visual resources in multimodal compositions in which the different modes complement and enhance each other. The following case is based on a larger research project on the translation of CSR in Austria (Höllerer, 2013; Meyer & Höllerer, 2016; Höllerer, Meyer, & Lounsbury, 2017). We draw especially on empirical material and findings from two studies on the multimodal construction of CSR (Höllerer et al., 2013; Jancsary et al., 2018). Upon outlining how these studies can be 'read' through the prism of legitimacy theory, we also suggest additional ways and complementary research designs conducive to how multimodality can inspire legitimacy research.

14.1 Multimodal Legitimation

Legitimation "explains the institutional order by ascribing cognitive validity to its objectivated meanings" and justifies it by "giving a normative dignity to its practical imperatives" (Berger & Luckmann, 1967, p. 111). In the simplest terms, legitimations answer the questions: "Why should we do this?" and "Why should we do this in this way?" (van Leeuwen, 2007, p. 93). Accordingly, legitimation encompasses the processes and strategies that have legitimacy (an attribution) as their goal. Questions of legitimacy govern the relationship between organizations and society, and legitimacy in the eyes of its stakeholders is what bestows upon organizations their 'licence to operate'. Research has distinguished between various levels of legitimation (from basic categories to complex symbolic systems; Berger & Luckmann, 1967) and different types of legitimacy (e.g. normative, moral, pragmatic; Suchman, 1995). In this case study, we are particularly interested in how legitimation is performed multimodally in discourse, that is, how actors try to construe legitimacy. Focusing on the verbal mode, such theoretical framework has already been fruitfully applied in research on immigration discourse (van Leeuwen & Wodak, 1999), discourse on climate change (Lefsrud & Meyer, 2012), communication in multinational corporations (Erkama & Vaara, 2010; Vaara & Tienari, 2008), the Eurozone crisis (Vaara, 2014), or public accounting reforms (Hyndman, Liguori, Meyer, Polzer, Rota, Seiwald, & Steccolini, 2018). *Authorization* means legitimation by reference to different bases of authority. Such authority can be personal (e.g. experts or role models) or impersonal (e.g. tradition or conformity). *Rationalization* involves reference to aims and utilities or to established knowledge. It is instrumental when actions and actors are legitimated by the purposes that they serve; it is theoretical, when it relates actors and actions to established versions of 'truth' through definitions, explanations, or predictions. A third type of legitimation strategy is *moral evaluation*, which legitimates by reference to particular value systems. This can be achieved through evaluation (i.e., assigning desirable qualities); normalization (i.e., arguing that certain actions are 'natural'); or abstraction (i.e., embedding actors and actions in abstract and desirable meanings, such as practices to freedom, love, etc.). Analogies compare specific actions to others that are commonly seen as morally appropriate. Finally, *mythopoesis* means legitimation conveyed through narratives. Such narrative forms link the past, present, and future, and, through their sequential structure, link actions to outcomes. Legitimating narratives often have a 'moral', meaning that outcomes reward legitimate action and punish non-legitimate action. The most frequent narrative types used for legitimation, accordingly, are moral tales and cautionary tales.

Each level, type or strategy may utilize different modalities; it may be constructed verbally, but also visually, aurally, olfactory, etc. In general, legitimacy and legitimation will include a variety of modes and their multimodal orchestrations. 'Incipient' legitimation, for instance, which means most basic assertions about reality (Berger & Luckmann, 1967), is built into the vocabulary we use, and supported by the apparent 'facticity' of visual or material evidence. Moral legitimacy can be suggested by depiction of prestigious figures and/or normatively laden symbols, whereas cognitive legitimacy may be facilitated by linking potentially problematic information with familiar, socially shared, and institutionalized categories stored not only words, but also in images, material artefacts, or spaces. The visual depiction of experts or the materiality of powerful figures in statues invokes authority; visually communicating de-personalization and objectification (for instance in charts and figures;

164 *Application*

see the case on diagrams in Chapter 11) communicates rationality, and visual metaphor and symbolism may confer moral evaluations. Normalization, may in particular build on the verisimilitude (i.e., 'truthlikeness') of photography, which makes artificially arranged perspectives seem factual. Visual storytelling and visual stereotypes (e.g. heroes, villains, etc.; see, for instance, van Leeuwen, 2007) also enhance legitimation, as can musical arrangements (van Leeuwen, 2018a). As a consequence, actors commonly use multimodal designs in their legitimacy work.

To study multimodal legitimation, researchers often analyse texts. Here, it is useful to consider the different 'strata' of multimodal social semiotics (see Chapter 2). In Goffman's (1981) terms: Who is the 'principle' whose meanings are communicated, who is the 'author' who makes the selection process, and who is the 'animator' who finally communicates? In social semiotics, such stratification is expressed as the differences between discourse, design, and media. *Design* means the translation of particular *discourses* (in our case, legitimation strategies) into one or several modes, whereas *media* encompass the materialization of designs in both production and distribution. Production, according to Kress and van Leeuwen (2001, p. 6) is "the organisation of the expression", the "actual material articulation of the semiotic event or the actual material production of the semiotic artefact". In addition to production media, there are also distribution media which allow designs to 'travel'.

Hence, multimodal legitimation strategies may manifest in a broad variety of texts, and, depending on the research question and the level of analysis, researchers have to carefully choose which media and concrete texts are best suited. Organizational legitimation efforts address diverse audiences, ranging from specifically targeted efforts (e.g. specific investors, big customers) to broad and diffuse audiences (e.g. society in general). In case of the latter, the specific media used are equally broadly available and accessible. Accordingly, annual reports, more specialized reporting documents, or 'integrated' reports are core media for publishing and communicating legitimate conduct multimodally. Additionally, websites are also becoming increasingly popular, not least due to their ability to communicate through a broad variety of semiotic modes simultaneously (see also Chapter 13). The studies discussed in this case focus on corporate reporting documents and the multimodal compositions used in these texts. In such reporting documents, the 'principal' (the organization) is often different from the 'author' (e.g. some public relations agency).

14.2 Corporate Social Responsibility as a Response to Issues of Legitimacy

Corporate (social) responsibility and corporate sustainability are two concepts that have strongly influenced discourses on the role of business in society over the past decades. As one of the most pronounced trends in corporate governance in the 2000s, they have substantially impacted organizational practice. Most generally, CSR refers to the social and societal challenges that come with the conduct of business. It propagates distinct values such as integrity, fairness, and transparency. CSR often invokes the idea of a 'triple bottom line' of business, including the acknowledgement of economic, social, and ecological objectives of the organization. The social dimension can be further differentiated into a variety of topics that encompass both internal (primarily employees) and external (for instance, marginalized groups in society, local communities, etc.) stakeholders. Internal aspects cover topics such as health and safety as well as equal opportunity employment; external aspects include corporate philanthropy, sponsoring, and being, in general, a good 'corporate citizen'.

However, despite a general understanding of what CSR means, more precise definitions remain elusive, partially due to shifts in meaning during its "long and varied history" (Carroll, 1999, p. 268), but also because—as a globally diffusing management idea—CSR has been translated into a variety of local contexts in different ways. In addition to such local variations, fierce debates have accompanied the concept's global diffusion, from broader societal and political debates to organizational practice and academia. This open meaning and contested nature make CSR a particularly interesting topic of study. Thus, CSR adoption and implementation has garnered strong attention in organization and management research (for further research in this area, see, for instance, Aras & Growther, 2010; Crane et al., 2008; Hiss, 2009; Höllerer, 2013; Kinderman & Lutter, 2018; Margolis & Walsh, 2003; Matten & Moon, 2008; Meyer & Höllerer, 2016; Thompson, 2008).

By providing a 'licence to operate', CSR and sustainability are, at their very core, responses to issues of legitimacy; that is, organizations adopt and communicate practices related to CSR and sustainability to ensure legitimacy in an increasingly demanding societal environment. This becomes a particularly complex issue in differentiated societies, where bases of assessing legitimacy are diverse, and different communities voice potentially contradictory expectations towards the organization. In communication media in which 'compartmentalization' of audiences into separate communication arenas is not possible (e.g. in corporate reports or websites), legitimacy becomes precarious and the unpacking of legitimation strategies a fruitful area for multimodal analysis.

Organizational legitimacy can be studied on different levels of analysis. With regard to CSR, the intra-organizational legitimation of one particular practice could be investigated, its proponents and opponents and the strategies they use; or the legitimation efforts of one organization towards one small but vocal audience; or alternatively, the legitimacy of a specific organization or organizational form over time.

166 *Application*

The new institutionalism in organizational analysis (see Greenwood, Oliver, Lawrence, & Meyer, 2017) suggests that rationalized myths in the organization's social environments influence what is seen as 'good' and 'rational' conduct (Meyer & Rowan, 1977). Conformity with the institutional environment increases organizational legitimacy and becomes a strong incentive for organizational action and design. Through their CSR communication, businesses work on the general impression that they are a valuable part of broader society and that their conduct is beneficial, rather than harmful for society. Although legitimation strategies of individual businesses differ and are not coordinated, they all reflect, in one way or another, the 'cultural myths' they are embedded in. Our case concerns the legitimacy of 'business' as a whole and we are interested in the interpretations of CSR that large organizations communicate to broader society as audience; our level of analysis is field-level discourse rather than the multimodal communication strategy of a single organization. We study a particular empirical context: one where typical Anglo-American interpretations of CSR do not immediately fall on 'legitimate grounds'.

14.3 Corporate Social Responsibility in Austrian Corporate Reporting

Austria has a long tradition of businesses accepting societal responsibilities—as indeed is true for most of continental Europe long before CSR as a concept and discourse gained ground. Different from instrumental 'business case' understandings of CSR, naïve egalitarian illusions, or corporate altruism, such implicit understanding of CSR involves "a certain conviction, claim, and even obligation to know better what is good for stakeholders—perhaps more so than they do themselves—and society as a whole" (Meyer & Höllerer, 2016, p. 376). Austria's distinct corporatist tradition includes a close link between the economic and political elite and implies a way of policymaking through institutionalized bargaining and compromise ('social partnership'). This involves a complex web of advisory boards, commissions, and task forces, which, as one downside, means a considerably secrecy and informality of political decision-making as well as a substantial politicization of the economy. Implicit notions of CSR are also furthered by the fact that an obligation to a stakeholder orientation in corporate governance is written into the Austrian Stock Corporations Act, which demands that the executive board acts in the best interest of the corporation, but also considers the interests of shareholders and employees, as well as the public good.

Due to such existing implicit notion of social and societal responsibility, Höllerer (2013) finds distinct adoption patterns of CSR in Austria that reveal an initial hesitation and reluctance, especially on part of the established business elite, to implement more 'explicit' understandings of

CSR. However, his study also shows that non-elite actors saw opportunities in the idea and embraced it more readily. In a later study comparing the adoption of both shareholder value (SHV) and CSR in Austria, Meyer and Höllerer (2016) show that CSR adoption increased at the same time as SHV lost legitimacy in the public view and it was endorsed especially by companies that had proclaimed their commitment to SHV in prior years. Both studies clearly suggest that CSR reporting became an important legitimation device, especially for non-elite actors in the Austrian economic arena.

14.3.1 Data and Sampling

The methodological and empirical illustrations in this section draw from two studies on the Austrian CSR discourse. Both are less interested in single multimodal texts or individual organizations, but use a more structural lens. The first study (Höllerer et al., 2013) reconstructs the structural dimensions of the CSR discourse on the field level to explore how CSR is translated by large for-profit companies into the Austrian local setting. In order to do so, a full sample of stand-alone annual CSR reports issued by Austrian publicly traded corporations between 2001 and 2008 was analysed. In total, this included 37 reports from 12 different corporations. Visuals—as well as their interactions with verbal headlines and image captions—were at the centre of the investigation; in total, 1,652 visuals (excluding schematic and technical visuals such as graphs, charts, and diagrams) were extracted from the reports. This first study, accordingly, exemplifies how visual (and multimodal) analysis can be conducted systematically for a larger set of texts.

The second study (Jancsary et al., 2018) foregrounds the idea that multimodal communication is always directed at an audience. It therefore explores the different subject positions that are assigned to these audiences multimodally. To do so, the authors develop the notion of modal registers as "collective adaptations of the meaning-making resources of a semiotic mode according to the specific social/institutional context of use" (Jancsary et al., 2018, p. 89). Building on social semiotics and functional linguistics, the article explores the 'gazes' that reports provide for audiences, thereby relating audiences to the subject matter (CSR) and to text producers (companies). For this explorative study, a sub-sample of the CSR reports included in the first study was analysed in more depth, focusing on the realization of the interpersonal metafunction (see Chapter 2). This sample consists of the first and the last report published by each organization between 2001 and 2008, as well as reports at regular intervals in between. In total, 25 reports from 11 corporations were investigated, encompassing 1,023 visuals overall. These data were analysed both for the content of representation as well as the embodied positions suggested for audiences, and the interaction between the two aspects.

168 *Application*

14.3.2 Analytical Procedures

In order to illustrate the coding of visual material, we briefly describe each interpretive step of the two studies and explain it on the basis of the concrete example shown in Figure 14.1.[1]

The first study was primarily concerned with the *meaning structures* of the corporate CSR discourse in Austria. Accordingly, the analysis focused on both the manifest and latent content of multimodal compositions, and on the institutionalized stocks of knowledge that such content invokes. In a first step of analysis, the authors inductively developed codes and categories to capture manifest and latent aspects of the visuals in maximal detail. Whereas coding for manifest content is more akin to visual content analysis (see Bell, 2001), reconstructing the latent aspects can be considered a more genuinely semiotic endeavour, as it concerns the question what the manifest content 'represents' in terms of meanings (van Leeuwen, 2001). This served to sensitize the researchers to the communicative efforts of text producers and created a better understanding of the specific visual vocabulary used (see also Kress & van Leeuwen, 2006). The coding resulted in a comprehensive 'dictionary' of 'symbolic devices' (Gamson & Lasch, 1983). Detailed coding in this step is important in order to assess elements of legitimation comprehensively. Symbolic devices may provide hints about what is legitimated: actions, actors

Figure 14.1 Children Playing at a Fountain
Source: Used under license from Shutterstock.com

involved, or even timing, location, tools and materials used. All of these may be legitimate or not, together, or separately.

> For the visual in Figure 14.1, the manifest visual codes are *children, female, cultural deviation*,[2] *immobile infrastructure (well), natural element (water), rural setting, personal interaction (playing)*. Manifest verbal codes (as drawn from the image caption in the report) were *social issues* and *human rights*. Latent codes were *fun, playfulness, aridity, development aid*, and *future generations*.

In the second step, patterns within and across individual visuals were analysed by using manifest and latent symbolic devices as sensitizing concepts. Through an adaptation of existing methods of hermeneutics and discourse analysis (Jancsary et al., 2016; Lueger, Sandner, Meyer, & Hammerschmid, 2005), the authors formulated a brief verbal paraphrase for each visual-verbal composition, answering the question "What are the claims the visual conveys?" Afterwards, the potential structural conditions ("Under what circumstances can such claims be perceived as reasonable and/or typical?") and hypothetical consequences ("What effects would such a claim typically have, and how would this impact on our understanding of CSR?") were assessed. The results were axially coded through constant comparison (Glaser & Strauss, 1967) which yielded a set of 154 distinct idea elements. Read through the prism of legitimation, the claims expressed through these idea elements are claims towards legitimate attitudes and conduct, as the idea elements reconstructed from the illustrative visual show.

> In our illustration, the idea elements resulting from such procedure are *appreciation of nature's wealth, global engagement through development aid, global orientation*, and *rendering sources of life accessible*.

The third step was dedicated to reconstructing the discourse-carrying dimensions (Greimas, 1983; Link, 1997) underlying these idea elements, and the polar oppositions that constitute and bound the respective dimensions. To do so, another round of constant comparison across idea elements was conducted. During this step the authors drew heavily on visual and material means to support their analysis (see use of multimodality in data analysis and theory development in the documenting approach in Chapter 8). In more detail, they created small cards containing individual idea elements and, through team interpretation, proceeded through multiple sessions of arranging and rearranging these cards until they were satisfied with the oppositions thus identified, and the dimensions thus revealed. The material properties of the cards allowed everybody to shift them back and forth, and the emerging configurations could be photographed, which meant that the team could always go back to previous stages if additional rearranging led nowhere. Eventually, idea elements were arranged in an emerging set of 21 different dimensions, such as, for instance, impetus (rational vs. emotional), connectivity (connection vs. separation), or capability (potency vs. impotency), among others. Whereas for some dimensions, both polarities can be assumed to be legitimate towards different audiences (e.g. rational vs. emotional), others clearly distinguish a legitimate from an illegitimate polarity (e.g. potency vs. impotency). Not surprisingly, but nonetheless revealing, illegitimate polarities (e.g. impotency, unprofessional, untrustworthy, deterioration, or separation) were basically absent from the discourse.

> The respective dimensions and polarities for our illustrative photograph are *value system* (other [non-economic] values), *human values* (both material and spiritual), *exchange* (giving/sharing), *locus* (universal/global), *impetus* (emotional), and *area of human influence* (both nature and technology).

In a fifth and final step, the authors used a network visualization software to plot the final opposites into a semantic network that visually revealed certain clusters of polarities, based on the co-occurrence of polarities in the data. From the clustering (Newman, 2006) of polarities in the network, different *topoi*—rhetorical standpoints within the overall discursive landscape regarding a specific issue (Wengeler, 2003)—were reconstructed and described in terms of their main storyline (see also Meyer & Höllerer, 2010). These topoi constitute argumentative bases that are considered legitimate (and legitimating) by text producers in the context of CSR in Austria. Each individual visual-verbal composition usually connected a variety of topoi, leading the authors to conclude that visuals act as a powerful 'bridging device'. Since this step of analysis builds on the interpretation of aggregated data, it cannot be adequately illustrated on the basis of our single example in Figure 14.1. A thorough discussion of methodological procedures can be found in Höllerer et al. (2013).

The second study focused on the interactional aspect of the visual register of the CSR discourse in Austria. In more detail, data were coded—inspired by Kress and van Leeuwen (2006)—for the interpersonal metafunction, first, in terms of the *contact* established between the visual and the viewer. *Strong contact* meant that there was direct eye contact or some other direct addressing of the viewer (e.g. finger pointing). *Weak contact* meant the absence of such direct contact, and *no contact* existed when no people were present, and there was no obvious interaction with physical objects. Second, interaction was also coded in terms of *social distance* between viewer and content of the visual, implying a particular 'gaze'. An *intimate* gaze was suggested when a person or object was shown at very close range, an *interpersonal* gaze showed the bigger part of a whole person (or small groups), and an *impersonal* gaze showed one or more people or objects from afar. Finally, vertical and horizontal angle were considered, with low vertical angle ('frog's eye view) implying *representation power* of the content, high vertical angle ('bird's eye view) suggesting *viewer power* over content, and eye-level perspectives suggesting *equality*. When the horizontal plane of the participants aligns with that of the viewer (frontal angle), this implies identification and *involvement* in the sense of 'belonging to the same world', whereas oblique angles in which the frontal plane of the participants and the viewer diverge from each other, suggest *detachment* and 'otherness'. Through combining contact, distance, power, and involvement, such gazes can (de-)legitimate both viewer and subject. The visual in our illustrative example is one in which the viewer is legitimated through the ascription of 'benevolence':

> The photograph in Figure 14.1 shows a strong case of 'otherness' in the depiction of the two children that aligns with their ethnic and cultural difference from the perspective of an Austrian audience. The visual creates *weak contact* in that it assigns the viewer a position as passive observer. The children are positioned at *interpersonal distance* from a high vertical angle suggesting a power difference in favour of the viewer (*viewer power*). Additionally, the photograph is shot from an oblique angle, in which the perspectives of the children are *detached* from the perspective of the viewer. This is a typical example of the *'benevolent gaze towards the human other'* which positions the viewer in a powerful and benevolent position towards the beneficiaries of CSR activities.

Of course, such interpretation is highly dependent on the broader context (CSR) in which a text is embedded. A gaze assigning the viewers power over the 'other', while detaching them from that 'other' could, in other contexts, be interpreted quite differently.

14.3.3 Central Findings

Legitimation strategies. Höllerer et al. (2013) reconstruct seven central topoi from their data. *Mastery* focuses on the organization itself and portrays it as strong, capable, and vigorous. The topos of *progress* links the past to the present and the future through positive trajectories, and technology to nature by claiming that modern technology actually helps preserve nature. *Local community* stresses the embeddedness of organizations in their societal environment on a local level, whereas *globalism* focuses on international business opportunities and increased global responsibilities. The topos of *values* emphasizes the importance of non-economic values, and *enterprise* brings visionary and spiritual thinking into the business realm. Finally, *credibility* addresses the viewer most

172 Application

directly. In contrast to the others, it does not primarily focus on presenting a particular understanding of CSR, but on bolstering the claims made by the organization, either by portraying its representatives as professional and trustworthy, or by drawing on highly legitimized external experts and opinion leaders that provide testimonials. That credibility is one of the most pervasive topoi in the discourse shows that CSR is at its core a response to legitimacy issues. The other topoi serve to legitimate the organization and its conduct by representing legitimate accounts of how the organization corresponds to the cultural myth of the global 'corporate citizen'.

Topoi are woven into various, and sometimes multiple legitimation strategies. *Authorization* is most clearly attempted through the *credibility* topos, since it draws heavily on the depiction of personal authority (e.g. the board of directors). Such images personalize the organization and 'give a face' to the otherwise 'faceless corporations'. These representations communicate trustworthiness, potency, and professionalism. Figure 14.2 provides examples of how managers are predominantly depicted in our data. The single portrait and the group portrait are two typical genres. Through direct eye contact, accountability is signalled. Also notice how in the group photograph, the male manager in the front turns towards the viewers and thereby 'opens up' the table for them. However, multimodal designs also create legitimacy 'spillovers' by connecting the organization to highly legitimate actors and ideas from its environment. Expert authority (e.g. testimonials of established scientists or internal experts and professionals) is often invoked, and so is role model authority (e.g. testimonials by political figures, actors, and/or advocacy groups). These testimonials are inherently multimodal, combining the visual effect of immediate recognition of prominent actors (such as non-governmental organization leaders) with their laudatory words for the organization or particular practices. Impersonal sources of authority include, for instance, the logo of the UN global compact. Such authorization strategies aim at

Figure 14.2 Examples for Authorization
Source: Used under license from Shutterstock.com

legitimating both the content of the report, as well as the organization more broadly, since highly prestigious and prominent figures and impersonal authorities lend their faces and words to be presented in conjunction with the organization and its CSR activities.

Rationalization is used throughout the reports in various forms and foci. *Mastery* supports rationalization by suggesting the potency and power of organizations (depicted as either impressive buildings or hard-working employees) is necessary to create a better and more sustainable tomorrow. *Progress* additionally provides explanations and predictions through linking past and future, for instance, by claiming that 'clean' technologies will eventually be able to overcome threats related to climate change (e.g. in charts and/or timelines). *Enterprise*, finally, suggests exploration and discovery as a necessary business model to anticipate the challenges of tomorrow.

Moral evaluation is the most dominant and most clearly visible legitimation strategy in the reports, and it cuts across a variety of topoi. These topoi anchor the conduct of the organization in 'higher', societally desirable values from family to community, religion, and nature, to the depiction of corporate actors in 'heroic' poses and settings. In the *mastery* topos, financial and market performance are abstracted as general potency and power to shape the future. Visuals are highly metaphorical and present such power through heroic poses of employees or a frog's eye perspective on corporate architecture. For instance, in the left photograph in Figure 14.3, heroism is portrayed in the form of a firefighter wearing protective clothing produced by the focal organization. *Progress* naturalizes doing business as part of a general process of continuous improvement, and portrays the relationship between nature and technology as unproblematic, for instance by showing industrial facilities surrounded by beautiful natural scenery. Both *local community* and *globalism* claim an altruistic, or at least 'fair' attitude of the organization, which implies giving back to global and local communities. The analogy

Figure 14.3 Examples for Moral Evaluation
Source: Used under license from Shutterstock.com

of the 'corporate citizen' is visually invoked, for instance, by board members interacting with representatives of the community, as is illustrated with the right-hand photograph in Figure 14.3. *Enterprise*, finally, taps into the positive values of curiosity and visionary thinking.

Mythopoesis is used throughout the reports by telling a general 'story' about how the organization is becoming increasingly sustainable and socially responsible. In some reports, visuals tell their own separate storyline that complements the verbal one, for instance in loosely linked 'photo narratives' represented by large, two-page visuals for each section headline, or through the use of explanatory boxes that—often visually—illustrate the more abstract descriptions in the relevant section. The topos most clearly linked to strategies of *mythopoesis* is progress, since it focuses on linking past, present, and future. Timelines and 'before-after' montages are used to illustrate a continuous process of improvement.

Subject positions of the viewer. According to Kress and van Leeuwen (2006), a specificity of visual grammar is that it provides perspectivity in a way other modes are unable to do. Jancsary et al. (2018), accordingly, argue that visual registers can usefully be characterized through the ways in which they create particular embodied positions for viewers and audiences. The way in which viewers are 'drawn into' a particular discourse may also affect their legitimacy judgments. In this way, visuals are able to create involvement much more directly and affectively than verbal text.

In their investigation of the register of the Austrian CSR discourse, Jancsary et al. (2018) find three distinct positions or 'gazes' that are offered to audiences. The *scrutinizing gaze towards ecological impact* has legitimating effects in the sense that it positions the viewer either at intimate distance or at impersonal distance to industrial facilities and processes. This implies transparency and overview, and suggests that the organization has nothing to hide and allows the viewer to 'observe' and 'investigate' their production and ecological impact. The left-hand image in Figure 14.4 shows an example of the impersonal 'overview' gaze,

Figure 14.4 Examples for the Scrutinizing Gaze Towards Ecological Impact
Source: Used under license from Shutterstock.com

stressing that the wind turbine is 'naturally' embedded in the agricultural landscape and does not constitute a 'foreign object'. It allows for scrutiny by stressing context instead of hiding it. Conversely, the right-hand image shows an extreme zoom-in into the structure of a product. Both gazes imply transparency. The viewer, through this gaze, becomes an investigator with access to all relevant information.

In contrast, the *partner-like gaze on management* attempts to create involvement and identification between the viewer and the management of the organization. Viewers are positioned as equals, at rather intimate (or at least interpersonal) distance to management actors. The photograph in Figure 14.5, for instance, creates a subject position for viewers which positions them literally 'at the table' with management. Interpersonal distance, strong eye contact, and frontal horizontal angle imply membership and identification. This suggests an alignment of interests and invites the viewer to adopt the rationalities of management, which welcomes them into their ranks.

Finally, the *benevolent gaze towards the human 'other'*, while also suggesting the perspective of management and the organization, is directed outward and constitutes a detached, but sympathetic position towards those in need of protection—whether this means actual people or abstract entities like 'nature'. In Figure 14.6, the children as beneficiaries of corporate philanthropy are shown from behind, from an oblique horizontal angle and from rather impersonal distance. All this creates detachment

Figure 14.5 Example for the Partner-Like Gaze on Management
Source: Used under license from Shutterstock.com

Figure 14.6 Example for the Benevolent Gaze Towards the Human 'Other'
Source: Used under license from Shutterstock.com

from the 'other' (much like in Figure 14.1). This perspective legitimates because the viewer can 'see' through the eyes of the organization how other people and the environment in general benefit from the organizations' actions. By proxy, the viewer as a supporter or even shareholder of the organization becomes an 'accomplice' in such responsible action.

Closer inspection of the images in the CSR reports, particularly of absences, point at elements that may also have de-legitimating effects. Regarding the ideational metafunction, for instance, management almost exclusively encompasses older white men in dark suits, white shirts, and ties. Female managers are the exception and do not constitute a clear visual type as male managers do. Ethnic diversity in management is basically non-existent. Additionally, in terms of actions and processes, managers in visuals do not actually do much work. Rather, they either simply pose for the camera or talk to each other. The visual type of the manager, accordingly, is a very general one that is similar across organizations and does not seem to relate much to the actual area of activity of the organization. Regarding the interpersonal metafunction, we find that the organization and management are mostly portrayed as the 'self', whereas the beneficiaries of CSR activities are cast as the 'other'. This questions the idea of the organizations as 'corporate citizen' and 'member of society'. Communication always potentially reveals more than the producer has intended, and this potential multiplies in multimodal communication.

14.4 Implications of Multimodality for Legitimacy Research

Discursive legitimation strategies can be understood as communicative action aimed at achieving or safeguarding (organizational) legitimacy. The discourse around CSR and corporate sustainability clearly constitutes such effort at legitimation in the face of increasing societal pressures that prompt organizations to clarify their role in society. We have presented insights from two empirical studies on the CSR discourse in Austria in more detail, and 'read' their findings in the light of legitimation. We have exemplified how both the ideational (first study) and the interpersonal (second study) metafunction of the visual mode can be utilized for legitimation strategies and have provided some suggestions on how to code for, and therefore empirically reconstruct, elements of legitimation from larger samples of multimodal data and aggregate them to field-level meaning structures.

Our efforts at conceptualizing legitimation as a multimodal endeavour resonates well with other studies that acknowledge the role of modes different from the verbal for the construction of CSR. Acknowledging that CSR is a major component in the stakeholder management of organizations, Breitbarth, Harris, and Insch (2010) suggest a typology of visuals and verbal text used in non-financial reporting in the UK and Germany. In terms of multimodal compositions, they observe that visuals may support text, appear unrelated to text, or distract from text. Visual information, they contend, is used to establish CSR as true and factual, which strongly aligns with issues of legitimation. Rämö (2011) investigated 153 companies from all over the world included in both the Dow Jones Sustainability Index (DJSI) and the Financial Times 4Good Global Index (FTSE4Good) for aspects of phronesis (i.e., wise and discerning values) that convey a desirable image of respectability and success. He concludes that visuals in corporate reports help "in shaping symbolic visual declarations; that of being a phronetic and responsible corporate citizen" (Rämö, 2011, p. 379).

This body of research suggests a strong relevance of multimodality for research on legitimacy and legitimation, and that each mode contributes differently to such objective. A growing number of authors (see, for instance, Jones et al., 2017; Lefsrud et al., 2018) have pointed out that the focus on verbal text in studies on legitimacy work and legitimation has resulted in a neglect of other modes that might be equally relevant. As Lefsrud et al. (2018, p. 133; emphasis in the original) contend in their study on legitimation and de-legitimation work in the discourse on the Alberta oil sands, these processes are "*dialogic* phenomena among diverse sets of stakeholders, *semiotic* phenomena fundamentally dependent on symbolic texts produced and interpreted by these stakeholders, and an *affective* process evoked through multimodal texts". For organizational scholars,

178 *Application*

this means a necessity to better understand how different modes—in our case the visual mode—contribute to legitimation strategies.

For multimodality studies, legitimacy and legitimation provide a vast 'playing field' for relevant and practically valuable research. Whereas CSR and corporate sustainability remain dominant discourses in the corporate world, issues of legitimation reach much further. The design of organizational spaces, press releases, advertisements, or public appearances of corporate executives all relate to legitimation. Since legitimacy is understood as the 'licence to operate' for any kind of organization or community, potential empirical applications for multimodality theory abound.

14.5 Other Research Approaches to Multimodal Legitimation

The research presented in this case study aligns with an *archaeological approach* (see Chapter 4), thereby reconstructing traces of social knowledge from multimodal artefacts in order to better understand what kind of social reality is manifested in these artefacts. Of course, other approaches to legitimation are possible.

An excellent example of a *strategic approach* is provided by Cho et al. (2009) who study the impact of media richness on viewer trust in the context of presenting CSR issues on corporate websites. They find that the richness of presentation positively influences the degree of trusting intentions (the willingness to depend on another party), but not trusting beliefs (the beliefs that another party has favourable qualities). More research on how multimodal CSR communication actually influences audiences' perceptions would be highly useful for organizational practice and provide insights on the effectiveness of legitimation strategies.

Dialogical approaches could take yet different avenues. For instance, photo elicitation interviews might uncover how organizational members make CSR claims part of their professional identities, and which visual and material aspects of the organization are perceived to exemplify a mind-set of CSR and sustainability most distinctively. Such approach might also contrast employees' and stakeholders' imageries of the sustainable organization with official corporate communication and inform on the fit between official and lived 'images' of CSR.

Finally, *practice approaches* could provide further insights into the actual 'crafting' of legitimation strategies. Such research would be highly sympathetic to existing streams of literature on strategy-as-practice (Vaara & Whittington, 2012) and investigate how different modes and media are utilized in 'doing' strategy (see, for instance, Gylfe et al., 2016 for the role of gestures). It could therefore enlighten organization theory both with regard to the ways in which multimodal artefacts are used internally to craft legitimation strategies, and the processes through which decisions are made about the multimodal artefacts employed to communicate CSR and corporate sustainability to audiences.

14.6 Conclusions

In this case study, we have shown how organizations mobilize multimodal legitimation strategies in their CSR and sustainability reporting in order to communicate a favourable and socially desirable role in society. The different contributions between the verbal and the visual mode in this endeavour are distinct and highly relevant. Whereas the verbal design of legitimation strategies has been researched in detail, less is currently known about the ways in which other modes support such communicative action (for ideas on musical legitimation, see van Leeuwen, 2018a). The studies discussed in our case suggest that *materializing* and *bridging* of themes and value spheres, as well as *embodied positioning* of viewers are central aspects through which visual text enhances the legitimating potential of verbal text. However, a triangulation of designs is needed for a more thorough understanding of the legitimating potential of multimodality, which means that archaeological designs should be complemented with strategic, dialogical, and practice approaches in order to study the micro-processes and the *in situ* use of multimodal artefacts in more detail.

Notes

1. While copyright restrictions prevent us from reprinting visuals from the actual data, we use visuals from the image database Shutterstock (www.shutterstock.com) for purposes of exemplification. The visuals in this chapter were chosen as to conform as closely as possible to those in the actual data set.
2. Meaning 'culturally and/or ethnically different from the context in which the report was produced' (Austria).

Part IV
Discussion

15 The Way Ahead
Discussion and Conclusion

The impetus for this book was the observation that both organization and multimodality studies are flourishing strands of research that have a lot to contribute to each other. Unfortunately, contact between the two research traditions has been sporadic at best. It has, therefore, been our intent to 'tear down the walls' between these two research communities and, in a collaborative effort, sketch and demarcate the overlaps and mutual areas of interest. After an introductory chapter (Chapter 1) arguing for the relevance and potential for cross-fertilization, we have provided a brief primer on social semiotics (Chapter 2) as a basis for conceptualizing multimodality. In Part II (Chapters 3–9), we have then reviewed several approaches to the study of multimodality in organizations and shown that multimodal artefacts can assume a multitude of roles in and around organizations, and even in research on organizations. Part III (Chapters 10–14) has in turn focused on presentations of in-depth case studies covering key aspects of organizations and multimodality. In this final chapter, we will summarize our insights and suggest potential avenues for fruitful future research at the intersection of the two disciplines, based on what we have learnt from writing this book. We also provide some ideas on how closer collaboration could be envisaged, and end with some tentative implications for practitioners.

15.1 Taking Stock: Ongoing Progress in Multimodal Organization Research

Our argument throughout this book has been that substantial synergies are to be expected from integrating organization research and multimodality research and sharing insights more substantially and vigorously. In Part II, especially, we have shown that such integration is already happening, and that researchers in organization and management theory have picked up insights from different disciplines and traditions concerned with modes other than the verbal. We therefore think it useful to briefly review and take stock of efforts that have been made so far and evaluate existing contributions to making organizational research more multimodal and multimodality research more organizational. Of necessity,

184 Discussion

such a review can never be fully complete but draws on selected examples and illustrations from existing research.

15.1.1 Growing Realization About the Multimodality of Contemporary Organization(s)

Our first conclusion is that multimodality or, at least, the acknowledgement that organizational reality is constructed through a multiplicity of modes, has gained momentum in organization and management research. Although it cannot yet be considered 'mainstream', it has produced multiple review articles (Bell & Davison, 2013; Davison, 2015, Meyer et al., 2013), edited books (Bell et al., 2014; Puyou et al., 2012), special issues in journals like *Accounting, Auditing & Accountability Journal* in 2009, *Qualitative Research in Organizations and Management* in 2012, *Organizational Research Methods* in 2018, *Research in the Sociology of Organizations* in 2018, and *Organization Studies* in 2018, as well as specialized tracks, symposia, and developmental workshops at major conferences of the field, such as the *Academy of Management Annual Conference* and the annual *EGOS Colloquium*.

Accordingly, it seems fair to say that visuality and multimodality are not an 'absent present' (Styhre, 2010) or a 'blind spot' (Davison & Warren, 2009) in organization studies anymore, as was true only a few years ago. Researchers have started to pay serious attention to modes different from the verbal, and to explore—and increasingly systematize—the novel insights made possible through such an expanded lens. Another sign that multimodality is becoming more central to organization and management research is that chapters on multimodality are starting to make it into the standard handbooks (see, for instance, Jones et al., 2017). The integration of visual and multimodal questions and insights into such readings on organizations means that the topic is slowly moving from being considered a 'niche' area to becoming part of the 'standard'.

To sum up: The cross-fertilization between multimodality research and organization studies is in full motion, and it seems unlikely that this trend will end anytime soon. However, the potential of such interdisciplinary work has hardly been exploited yet, and while consolidation is desirable, declaring maturity too early risks the loss of additional insights that could be gained through further exploration. We will discuss some of the unrealized potentials in the next section of this chapter.

15.1.2 Engagement With a Broad Spectrum of Topics and Issues

In addition to the strong trend towards becoming a core topic in organization and management research, there is increasing acknowledgement of the importance of multimodality for a vast spectrum of organizational topics. While initially focusing on accounting issues (Davison, 2015;

Quattrone, 2009), the range of multimodal aspects of organizations that has been considered has become much broader (Meyer et al., 2013). Some of these topics seem of particular strength and fertility.

A first topic area is *strategy* and *strategizing*. Practices of strategizing are becoming increasingly multimodal, including forms of expression such as gesture, speech, visualization, layout, and colour. Visual charts and maps (see Chapter 11) and material artefacts support strategizing (Cummings & Wilson, 2003; Heracleous & Jacobs, 2008) by making emergent strategies more tangible and comprehensible, and video methods are better at capturing the multimodal nature of strategy making (Gylfe et al., 2016). Second, studies of *identities* in, around, and of organizations rely heavily on multimodal data (see Chapter 12). Both individuals (Shortt & Warren, 2012) and organizations (Oberg et al., 2018) communicate their identities visually, spatially, and multimodally. Such research further expands our insights into the multifaceted nature of individual and collective identities in organizational contexts. Multimodal data provide cues that purely verbal accounts cannot, and enriches both findings and new theories. A third area of research is the broad area of *marketing*, both of products and the organization itself (i.e., its public image). Such research strongly focuses on the interface between organizations and customers (see Chapter 13). Visual and multimodal communication is employed to convey favourable images of products (Scott & Vargas, 2007) and construct brands (Schroeder, 2012). Specific modes offer different ways of communicating with customers and audiences. Fourth, multimodality has also been considered in research on *legitimacy and legitimation* (see Chapter 14). Visuals may suggest authenticity (Guthey & Jackson, 2005), and integrate seemingly contradictory expectations to protect organizational legitimacy (Höllerer et al., 2013). This concerns audience communication that goes beyond immediate customers but relates to the broader role of organizations in society.

These are only four areas of application of multimodal theory and data in organization and management research. Other studies have, for instance, drawn on multimodality to explain theorization (Cartel, Colombero, & Boxenbaum, 2018), sensemaking (Höllerer, Jancsary, & Grafström, 2018), innovation (Pershina & Soppe, 2018), organizational actorhood (Halgin et al., 2018), framing (Christiansen, 2018), power and resistance (Bell, 2012), and field-level change (Croidieu et al., 2018). The general agreement seems to be that multimodality is relevant throughout all areas and aspects of organization.

15.1.3 Increasing Sophistication in the Conceptualization of Modes

In addition to increasing legitimacy and breadth, multimodality research in organization and management studies is gaining in terms of conceptual depth. That is, research has started to tackle more systematically what different modes—and multimodality—actually do in organizations, as well as how and why. Different approaches to multimodality in organizations (see Part II) emphasize different *roles* of multimodal artefacts and help to more systematically understand the relevance of multimodality for organizational questions.

A complementary stream of research has started to 'dissect' modes. Primarily building on the social semiotic foundations of Kress and van Leeuwen (2006), but also borrowing from cognitive psychology and institutional theory, Meyer et al. (2018) suggest characterizing modes based on their *constitutive features*. These features distinguish modes from each other based on semiotic, cognitive, and cultural characteristics that are valid for a given time and place. When manifested in media or texts, modes then gain certain affordances, defined as potentials for meaning-making that need to be realized in specific social situations. Whereas Meyer et al. (2018) have elaborated constitutive features and affordances primarily for verbal and visual text, Oliveira et al. (2018) disentangle materiality. They suggest that material artefacts encompass what they call three *imaginaries* that represent the entanglement of the material and the discursive. In more detail, they suggest that materiality is 'concrete' in the sense that artefacts can be used by individuals for certain kind of actions; it is semiotic in the sense that artefacts are carriers of social and organizational meanings through symbolic functions; and it is mimetic in the sense that artefacts represent embodied metaphors and analogies due to their material arrangements. Such research unpacks modes from different theoretical angles, showing that modes are not monolithic and can work differently depending on context and usage. Finally, Jancsary et al. (2018) draw on the idea of registers (Matthiessen, 2015) and suggest the existence of 'modal' registers that represent and reproduce specific meaning spheres. The implication is that specific zones of meaning in and around organizations are reproduced through multiple modes in specific ways, with each mode providing its own register of cultural and linguistic resources for meaning-making. They, however, leave open the question of whether genuinely multimodal registers that integrate resources from multiple modes exist.

15.1.4 Doing Research Multimodally

Finally, engagement with the multimodal character of organizations has also triggered a discussion about the use of multimodal resources and techniques in the research process itself. As Ravasi (2017, p. 241) notes: "If visualization is so fundamental to our experience, and if so many of us have recognized and implemented visual techniques in our teaching and learning, why have we so underplayed its role in doing empirical research?" He then goes on to provide a number of recommendations for using visualization to support and stimulate the *interpretation* of qualitative data. However, research not only benefits in terms of enhanced interpretation. Data *collection* can also draw on multimodal techniques, such as photo elicitation (Warren, 2002), or triggering interviewee responses through smells (Riach & Warren, 2015). Similarly, photo diaries (Czarniawska, 2010) or video ethnographies (Smets, Burke, Jarzabkowski, & Spee, 2014) are multimodally enhanced ways of collecting and storing data. Of course, multimodality is also relevant for the *presentation* of findings and insights. Researchers have, for instance, created network graphs as innovative ways to present the emergence of novel fields in ways that the verbal mode would be unable to do (Powell, Oberg, Korff, Oelberger, & Kloos, 2017). More conventional multimodal resources such as diagrams (Kvåle, 2016; Ledin & Machin, 2016) or photo essays (Jewitt et al., 2011; Preston & Young, 2000) have also been discussed.

One strong inhibitor of more multimodal presentations of research is the current template for publishing journal articles in organization and management research. However, new journals like the *Academy of Management Discoveries* are already playing with non-traditional publication formats allowing, among other things, for the integration of videos. We are therefore hopeful that future organization research will take its own insights to heart and become itself more multimodal, thereby increasing its impact on lay audiences.

15.2 Unrealized Potentials and Avenues for Future Research

Despite the increasing engagement between disciplines, there is still a lot of unrealized potential for learning from each other and taking the two fields of research further. As have others (Bell & Davison, 2013; Boxenbaum et al., 2018; Höllerer, Daudigeos, & Jancsary, 2018), we chime in to sketch what we regard as the most substantial gaps and most promising avenues for future research at the intersection of organization research and multimodality research. Some of our observations result in warnings against overly simplistic understandings of central concepts and all-too-easy ways of integrating insights, others imply suggestions for novel research that can only develop in the overlaps between the two fields. Often, dangers and potentials go hand in hand. We hope that our ideas will inspire future research to come up with even more innovative approaches and contributions.

15.2.1 More Sophisticated Understandings of Modal Orchestrations/Amalgamations

In Chapter 2, we have outlined that multimodality research in the social semiotic tradition has known three broad 'phases': A first phase, in which modes are viewed in isolation, and the specific 'language' of each mode is characterized and utilized; a second phase, in which the interplay between multiple modes is at the centre of interest and in which modes—although still seen as largely separate—affect each other in complex ways in the construction of meaning; and a third phase, in which modes as meaning-making systems 'unite' in complex combined acts of meaning, and in which meanings are only fully comprehensible when modal amalgamations are understood as strongly integrated.

In organization studies, research relating to the first two phases is still dominant. We do not wish to say that later phases are inherently more valuable than earlier ones. However, the amalgamation of modes is still strongly under-researched in organization and management studies. Sometimes it is only through the textual composition of multiple, strongly integrated modes—where no single mode needs to fulfil all metafunctions—that a message becomes complete. Such understanding is distinctly different from multimodal compositions (Bullinger, 2018; Lefsrud et al., 2018) in which the interplay between modes creates new, additional meanings. Organization studies can learn from recent developments in social semiotics in this area. In turn, it can provide social semioticians with a plethora of multimodal phenomena to explore and test their theories on. However, taking such 'radical multimodality' seriously involves methodological challenges.

15.2.2 Developing Systematic Methodologies to Tackle Multimodality

One important area for future research is the further development of multimodal methodology allowing for a more systematic analysis of multimodal data in organizational research. Here, we wish to stress two particularly salient issues: the analysis of integrated multimodal 'orchestrations' (Kress, 2010), and the analysis of larger samples of multimodal data.

Despite the growing interest and conceptual sophistication of multimodal research in organization studies, authors often bemoan the lack of a clear methodological 'toolbox'. This issue is particularly salient when genuinely multimodal data are under scrutiny, that is, data, where only the combined analysis of multiple modes simultaneously yields sufficient insight (see, for instance, Forgues & May's [2018] study on whisky bottles). Although detailed analytical methods are now available for a wide range of semiotic modes, our case studies have shown that they have to be selected, combined and adapted to suit the research topics and questions at hand. While this can be challenging for researchers, it does guarantee the flexibility and fertility of multimodal approaches to organization research.

Most multimodal research on organizations draws on methodologies that reconstruct meaning from a limited set of data. Advances in organization studies, however, have recently created a trend towards 'big data' and the use of models and methods to analyse larger quantities of verbal text (for example, correspondence analysis, network techniques, topic modelling). For multimodal data, no such methodologies exist as yet, to our knowledge. Some studies (see also Chapter 14) have attempted to use the principles of social semiotics to code mid-sized samples of visuals. However, more work is needed to provide ideas on how to analyse larger samples without losing the specificities of meaning-making for each mode, and their orchestrations.

15.2.3 Systematizing the 'Omelette' of Concepts and Theories

Ideas regarding multimodality have been fermenting in organization research for a long time (see, for instance, Meyer, 1991). The initial phase has been characterized by researchers looking to other, related disciplines for conceptual and methodological guidance, and to a large degree, this is still the state of affairs today. While conceptual and methodological pluralism is desirable, the combination of a small group of researchers and a broad spectrum of conceptual lenses has led to cross-citation of works from very different traditions, often without proper discussion of how they fit together in their basic assumptions. For instance, even within the field of semiotics, organizational research has built on the semiotics of Barthes (Davison, 2011), Peirce (Zhao, 2018), and social semiotics (Höllerer et al., 2013), whereas others have usefully drawn on the philosophical ideas of Lefebvre (Wasserman & Frenkel, 2011), Levinas (Campbell, McPhail, & Slack, 2009), or Derrida (Campbell, 2012).

We ourselves had to realize the level of painstaking detail and in-depth knowledge necessary to make different approaches speak to each other in research on multimodality. There is a certain danger in borrowing and combining conceptual elements from traditions that do not strictly speak well to each other—is the 'theoretical omelette' still comprehensible? With our distinct social semiotic background, we believe to have provided a solid conceptual basis for analysing multimodality. However, we do not advocate a 'dominant paradigm' in multimodal organization research; instead, we suggest that future research should become even more aware of the theoretical differences between traditions, and of the fact that modes, too, are social and cultural constructions whose meanings, boundaries, and potentials are dependent on the particular theory that constitutes their foundation.

15.2.4 Acknowledging the Cultural Construction of Modes

The constructed nature of modes is an additional issue that we suggest must not be forgotten. Van Leeuwen (2018b, pp. 239–240) warns that some organization research "ascribes essential qualities to the visual" and notes that "just as images and other visual can depict rational ideas and structures as well as delight the senses, so too, can language be sensual as well as rational". This is a potent warning against an 'essentialist' view on semiotic modes that organization scholars should take to heart. Modes are socially constructed and culturally and temporally bound (Kress & van Leeuwen, 2006). This means that any potentials or affordances of a mode are only valid within a particular spatio-temporal context, in which there is agreement about the uses and boundaries of that mode. For instance, visuals are only able to 'fly under the radar' of discursive control (Meyer et al., 2018) when the visual is culturally subordinated to the verbal, as is currently the case in most Western societies (Kress & van Leeuwen, 2006). In other cultural contexts, the visual may be even more regulated than the verbal.

While this poses certain restrictions for the ascription of particular qualities to modes, it also opens up interesting avenues for further inquiry within organization research. First, we call for more cross-cultural studies about the use of multimodal artefacts in organizations. Cultural spheres with a stronger visual tradition than the West might be wellsprings of additional insights into the visual mode. Equally interesting may be research that compares organizational practices across cultures with specific 'modal taboos', i.e. restrictions on communication in any one particular mode. If modes are unequally regulated in society, then research could also look for the appropriation of certain modes in marginalized communities. Bell (2012) shows that resistance in organizations is often framed visually. More research in this direction may uncover the realities experienced by groups without formal 'voice' (Slutskaya et al., 2012). Second, further research could extend our insights into the 'careers' of modes in organizations and fields. Since developments in literature on multimodality were often reactions to major social and cultural changes (van Leeuwen, 2018b), organizations and their members can be expected to constantly experiment with multimodal designs, following—and shaping—broader trends that make some modes come into fashion and others fall from grace. Such research could ask how modes become (ir)relevant in and around organizations, and how the understanding of modes changes over time. An interesting pioneering study is provided by Eisenman (2018) who shows how aesthetic properties of personal computers emerged as dominant design strategies at a critical juncture in the development of the market. Capturing the development of modes and multimodal designs as 'dependent' variable has the potential to enrich both literature in organization studies and multimodality research equally.

15.2.5 Avoiding 'Cherry-Picking' of Modes Under Study

As outlined in the introduction to this book, multimodality found its way into organization research primarily through increasing attention to visual and material aspects of organizations. As a consequence, the visual and material modes are still very dominant in organization studies, although more recent articles have started to examine the interaction of multiple modes, primarily the visual and the verbal.

There is, accordingly, a certain danger of narrowing the field prematurely. The more 'standard' research on the visuality and materiality of organization(s) becomes, the more researchers will be drawn towards these topics. Hence, while we are constantly deepening our insights about the visual, material, and verbal modes, other modes—and their orchestrations—are still underrepresented. We therefore call for including additional modes in organization research. Work into the crucial role of scent (Gümüsay et al., 2018; Islam et al., 2016; Riach & Warren, 2015) has the potential to substantially alter the way we understand organizations and organizational behaviour. The same is true for a more systematic acknowledgement of sound (Pinch & Bijsterveld, 2012). Tackling modes that are less easily conceptualized in and around organizations will also enable a better understanding of both the boundaries and the amalgamation of modes.

15.3 Towards a Joint Way Forward

It is our firm conviction that multimodality is not just another source of data for organizational scholars, nor are organizations simply an additional research context for multimodality scholars. Multimodality provides additional ways of thinking about organization that have considerable potential to change the way organization scholars see their subject matter; and studies of organizational communication practices can enhance what multimodal research can mean and achieve. This is not to say that integration and collaboration are necessarily easy. There are subtle (and less subtle) differences in approaches to the object of research, to writing, and to what is considered a contribution. However, we feel that there is much promise in engaging with these differences.

We believe to have shown that there are substantial similarities in the issues that the two disciplines address; however, there are also important differences in their approach to these issues. The strength of multimodality studies lies in the systematic analytical frameworks that they apply to data sets. Based on rigorous theoretical knowledge about multimodality, these analytical frameworks are well-suited to finding patterns and generalities that have the potential to create substantial theoretical contributions. The risk, however, is that such meaningful patterns are not found, which may lead to mostly descriptive findings with few novel insights into the social. In organization and management research, by contrast, research often starts with a theoretical issue or a small taxonomy, which frames the perspective on the data. This ensures relevance for the topic at hand but entails the risk of narrowing the perspective too soon, thereby hiding what that lens fails to show.

Combining theoretical issues with systematic multimodal analysis yields the most promising results. The implication is clearly that organization studies and multimodality research bring different strengths to the table, which may create considerable synergies in enabling a better understanding of the role and impact of multimodality on social and organizational life. On the one hand, organization theory can provide conceptual frameworks that may help multimodality scholars better interpret and contextualize their in-depth findings and connect them to established stocks of knowledge, so increasing the reach of their findings and facilitating dissemination into other research areas. Multimodality theory, on the other hand, can provide organization theory with the methodological finesse and conceptual depth that will help organization scholars to better understand what is actually happening in the empirical field when actors create, manipulate, and use multimodal artefacts in their daily organizational practices. Since research on the multimodal character of organizations is still a relatively recent development, the conceptual foundations which multimodality research has established are highly valuable for organization scholars, and can help them legitimize their research and get it published.

To make such synergies a reality, we also suggest that scholars across the two research fields collaborate more directly and intensively with each other. That is, whereas *reading* each other is already a promising start, *working* with each other is what creates the best and most foundational new insights. Through direct collaboration, fault lines also become more visible, so the risk of misunderstanding and misappropriating each other's theories and concepts is less pronounced. This means organizing and participating in interdisciplinary workshops and conferences where thoughts and ideas flow more freely. This book is a first step. We hope that many more projects will follow in its wake.

15.4 Implications for Organizational Practice

Although this book is primarily written for researchers, the topic of multimodality should be of considerable interest to practitioners in and around organizations. Since multimodality is such an omnipresent characteristic of organizational life, the skills and literacies to deal with multimodal discourse are of utmost importance in many everyday situations. A thorough appreciation of the value of multimodal organization theory for practitioners is beyond the scope of this book. However, we briefly sketch two areas of insight that should be particularly interesting for organizational practice.

15.4.1 Increasing Attention and Literacy

Although organizations and their members often communicate multimodally, they are not always doing so consciously and reflectively. Multimodal organization research can therefore help sensitize practitioners to multimodal communication and help them better understand their own communication practices as well as those of relevant audiences. For instance, offices and other organizational spaces are often designed with certain objectives in mind, but actual usage may deviate from, or even counteract intended usage (Wasserman & Frenkel, 2011). The material set-up of organizations is both communicative and performative. More critical awareness of how multimodal texts can be interpreted and impact on organizational members can help to create better designs. The same applies to external communication. In our case studies (Part III), we have focused on four areas of organizational communication that are inherently multimodal: organizational structure as manifested in graphs and charts, organizational identity as communicated in logos, customer interfaces as designed on websites, and corporate social responsibility (CSR) as communicated in annual corporate reports. All of these organizational facets are crucial for the long-term success of organizations. Multimodality research can help practitioners to better assess the potential impact of their communication, and help them design multimodal artefacts more consciously and craftily.

15.4.2 Expanding the Communicative Toolbox

In addition to strengthening the ability of organizations and their members to adequately interpret and deal with multimodal artefacts, multimodality research can also provide organizations with additional tools to deal with common organizational issues and challenges. For instance, research employing archaeological and practice approaches to multimodal artefacts suggests relevant ways in which multimodality can be utilized to *store and retrieve tacit and elusive knowledge*. By encoding information in ways that go beyond the written and spoken word, knowledge that is otherwise hard or impossible to manifest can be stored and transmitted (Toraldo et al., 2018). Sketches, prototypes, and infographs, for instance, are visual and material ways of embodying knowledge that would be difficult if not impossible to verbalize. Organizations therefore need to learn their specific 'language' to maximize their potential. Further, research from the strategic and dialogical approaches provide vital insights into how multimodality can be utilized to elicit cognitive and affective responses from audiences. Since some modes increase attention, memory, and attitudes more immediately than others, multimodality becomes directly relevant not only for marketing and advertising, but also for issues of health and safety, and for human resource management generally. Different ways of multimodal 'nudging' may lead to more sustainability and safety in organizations than hard regulation. Finally, multimodality is a great resource for *communicating across language barriers*. Although modes are also context-dependent, research has found that visual text is less often localized than verbal text, so that visual text emerges as a more or less global language (Machin, 2004). In the same way multimodal artefacts may serve as boundary objects, connecting disparate communities and communities with very different cultures (Justesen & Mouritsen, 2009). The potential breadth of multimodal organization research will certainly provide many more interesting and important insights for practitioners that wish to improve different aspects of their organization.

References

Aaron, M. (2007). *Spectatorship: The power of looking on*. London: Wallflower Press.

Adler, P., Du Gay, P., Morgan, G., & Reed, M. (Eds.) (2014). *The Oxford handbook of sociology, social theory, & organization studies*. Oxford: Oxford University Press.

Aghekyan-Simonian, M., Forsythe, S., Kwon, W. S., & Chattaraman, V. (2012). The role of product brand image and online store image on perceived risks and online purchase intentions for apparel. *Journal of Retailing and Consumer Service*, *19*(3), 325–331.

Aiello, G. (2017). Losing to gain: Balancing style and texture in the Starbucks logo. In C. M. Johannesen & T. van Leeuwen (Eds.), *The materiality of writing: A trace-making perspective* (pp. 195–210). London: Routledge.

Aiello, G., & Dickinson, G. (2014). Beyond authenticity: A visual-material analysis of locality in the global redesign of Starbuck stores. *Visual Communication*, *13*(3), 303–322.

Alvesson, M., & Kärreman, D. (2000). Taking the linguistic turn in organizational research: Challenges, responses, consequences. *The Journal of Applied Behavioral Science*, *36*(2), 136–158.

Andersen, T. H. (2007). *Sæt ord på!* Odense: Syddansk Universitätsverlag.

Andersen, T. H., & Boeriis, M. (2012). Relationship/Participant focus in multimodal market communication. *Hermes*, *25*(48), 75–94.

Andersen, T. H., & Boeriis, M. (2015). Multimodal register. In N. Nørgaard (Ed.), *Key terms in multimodality: Definitions, issues, discussions*. Retrieved from https://multimodalkeyterms.wordpress.com/.

Andersen, T. H., Boeriis, M., Maagerø, E., & Tønnesen, E. S. (Eds.) (2015). *Social semiotics: Key figures, new directions*. London: Routledge.

Andersen, T. H., & Holsting, A. (2015). *Teksten i grammatikken*. Odense: Syddansk Universitetsforlag.

Anderson, C. J., & Imperia, G. (1992). The corporate annual report: A photo analysis of male and female portrayals. *The Journal of Business Communication*, *29*(2), 113–128.

Andersen, T. H., & van Leeuwen, T. (2017). Genre crash: The case of online shopping. *Discourse, Context and Text*, *20*, 191–203.

Aras, G., & Growther, D. (Eds.) (2010). *A handbook of corporate governance and social responsibility*. Farnham: Gower Publishing.

Arjaliès, D.-L., & Bansal, P. (2018). Beyond numbers: How investment managers accommodate societal issues in financial decisions. *Organization Studies*, 39(5–6), 691–719.

Arminen, I. (2005). *Institutional interaction: Studies of talk at work*. Aldershot: Ashgate Publishing Ltd.

Arnheim, R. (1974). *Art and visual perception: A psychology of the creative eye*. London: University of California Press.

Arnheim, R. (1982). *The power of the center*. Berkeley, CA: University of California Press.

Ashcraft, K. L., Kuhn, T. R., & Cooren, F. (2009). Constitutional amendments: 'Materializing' organizational communication. *The Academy of Management Annals*, 3(1), 1–64.

Aspara, J., Aula, H.-M., Tienari, J., & Tikkanen, H. (2014). Struggles in organizational attempts to adopt new branding logics: The case of a marketizing university. *Consumption Markets & Culture*, 17(6), 522–552.

Atkinson, R. C., & Shiffrin, R. M. (1968). Human memory: A proposed system and its control processes. In K. W. Spence & J. T. Spence (Eds.), *Psychology of learning and motivation* (Vol. 2, pp. 89–195). Cambridge, MA: Academic Press.

Aula, H.-M. (2016). *Constructing reputation in a university merger* (Doctoral Dissertation). Aalto University School of Business.

Aula, H.-M., & Tienari, J. (2011). Becoming 'world-class'? Reputation-building in a university merger. *Critical Perspectives on International Business*, 7(1), 7–29.

Aula, H.-M., Tienari, J., & Wæraas, A. (2015). The university branding game: Players, interests, politics. *International Studies of Management & Organization*, 45(2), 164–179.

Azar, S., Khan, S. N., & Shavaid, J. (2015). Familiarity with online retailing. *The Journal of Developing Areas*, 49(6), 133–144.

Baldry, A., & Thibault, P. J. (2006). *Multimodal transcription and text analysis: A multimodal toolkit and coursebook with associated on-line course*. London: Equinox.

Balogun, J., Jacobs, C., Jarzabkowski, P., Mantere, S., & Vaara, E. (2014). Placing strategy discourse in context: Sociomateriality, sensemaking, and power. *Journal of Management Studies*, 51(2), 175–201.

Bambauer-Sachse, S., & Gierl, H. (2009). Effects of nostalgic advertising through emotions and the intensity of the evoked mental images. *Advances in Consumer Research*, 36, 391–398.

Banks, M. (2001). *Visual methods in sociological research*. Thousands Oaks, CA: Sage Publications.

Barnet, B. (2014). *Memory machines: The evolution of hyptertext*. London and New York, NY: Anthem Press.

Barnhurst, K. G., Vari, M., & Rodríguez, Í. (2004). Mapping visual studies in communication. *Journal of Communication*, 54(4), 616–644.

Barthes, R. (1967). *Elements of semiology*. London: Jonathan Cape.

Barthes, R. (1973). *Mythologies*. London: Jonathan Cape.

Barthes, R. (1975). *The pleasure of the text*. New York, NY: Wang & Hill.

Barthes, R. (1977). *Image, music, text*. London: Paladin.

Barthes, R. (1980). *La chambre claire*. Paris: Le Seuil.

Barthes, R. (1982). *L'obvie et l'obtus*. Paris: Le Seuil.
Barthes, R. (1983). *The system of fashion*. New York, NY: Hill and Wang.
Barthes, R. (2013 [1960]). *The language of fashion*. London and New York, NY: Bloomsbury.
Bateman, J. A. (2008). *Multimodality and genre: A foundation for the systematic analysis of multimodal discourse*. London: Palgrave Macmillan.
Bateman, J. A. (2014). *Text and image: A critical introduction to the visual/verbal divide*. London: Routledge.
Bateman, J. A. (2017). The place of systemic functional linguistics as a linguistic theory in the twenty-first century. In T. Bartlett & G. O'Grady (Eds.), *The Routledge handbook of systemic functional linguistics* (pp. 11–26). London: Routledge.
Bateman, J. A., & Schmidt, K.-H. (2012). *Multimodal film analysis*. London: Routledge.
Bateman, J. A., Wildfeuer, J., & Hiippala, T. (2017). *Multimodality: Foundations, research and analysis: A problem-oriented introduction*. Berlin: De Gruyter.
Becker, H. S. (1974). Photography and sociology. *Studies in the Anthropology of Visual Communication*, 1(1), 3–26.
Becker, H. S. (1998). Visual sociology, documentary photography, and photo-journalism: It's (almost) all a matter of context. In J. Prosser (Ed.), *Image-based research: A sourcebook for qualitative researchers* (pp. 84–96). London: Falmer Press.
Becker, W. S., & Burke, M. J. (2012). The staff ride: An approach to qualitative data generation and analysis. *Organizational Research Methods*, 15(2), 316–335.
Bell, E. (2012). Ways of seeing organisational death: A critical semiotic analysis of organisational memorialisation. *Visual Studies*, 27(1), 4–17.
Bell, E., & Davison, J. (2013). Visual management studies: Empirical and theoretical approaches. *International Journal of Management Reviews*, 15(2), 167–184.
Bell, E., Warren, S., & Schroeder, J. E. (Eds.) (2014). *The Routledge companion to visual organization*. Abingdon and New York, NY: Routledge.
Bell, P. (2001). Content analysis of visual images. In T. van Leeuwen & C. Jewitt (Eds.), *Handbook of visual analysis* (pp. 10–34). London: Sage Publications.
Benn, Y., Webb, T. L., Chang, B. P., & Rediy, J. (2015). What information do consumers consider, and how do they look for it, when shopping for groceries online? *Appetite*, 89, 265–273.
Berger, J. (1972). *Ways of seeing*. London: British Broadcasting Corporation and Penguin Books.
Berger, P. L., & Kellner, H. (1984). *Für eine neue Soziologie. Ein Essay über Methode und Profession*. Frankfurt/Main: Fischer.
Berger, P. L., & Luckmann, T. (1967). *The social construction of reality: A treatise in the sociology of knowledge*. New York, NY: Anchor Books.
Bernat, E., Patrick, C. J., Benning, S. D., & Tellegen, A. (2006). Effects of picture content and intensity on affective physiological response. *Psychophysiology*, 43(1), 93–103.
Bernstein, B. (1990). *The structure of pedagogic discourse: Class, codes and control* (Vol. IV). London: Routledge.
Bertin, J. (1983). *Semiology of graphics: Diagrams, networks, maps*. Madison, WI: University of Wisconsin Press.

Biiker, W., Hughes, T., & Pinch, T. (Eds.) (1987). *The social construction of technological systems: New directions in the sociology and history of technology*. Cambridge, MA: MIT Press.

Bitektine, A., Lucas, J., Schilke, O. (2018). Institutions under a microscope: Experimental methods in institutional theory. In A. Bryman & D. A. Buchanan (Eds.), *Unconventional methodology in organization and management research* (pp. 147–167). Oxford: Oxford University Press.

Björkvall, A. (2009). Practical function and meaning: A case study of IKEA tables. In C. Jewitt (Ed.), *The Routledge handbook of multimodal analysis* (pp. 342–353). London: Routledge.

Björkvall, A. (2012). Artefakters betydelsepotentialer: En presentation av den sociosemiotiska etnografin som teori och metod. In T. H. Andersen & M. Boeriis (Eds.), *Nordisk socialsemiotik* (pp. 59–88). Odense: Odense Universitetsforlag.

Blazquez, M. (2014). Fashion shopping in multichannel retail: The role of technology in enhancing the customer experience. *International Journal of Electronic Commerce, 18*(4), 97–116.

Boehm, G. (1994). Die Wiederkehr der Bilder. In G. Boehm (Ed.), *Was ist ein Bild?* (pp. 11–38). Munich: Fink.

Boeriis, M. (2009). *Multimodal socialsemiotik & levende billeder* (PhD Thesis). Institute of Language and Communication. Odense: University of Southern Denmark.

Boeriis, M., & Holsanova, J. (2012). Tracking visual segmentation: connecting semiotic and cognitive perspectives. *Visual Communication, 12*(3), 259–281.

Boeriis, M., & van Leeuwen, T. (2016). Vectors. In O. Seizov & J. Wildfeuer (Eds.), *New studies in multimodality: Conceptual and methodological elaborations* (pp. 15–35). London: Bloomsbury.

Bogatyrev, P. (1971 [1937]). *The function of folk costume in Moravian Slovakia*. The Hague: Mouton de Gruyter.

Bohnsack, R. (2008). The interpretation of pictures and the documentary method [64 paragraphs]. *Forum Qualitative Sozialforschung/Forum: Qualitative Social Research, 9*(3), Art. 26.

Bolton, A., Pole, C., & Mizen, P. (2001). Picture this: Researching child workers. *Sociology, 35*(2), 501–518.

Borah, P. (2009). Comparing visual framing in newspapers: Hurricane Katrina versus tsunami. *Newspaper Research Journal, 30*(1), 50–57.

Bourdieu, P. (1977). *Outline of a theory of practice*. Cambridge: Cambridge University Press.

Bourdieu, P. (1990). *Photography: A middle-brow art* (translated by S. Whiteside). Cambridge: Polity Press.

Bourdieu, P. (2004). The peasant and photography. *Ethnography, 5*(4), 601–616.

Bowcher, W. (2012). *Multimodal texts from around the world*. London: Palgrave Macmillan.

Boxenbaum, E. (2006). Lost in translation: The making of Danish diversity management. *American Behavioral Scientist, 49*(7), 939–948.

Boxenbaum, E., Jones, C., Meyer, R. E., & Svejenova, S. (2018). Towards an articulation of the material and visual turn in organization studies. *Organization Studies, 39*(5–6), 597–616.

Breitbarth, T., Harris, P., & Insch, A. (2010). Pictures at an exhibition revisited: Reflections on a typology of images used in the construction of corporate social responsibility and sustainability in non-financial corporate reporting. *Journal of Public Affairs, 10*(4), 238–257.

Bryans, P., & Mavin, S. (2006). Visual images: A technique to surface conceptions of research and researchers. *Qualitative Research in Organizations and Management: An International Journal, 1*(2), 113–128.

Buchanan, D. A. (1998). Representing process: The contribution of a re-engineering frame. *International Journal of Operations & Production Management, 18*(12), 1163–1188.

Buchanan, D. A. (2001). The role of photography in organization research: A Reengineering case illustration. *Journal of Management Inquiry, 10*(2), 151–164.

Bullinger, B. (2018). Companies on the runway: Fashion companies' multimodal presentation of their organizational identity in job advertisements. *Research in the Sociology of Organizations, 54*(B), 145–177.

Caffarel, A. (1992). Interacting between a generalized tense semantics and register-specific semantic tense systems: A bi-stratal exploration of the semantics of French tense. *Language Sciences, 14*(4), 385–418.

Caldas-Coulthard, A. R., & van Leeuwen, T. (2003). Teddy bear stories. *Social Semiotics, 13*(1), 5–28.

Callon, M. (Ed.). (1998). *The laws of the markets*. Oxford: Blackwell Publishers.

Campbell, D., McPhail, K., & Slack, R. (2009). Face work in annual reports. A study of the management of encounter through annual reports, informed by Levinas and Bauman. *Accounting, Auditing & Accountability Journal, 22*(6), 907–932.

Campbell, N. (2012). Regarding Derrida: The tasks of visual deconstruction. *Qualitative Research in Organizations and Management: An International Journal, 7*(1), 105–124.

Caple, H. (2013). *Photojournalism: A social semiotic approach*. London: Palgrave Macmillan.

Carlile, P. R., Nicolini, D., Langley, A., & Tsoukas, H. (2013). How matter matters: Objects, artifacts, and materiality in organization studies: Introducing the third volume of 'perspective on organization studies'. In P. R. Carlile, D. Nicolini, A. Langley, & H. Tsoukas (Eds.), *How matter matters: Objects, artifacts, and materiality in organization studies*. Oxford: Oxford University Press.

Carroll, A. B. (1999). Corporate social responsibility. Evolution of a definitional construct. *Business & Society, 38*(3), 268–295.

Cartel, M., Colombero, S., & Boxenbaum, E. (2018). Towards a multimodal model of theorization processes. *Research in the Sociology of Organizations, 54*(A), 153–182.

Chaney, D. (1996). *Lifestyles*. London: Routledge.

Chaplin, E. (1994). *Sociology and visual representations*. New York, NY: Routledge.

Cheema, A., & Bagchi, R. (2011). The effect of goal visualization on goal pursuit: Implications for consumers and managers. *Journal of Marketing, 75*(2), 109–123.

Cho, C. H., Phillips, J. R., Hageman, A. M., & Patten, D. M. (2009). Media richness, user trust, and perceptions of corporate social responsibility. *Accounting, Auditing & Accountability Journal, 22*(6), 933–952.

Christiansen, L. H. (2018). The use of visuals in issue framing: Signifying responsible drinking. *Organization Studies, 39*(5-6), 665–689.

Christianson, M. K. (2018). Mapping the terrain. The use of video-based research in top-tier organizational journals. *Organizational Research Methods*, 21(2), 261–287.

Christmann, G. B. (2008). The power of photographs of buildings in the Dresden urban discourse. Towards a visual discourse analysis [29 paragraphs]. *Forum Qualitative Sozialforschung/Forum: Qualitative Social Research*, 9(3), Art. 11.

Clark, S. M., Gioia, D. A., Ketchen, D. J., & Thomas, J. B. (2010). Transitional identity as a facilitator of organizational identity change during a merger. *Administrative Science Quarterly*, 55(3), 397–438.

Classen, C. (1993). *Worlds of sense: Exploring the senses in history and across cultures*. London: Routledge.

Classen, C., Howes, D., & Synnott, A. (1994). *Aroma: The cultural history of smell*. London: Routledge.

Collier, J. (1957). Photography in anthropology: A report on two experiments. *American Anthropologist*, 59(5), 843–859.

Collier, J., & Collier, M. (1986). *Visual anthropology: Photography as a research method*. Albuquerque, NM: University of New Mexico Press.

Collier, M. (2001). Analysis in visual anthropology. In T. van Leeuwen & C. Jewitt (Eds.), *Handbook of visual analysis* (pp. 35–60). London: Sage Publications.

Congdon, E. L., Novack, M. A., & Goldin-Meadow, S. (2018). Gesture in experimental studies: How videotape technology can advance psychological theory. *Organizational Research Methods*, 21(2), 489–499.

Cornelissen, J. P., Durand, R., Fiss, P. C., Lammers, J. C., & Vaara, E. (2015). Putting communication front and center in institutional theory and analysis. *Academy of Management Review*, 40(1), 10–27.

Cornelissen, J. P., Holt, R., & Zundel, M. (2011). The role of analogy and metaphor in the framing and legitimization of strategic change. *Organization Studies*, 32(12), 1701–1716.

Couldry, N., & Hepp, A. (2017). *The mediated construction of reality*. Cambridge, UK and Malden, MA: Polity Press.

Crane, A., McWilliams, A., Matten, D., Moon, J., & Siegel, D. S. (Eds.) (2008). *The Oxford handbook of corporate social responsibility*. New York, NY: Oxford University Press.

Creed, W. E. D., Hudson, B. A., Okhuysen, G. A., & Smith-Crowe, K. (2014). Swimming in a sea of shame: Incorporating emotion into explanations of institutional reproduction and change. *Academy of Management Review*, 39(3), 275–301.

Creed, W. E. D., Scully, M. A., & Austin, J. R. (2002). Clothes make the person? The tailoring of legitimating accounts and the social construction of identity. *Organization Science*, 13(5), 475–496.

Croidieu, G., Soppe, B., & Powell, W. W. (2018). Cru, glue, and status: How wine labels helped ennoble Bordeaux. *Research in the Sociology of Organizations*, 54(B), 37–70.

Cummings, S., & Wilson, D. (2003). Images of strategy. In S. Cummings & D. Wilson (Eds.), *Images of strategy* (pp. 1–40). Malden, MA: Blackwell.

Czarniawska, B. (1997). *Narrating the organization: Dramas of institutional identity*. Chicago, IL and London: The University of Chicago Press.

Czarniawska, B. (2010). Translation impossible? Accounting for a city project. *Accounting, Auditing & Accountability Journal*, 23(3), 420–437.

Czarniawska, B., & Joerges, B. (1996). Travel of ideas. In B. Czarniawska & G. Sevón (Eds.), *Translating organizational change* (pp. 13–48). Berlin and New York, NY: de Gruyter.
Dameron, S., Lê, J. K., & LeBaron, C. (2015). Materializing strategy and strategizing material: Why matter matters. *British Journal of Management*, 26(S1), S1–S12.
Davies, W. (2016). *The happiness industry*. London: Verso.
Davison, J. (2007). Photographs and accountability: Cracking the code of an NGO. *Accounting, Auditing & Accountability Journal*, 20(1), 133–158.
Davison, J. (2008). Rhetoric, repetition, reporting and the 'dot.com' era: Words, pictures, intangibles. *Accounting, Auditing & Accountability Journal*, 21(6), 791–826.
Davison, J. (2011). Barthesian perspectives on accounting communication and visual images of professional accountancy. *Accounting, Auditing & Accountability Journal*, 24(2), 250–283.
Davison, J. (2015). Visualising accounting: An interdisciplinary review and synthesis. *Accounting and Business Research*, 45(2), 121–165.
Davison, J., McLean, C., & Warren, S. (2012). Guest editorial: Exploring the visual in organizations and management. *Qualitative Research in Organizations and Management: An International Journal*, 7(1), 5–15.
Davison, J., & Warren, S. (2009). Imag[in]ing accounting and accountability. *Accounting, Auditing & Accountability Journal*, 22(6), 845–857.
Deephouse, D. L., Bundy, J., Tost, L. P., & Suchman, M. C. (2017). Organizational legitimacy: Six key questions. In R. Greenwood, C. Oliver, T. B. Lawrence, & R. E. Meyer (Eds.), *The Sage handbook of organizational institutionalism* (2nd ed., pp. 27–54). Los Angeles, CA: Sage Publications.
Deetz, S. (1992). *Democracy in an age of corporate colonization: Developments in communication and the politics of everyday life*. Albany, NY: State University of New York Press.
Deetz, S. (2003). Reclaiming the legacy of the linguistic turn. *Organization*, 10(3), 421–429.
Dellinger, K. (2002). Wearing gender and sexuality 'on your sleeve': Dress norms and the importance of occupational and organizational culture at work. *Gender Issues*, 20(1), 3–25.
Derrida, J. (1987). *The truth in painting* (translated by G. Benningto & I. McLeod). Chicago, IL: University of Chicago Press.
Derrida, J. (1993). *Memoirs of the blind: The self-portrait and other ruins*. Chicago, IL: University of Chicago Press.
Diem-Wille, G. (2001). A therapeutic perspective: The use of drawings in child psychoanalysis and social science. In T. van Leeuwen & C. Jewitt (Eds.), *Handbook of visual analysis* (pp. 119–133). London: Sage Publications.
Djonov, E. (2008). Website hierarchy and the interaction between content organization, webpage and navigation design: A systemic-functional hypermedia discourse analysis perspective. *Information Design Journal*, 15(2), 144–161.
Djonov, E., & van Leeuwen, T. (2011). The semiotics of texture: From tactile to visual. *Visual Communication*, 10(4), 541–564.
Djonov, E., & van Leeuwen, T. (2013). Bullet points, new writing and the marketization of public discourse. In E. Djonov & S. Zhao (Eds.), *Critical multimodal studies of popular discourse* (pp. 232–250). London: Routledge.

Djonov, E., & van Leeuwen, T. (2015). Notes towards a semiotics of kinetic typography. *Social Semiotics*, 25(2), 244–253.

Djonov, E., & van Leeuwen, T. (2018). Social media as semiotic technology and social practice: the case of ResearchGate's design and its potential to transform social practice. *Social Semiotics*, 28(5), 641–664.

Djonov, E., & Zhao, S. (Eds.) (2014). *Critical multimodal studies of popular discourse*. London: Routledge.

Dourish, P., & Mazmanian, M. (2012). Media as material: Information representations as material foundations for organizational practice. In P. Carlile, D. Nicolini, A. Langley, & H. Tsoukas (Eds.), *How matter matters: Objects, artifacts and materiality in organization studies* (pp. 92–118). Oxford: Oxford University Press.

Drori, G. S., Delmestri, G., & Oberg, A. (2016). The iconography of universities as institutional narratives. *Higher Education*, 71(2), 163–180.

Drori, I., Wrzesniewski, A., & Ellis, S. (2013). One out of many? Boundary negotiation and identity formation in postmerger integration. *Organization Science*, 24(6), 1717–1741.

Du Gay, P., & Vikkelsø, S. (2017). *For formal organization: The past in the present and future of organization theory*. Oxford: Oxford University Press.

Durand, J. (1970). Rhétorique et image publicitaire, *Communications*, 15(1), 70–93.

Durand, J. (1983). Rhetoric of the advertising image. *Australian Journal of Cultural Studies*, 1(2), 29–61.

Dusto, A. (2012). *Internet RETAILER homepage*. Retrieved from www.internetretailer.com/2012/10/26/shoppers-solve-try-it-problem-ordering-multiple-sizes.

Dyer, G. (1982). *Advertising as communication*. London: Methuen.

Eisenman, M. (2013). Understanding aesthetic innovation in the context of technological evolution. *Academy of Management Review*, 38(3), 332–351.

Eisenman, M. (2018). A multimodal investigation of the industrialization of aesthetic design as a dimension of competition in the pc industry. *Research in the Sociology of Organizations*, 54(A), 183–217.

Elkins, J. (2000). *How to use your eyes*. New York, NY: Routledge.

Elleström, L. (2010). *Media borders, multimodality and intermediality*. London: Palgrave Macmillan.

Elliott, C., & Stead, V. (2018). Constructing women's leadership representation in the UK press during a time of financial crisis: Gender capitals and dialectical tensions. *Organization Studies*, 39(1), 19–45.

Elsbach, K. D., & Pratt, M. G. (2007). The physical environment in organizations. *The Academy of Management Annals*, 1(1), 181–224.

Endo, S., Yang, J., & Park, J. (2012). The investigations on dimensions of e-satisfication for online shoes retailing. *Journal of Retailing and Consumer Services*, 19(4), 398–405.

Erkama, N., & Vaara, E. (2010). Struggles over legitimacy in global organizational restructuring: A rhetorical perspective on legitimation strategies and dynamics in a shutdown case. *Organization Studies*, 31(7), 813–839.

Ewenstein, B., & Whyte, J. (2007). Beyond words: Aesthetic knowledge and knowing in organizations. *Organization Studies*, 28(5), 689–708.

Ewenstein, B., & Whyte, J. (2009). Knowledge practices in design: The role of visual representations as 'epistemic objects'. *Organization Studies*, 30(1), 7–30.

Fahmy, S. (2010). Contrasting visual frames of our times: A framing analysis of English- and Arabic-language press coverage of war and terrorism. *International Communication Gazette*, 72(8), 695–717.
Fahmy, S., Kelly, J. D., & Kim, Y. S. (2007). What Katrina revealed: A visual analysis of the hurricane coverage by news wires and U.S. newspapers. *Journalism & Mass Communication Quarterly*, 84(3), 546–561.
Fairclough, N. (1992). *Discourse and social change*. Cambridge: Polity Press.
Fairclough, N. (2003). *Analyzing discourse: Textual analysis for social research*. London: Routledge.
Fauconnier, G., & Turner, M. (2002). *The way we think*. New York, NY: Basic Books.
Fellmann, F. (1995). Innere Bilder im Licht des imagic turn. In K. Sachs-Hombach (Ed.), *Bilder im Geiste: Zur kognitiven und erkenntnistheoretischen Funktion piktorialer Repräsentationen* (pp. 21–38). Amsterdam/Atlanta: Rodopi.
Felt, U., Fouché, R., Miller, C. A., & Smith-Doerr, L. (Eds.) (2017). *The handbook of science and technology studies* (4th ed.). Cambridge, MA: MIT Press.
Firth, J. R. (1957). *Papers in linguistics, 1934–1951*. London: Oxford University Press.
Firth, J. R. (1968). *Selected papers of J.R. Firth, 1952–59*. London: Longmans.
Flewitt, R., Hampel, R., Hauck, M., & Lancaster, L. (2009). What are multimodal data and transcription? In C. Jewitt (Ed.), *The Routledge handbook of multimodal analysis* (pp. 44–59). London: Routledge.
Floch, J. M. (2000). *Visual identities*. London: Continuum.
Fontaine. L., Bartlett, T., & O'Grady, G. (Eds.) (2015). *Systemic functional linguistics: Exploring choice*. Cambridge: Cambridge University Press.
Forceville, C. (1996). *Pictorial metaphor in advertising*. London: Routledge.
Forgues, B., & May, T. (2018). Message in a bottle: Multiple modes and multiple media in market identity claims. *Research in the Sociology of Organizations*, 54(B), 179–202.
Foucault, M. (1979). *Discipline and punish: The birth of the prison*. New York, NY: Vintage Books.
Freeman, L. C. (2004). *The development of social network analysis*. Vancouver: Empirical Press.
Fresnault-Deruelle, P. (1977). *La chambre à bulles*. Paris: 10/18.
Friedland, R., & Alford, R. R. (1991). Bringing society back in: Symbols, practices, and institutional contradictions. In W. W. Powell & P. J. DiMaggio (Eds.), *The new institutionalism in organizational analysis* (pp. 232–263). Chicago, IL: University of Chicago Press.
Friedland, R., Mohr, J. W., Roose, H., & Gardinali, P. (2014). The institutional logics of love: Measuring intimate life. *Theory and Society*, 43(3–4), 333–370.
Gamson, W. A., & Lasch, K. E. (1983). The political culture of social welfare policy. In S. E. Spiro & E. Yuchtman-Yaar (Eds.), *Evaluating the welfare state: Social and political perspectives* (pp. 397–415). New York, NY: Academic Press.
Garfinkel, H. (1967). *Studies in ethnomethodology*. Cambridge: Polity Press.
Garvin, P. L. (1964). *A Prague school reader on esthetics, literary structure and style*. Washington, DC: Georgetown University Press.
Geertz, C. (1973). *The interpretation of cultures*. New York, NY: Basic books.
Gehman, J., & Grimes, M. (2017). Hidden badge of honor: How contextual distinctiveness affects category promotion among certified B corporations. *Academy of Management Journal*, 60(6), 2294–2320.

Gibson, J. J. (1986). *The ecological approach to visual perception*. New York, NY and Hove: Psychology Press.

Gioia, D. A., Patvardhan, S. D., Hamilton, A. L., & Corley, K. G. (2013). Organizational identity formation and change. *The Academy of Management Annals, 7*(1), 123–192.

Glaser, B. G., & Strauss, A. L. (1967). *The discovery of grounded theory: Strategies for qualitative research*. New York, NY: De Gruyter.

Goffman, E. (1981). *Forms of talk*. Oxford: Blackwell.

Goldberg, D. T., & Hristova, S. (2007). Blue velvet—Re-dressing New Orleans in Katrina's wake. *Vectors, Journal of Culture and Technology in Dynamic Vernacular*. Retrieved from www.vectorsjournal.org

Gombrich, E. H. (1960). *Art and illusion: A study in the psychology of pictorial representation*. Princeton, NJ: Princeton University Press.

Goodwin, C. (2001). Practices of seeing visual analysis: An ethnomethodological approach. In T. van Leeuwen & C. Jewitt (Eds.), *Handbook of visual analysis* (pp. 157–182). London: Sage Publications.

Graakjær, N. J. (2012). Dance in the store: On the use and production of music in Abercrombie & Fitch. *Critical Discourse Studies, 9*(4), 393–406.

Grady, J. (1996). The scope of visual sociology. *Visual Sociology, 11*(2), 10–24.

Graebner, M., Heimeriks, K., Huy, Q., & Vaara, E. (2017). The process of post-merger integration: A review and agenda for future research. *Academy of Management Annals, 11*(1), 1–32.

Grant, D., Hardy, C., Oswick, C., & Putnam, L. (Eds.) (2004). *The Sage handbook of organizational discourse*. London: Sage Publications.

Graves, O. F., Flesher, D. L., & Jordan, R. E. (1996). Pictures and the bottom line: The television epistemology of U.S. annual reports. *Accounting, Organizations and Society, 21*(1), 57–88.

Green, S. E. (2004). A rhetorical theory of diffusion. *The Academy of Management Review, 29*(4), 653–669.

Green, S. E., Jr., Li, Y., & Nohria, N. (2009). Suspended in self-spun webs of significance: A rhetorical model of institutionalization and institutionally embedded agency. *Academy of Management Journal, 52*(1), 11–36.

Greenwood, M., Jack, G., Haylock, B. (2018). Toward a methodology for analyzing visual rhetoric in corporate reports. *Organizational Research Methods*. doi:10.1177/1094428118765942.

Greenwood, R., Oliver, C., Lawrence, T. B., & Meyer, R. E. (Eds.) (2017). *The Sage handbook of organizational institutionalism*. Los Angeles, CA: Sage Publications.

Greimas, A. J. (1983). *Structural semantics: An attempt at method*. Lincoln, NE: University of Nebraska Press.

Gümüsay, A. A. (2012). Boundaries and knowledge in a Sufi Dhikr Circle. *Journal of Management Development, 31*(10), 1077–1089.

Gümüsay, A. A., Höllerer, M. A., & Meyer, R. E. (2018). Organizational Scent. *M@n@gement, 21*(4), 1424–1428.

Guthey, E., & Jackson, B. (2005). CEO portraits and the autheticity paradox. *Journal of Management Studies, 42*(5), 1057–1082.

Gylfe, P., Franck, H., Lebaron, C., & Mantere, S. (2016). Video methods in strategy research: Focusing on embodied cognition. *Strategic Management Journal, 37*(1), 133–148.

Halgin, D. S., Glynn, M. A., & Rockwell, D. (2018). Organizational actorhood and the management paradox: A visual analysis. *Organization Studies, 39*(5–6), 645–664.

Hall, S. (1999). Introduction: Looking and subjectivity. In J. Evans & S. Hall (Eds.), *Visual culture: The reader* (pp. 309–314). London: Sage Publications.

Halliday, M. A. K. (1966). Some notes on 'deep' grammar. In M. A. K. Halliday (Ed.) (2002), *On grammar: Collected works of M.A.K. Halliday* (Vol. 1, pp. 106–117). London: Continuum.

Halliday, M. A. K. (1973). *Explorations in the functions of language*. London: Arnold.

Halliday, M. A. K. (1977). Text as semantic choice in social contexts. In J. Webster (Ed.) (2002), *Linguistic studies of text and discourse* (pp. 23–81). London: Continuum.

Halliday, M. A. K. (1978). *Language as social semiotic*. London: Arnold.

Halliday, M. A. K. (1979). Modes of meaning and modes of expression: Types of grammatical structure and their determination by different semantic functions. In D. J. Allerton, E. Coney, & D. Holdcroft (Eds.), *Function and context in linguistic analysis: A festschrift for William Haas*. Cambridge: Cambridge University Press.

Halliday, M. A. K. (1984a). On the ineffability of grammatical categories. In M. A. K. Halliday (Ed.) (2002), *On grammar: Collected works of M.A.K. Halliday* (Vol. 1, pp. 291–322). London: Continuum.

Halliday, M. A. K. (1984b). Language as code and language as behaviour: A systemic-functional interpretation of the nature and ontogenesis of dialogue. In R. P. Fawcett, M. A. K. Halliday, S. M. Lamb, & A. Makkai (Eds.), *The semiotics of culture and language* (Vol. 1, pp. 3–36). London and Dover, NH: Frances Pinter.

Halliday, M. A. K. (1985a). *An introduction to functional grammar*. London: Arnold.

Halliday, M. A. K. (1985b). Systemic Background. In M. A. K. Halliday (2003), *On language and linguistics: Collected Works of M.A.K. Halliday* (Vol. 3, pp. 185–198). London and New York, NY: Continuum.

Halliday, M. A. K. (1992). How do you mean. In M. A. K. Halliday (2002), *On grammar: Collected works of M.A.K. Halliday* (Vol. 1, pp. 352–368). London and New York, NY: Continuum.

Halliday, M. A. K. (1994). *An introduction to functional grammar* (2nd ed.). London: Arnold.

Halliday, M. A. K. (1995). On language in relation to fuzzy logic and intelligent computing. In M. A. K. Halliday (Ed.) (2005), *Computational and quantitative studies: Collected works of M.A.K. Halliday* (Vol. 6, pp. 196–212). London and New York, NY: Continuum.

Halliday, M. A. K. (1996). 'Introduction', language as social semiotic: The social interpretation of language and meaning. In P. Cobley (Ed.), *The communication theory reader* (pp. 88–93). London: Routledge.

Halliday, M. A. K. (1998). Grammar and daily life: Concurrence and complementarity. In M. A. K. Halliday (2002), *On grammar: Collected works of M.A.K. Halliday* (Vol. 1, pp. 369–383). London: Continuum.

Halliday, M. A. K., & Hasan, R. (1976). *Cohesion in English*. London: Longman.

Halliday, M. A. K., & Hasan, R. (1985). *Language, context and text: Aspects of language in a social-semiotic perspective*. Geelong, VIC: Deakin University Press.

Halliday, M. A. K., & Matthiessen, C. M. I. M. (1999). *Construing experience through meaning*. London: Continuum.
Halliday, M. A. K., & Matthiessen, C. M. I. M. (2013). *Halliday's introduction to functional grammar* (4th ed.). London: Routledge.
Hardy, C., & Phillips, N. (1999). No joking matter: Discursive struggle in the Canadian refugee system. *Organization Studies*, 20(1), 1–24.
Harper, D. (2002). Talking about pictures: A case for photo elicitation. *Visual Studies*, 17(1), 13–26.
Hasan, R. (2005). *Language, society and consciousness*. London: Equinox.
Hassard, J., Burns, D., Hyde, P., & Burns, J.-P. (2018). A visual turn for organizational ethnography: Embodying the subject in video-based research. *Organization Studies*, 39(10), 1403–1424.
Heath, R. (2001). *The hidden power of advertising: How low involvement processes influence the way we choose brands*. Henley-on-Thames: Admaps Publications.
Heckler, S. E., & Childers, T. L. (1992). The role of expectancy and relevancy in memory for verbal and visual information: What is incongruency? *Journal of Consumer Research*, 18(4), 475–492.
Henderson, K. (1991). Flexible sketches and inflexible data bases: Visual communication, conscription devices, and boundary objects in design engineering. *Science, Technology, & Human Values*, 16(4), 419–447.
Henderson, K. (1995). The political career of a prototype: Visual representation in design engineering. *Social Problems*, 42(2), 274–299.
Heracleous, L., & Jacobs, C. D. (2008). Crafting strategy: The role of embodied metaphors. *Long Range Planning*, 41(3), 309–325.
Hernes, T. (2014). *A process theory of organization*. Oxford: Oxford University Press.
Higgins, E., Leinenger, M., & Rayner, K. (2014). Eye movement when viewing advertisements. *Frontiers in Psychology*, 5(210), 1–15.
Hill, C. A., & Helmers, M. (Eds.) (2004). *Defining visual rhetorics*. Mahwah, NJ and London: Lawrence Erlbaum Associates.
Hindmarsh, J., & Llewellyn, N. (2018). Video in sociomaterial investigations: A solution to the problem of relevance for organizational research. *Organizational Research Methods*, 21(2), 412–437.
Hinings, B., & Meyer, R. E. (2018). *Starting points: Intellectual and institutional foundations of organization theory*. Cambridge: Cambridge University Press.
Hiss, S. (2009). From implicit to explicit corporate social responsibility: Institutional change as a fight for myths. *Business Ethics Quarterly*, 19(3), 433–451.
Hodge, B. (2003). How the medium is the message in the unconscious of 'America Online'. *Visual Communication*, 2(3), 341–353.
Hodge, B. (2017). *Social semiotics for a complex world: Analysing language and social meaning*. Cambridge, UK and Malden, MA: Polity Press.
Hodge, R., & Kress, B. (1988). *Social semiotics*. Cambridge: Polity Press.
Höllerer, M. A. (2013). From taken-for-granted to explicit commitment: The rise of CSR in a corporatist country. *Journal of Management Studies*, 50(4), 573–606.
Höllerer, M. A., Daudigeos, T., & Jancsary, D. (2018). Multimodality, meaning, and institutions: Editorial. *Research in the Sociology of Organizations*, 54(A), 1–24.

Höllerer, M. A., Jancsary, D., & Grafström, M. (2018). 'A picture is worth a thousand words': Multimodal sensemaking of the global financial crisis. *Organization Studies*, 39(5–6), 617–644.

Höllerer, M. A., Jancsary, D., Meyer, R. E., & Vettori, O. (2013). Imageries of corporate social responsibility: Visual recontextualization and field-level meaning. *Research in the Sociology of Organizations*, 39(B), 139–174.

Höllerer, M. A., Meyer, R. E., & Lounsbury, M. (2017). Constructing domains of corporate social responsibility: A politicization of corporations at the expense of a de-politicization of society? In G. Krücken, C. Mazza, R. E. Meyer, & P. Walgenbach (Eds.), *New themes in institutional analysis: Topics and issues from European research* (pp. 194–223). Cheltenham and Northampton: Edward Elgar.

Holmes, J. (1992). *An introduction to sociolinguistics*. London: Longman.

Holmes, W. E. (2005). Staff rides: A new concept in training future leaders? Or older leaders? *California Fire Service*, 38, 26–27.

Holsanova, J., Rahm, H., & Holmqvist, K. (2006). Entry points and reading paths on newspaper spreads: Comparing semiotic analysis with eye-tracking measurements. *Visual Communication*, 5(1), 65–93.

Hood, S. (2011). Body language in face-to-face teaching. In S. Dreyfus, S. Hood, & M. Stenglin (Eds.), *Semiotic margins: Meaning in multimodalities* (pp. 31–52). London: Continuum.

Hood, S. (2017). Live lectures: The significance of presence in building disciplinary knowledge. *Onomazein*, 179–208. doi:10.7764/onomazein.sfl.07

Houston, M. J., Childers, T. L., & Heckler, S. E. (1987). Picture-word consistency and the elaborative processing of advertisements. *Journal of Marketing Research*, 24(4), 359–369.

Huang, G., Korfiatis, N., & Chang, C. (2018). Mobile shopping cart abandonment: The roles of conflicts, ambivalence and hesitation. *Journal of Business Research*, 85, 165–174.

Hyndman, N., Liguori, M., Meyer, R. E., Polzer, T., Rota, S., Seiwald, J., & Steccolini, I. (2018). Legitimating change in the public sector: The introduction of (rational?) accounting practices in the United Kingdom, Italy and Austria. *Public Management Review*, 20(9), 1374–1399.

ICOM (2016). *The 8th international conference on multimodality: Programme and abstracts*. Cape Town: University of Cape Town.

Iedema, R. (2001). Resemiotization. *Semiotica*, 137(1/4), 23–40.

Iedema, R. (2003a). 'Multimodality, resemiotization: Extending the analysis of discourse as multi-semiotic practice. *Visual Communication*, 2(1), 29–57.

Iedema, R. (2003b). *Discourses of post-bureaucratic organization*. Amsterdam: John Benjamins.

Iedema, R. (2015). A participatory approach to 'analysing' visual data: Involving practitioners in visual feedback. In S. Norris & C. D. Maier (Eds.), *Interactions, images and texts: A reader in multimodality* (pp. 195–212). Berlin: Mouton de Gruyter.

Islam, G., Endrissat, N., & Noppeney, C. (2016). Beyond 'the eye' of the beholder: Scent innovation through analogical reconfiguration. *Organization Studies*, 37(6), 769–795.

Jackson, D. M. (2003). *Sonic branding: An introduction*. London: Palgrave Macmillan.

Jakobson, R. (1960a). Closing statement: Linguistics and poetics. In T. A. Sebeok (Ed.), *Style in language*. Cambridge, MA: MIT Press.
Jakobson, R. (1960b). Lingvistik og poetik. *Vindrosen*, 7, 41–52.
Jakubowicz, A., & van Leeuwen, T. (2010). The Goldberg variations 1: Assessing the academic quality of multidimensional linear texts and their re-emergence in multimedia publications. *Discourse & Communication*, 4(4), 361–378.
Jancsary, D. (2013). *Die rhetorische Konstruktion von Führung und Steuerung: Eine argumentationsanalytische Untersuchung deutschsprachiger Führungsgrundsätze*. Frankfurt a. M.: Peter Lang.
Jancsary, D., Höllerer, M. A., & Meyer, R. E. (2016). Critical analysis of visual and multimodal texts. In R. Wodak & M. Meyer (Eds.), *Methods of critical discourse studies* (3rd ed., pp. 180–204). Los Angeles, CA: Sage Publications.
Jancsary, D., Meyer, R. E., Höllerer, M. A., & Boxenbaum, E. (2018). Institutions as multimodal accomplishments: Towards the analysis of visual registers. *Research in the Sociology of Organizations*, 54(A), 87–117.
Jarzabkowski, P., & Pinch, T. (2013). Sociomateriality is 'the new black': Accomplishing repurposing, reinscripting and repairing in context. *M@n@gement*, 16(5), 579–592.
Jewitt, C. (2006). *Technology, literacy and learning: A multimodal approach*. London: Routledge.
Jewitt, C. (Ed.) (2014). *The Routledge handbook of multimodal analysis* (2nd ed.). London: Routledge.
Jewitt, C., Bezemer, J., & O'Halloran, K. (2016). *Introducing multimodality*. London: Routledge.
Jewitt, C., van Leeuwen, T., Triggs, T., & Longford, M. (2011). The visual essay (Special issue). *Visual Communication*, 10(3).
Johannessen, C. M. (2017). Experiential meaning potential in the Topaz Energy logo: A framework for graphemic and graphetic analysis of graphic logo design. *Social Semiotics*, 27(1), 1–20.
Johannessen, C. M., & van Leeuwen, T. (Eds.) (2017). *The materiality of writing*. London: Routledge.
Jones, C., Anthony, C., & Boxenbaum, E. (2013). *Let's get physical: Materiality and institutional theory*. Paper presented at the EGOS Colloquium in Montreal, Canada, July 3–6.
Jones, C., Boxenbaum, E., & Anthony, C. (2013). The immateriality of material practices in institutional logics. *Research in the Sociology of Organizations*, 39(A), 51–75.
Jones, C., Maoret, M., Massa, F. G., & Svejenova, S. (2012). Rebels with a cause: Formation, contestation, and expansion of the de novo category 'modern architecture,' 1870–1975. *Organization Science*, 23(6), 1523–1545.
Jones, C., Meyer, R. E., Jancsary, D., & Höllerer, M. A. (2017). The material and visual basis of institutions. In R. Greenwood, C. Oliver, R. E. Meyer, & T. Lawrence (Eds.), *The Sage handbook of organizational institutionalism* (2nd ed., pp. 621–646). Los Angeles, CA: Sage Publications.
Jones, C., & Svejenova, S. (2018). The architecture of city identities: A multimodal study of Barcelona and Boston. *Research in the Sociology of Organizations*, 54(B), 203–234.

Jones, C., & Ventola, E. (Eds.) (2008). *From language to multimodality: New developments in the study of ideational meaning.* London: Equinox.

Justesen, L., & Mouritsen, J. (2009). The triple visual. Translations between photographs, 3-D visualizations and calculations. *Accounting, Auditing & Accountability Journal, 22*(6), 973–990.

Kamla, R., & Roberts, C. (2010). The global and the local: Arabian Gulf states and imagery in annual reports. *Accounting, Auditing & Accountability Journal, 23*(4), 449–481.

Kaplan, R. S., & Norton, D. P. (2004). *Strategy maps: Converting intangible assets into tangible outcomes.* Boston, MA: Harvard Business School.

Kaplan, S. (2011). Strategy and PowerPoint: An inquiry into the epistemic culture and machinery of strategy making. *Organization Science, 22*(2), 320–346.

Karhunen, S., Jyrämä, A., & Knuutinen, L. (2012). *Genius loci: School of economics: Its architecture, design and art.* Helsinki: Aalto University publication series BUSINESS + ECONOMY.

Karlsson, A.-M. (2009). Fixing meaning: On the semiotic and interactional role of written texts in a risk analysis meeting. *Text & Talk, 29*(4), 415–438.

Karlsson, A.-M. (2012). Multimodaliteten och språket. Om lexikogrammatikens styrkor och begränsningar i förhållande till några arbetslivsdiskurser. In T. H. Andersen & M. Boeriis (Eds.), *Nordisk socialsemiotik* (pp. 17–38). Odense: Odense Universitetsforlag.

Kessler, S. (2014). *The next (sound) wave in branding: How AT&T created its new sonic identity.* Retrieved from www.fastcodedesign.com/1671164/the-next-sound-wave-in-branding-how-att-created-its-new-sonic-identity/.

Kim, J., & Forsythe, S. (2009). Adoption of sensory enabling technology for online apparel shopping. *European Journal of Marketing, 43*(9–10), 1101–1120.

Kim, K. J., & Sundar, S. S. (2016). Mobile persuasion: Can screen size and presentation mode make a difference to trust? *Human Communication Research, 42*(1), 45–70.

Kinderman, D., & Lutter, M. (2018). *Explaining the growth of CSR within OECD countries. The role of institutional legitimacy in resolving the institutional mirror vs. substitute debate.* MPIfG Discussion Paper 18/2.

Knox, J. S. (2007). Visual-verbal communication on online newspaper home pages. *Visual Communication, 6*(1), 19–53.

Kongsberg Maritime (2017). *Kongsberg Maritime established cybernetics R&D group.* Retrieved from km.kongsberg.com/ks/web/nokbg0238.nsf/AllWeb/DEDAB2A5E1391F4AC12579D0002CB585?OpenDocument.

Koskela, I., Arminen, I, & Palukka, H. (2013). Centres of coordination as a nexus of aviation. In P. Haddington, L. Mondada, & M. Nevile (Eds.), *Interaction and mobility* (pp. 245–276). Berlin: De Gruyter.

Kress, G. (2005). Gains and losses: New forms of text, knowledge and learning. *Computers and Composition, 22*(1), 4–22.

Kress, G. (2010). *Multimodality: A social-semiotic approach to contemporary communication.* London: Routledge.

Kress, G., & van Leeuwen, T. (1996). *Reading images: The grammar of visual design.* London: Routledge.

Kress, G., & van Leeuwen, T. (2001). *Multimodal discourse: The modes and media of contemporary communication.* London: Arnold.

Kress, G., & van Leeuwen, T. (2006). *Reading images: The grammar of visual design* (2nd ed.). London: Routledge.

Kress, G., Jewitt, C., Ogborn, J., & Tsatsarelis, C. (2001). *Multimodal teaching and learning: The rhetorics of the science classroom.* London: Continuum.

Kukar-Kinney, M., & Close, A. G. (2010). The determinants of consumers' online shopping cart abandonment. *Journal of the Academy of Marketing Science, 38*(2), 240–250.

Kunter, A., & Bell, E. (2006). The promise and potential of visual organizational research. *M@n@gement, 9*(3), 177–197.

Kvåle, G. (2016). Software as ideology: A multimodal critical discourse analysis of Microsoft Word and SmartArt. *Journal of Language and Politics, 15*(3), 259–273.

Labrecque, L. I., Patrick, V. M., & Milne, G. R. (2013). The marketers' prismatic palette: A review of color research and future directions. *Psychology & Marketing, 30*(2), 187–202.

Lakoff, G., & Johnson, M. (1980). *Metaphors we live by.* Chicago, IL: University of Chicago Press.

Latour, B. (1986). Visualization and cognition: Thinking with eyes and hands. In H. Kuklick (Ed.), *Knowledge and society: Studies in the sociology of culture. Past and present* (Vol. 6, pp. 1–40). London: Jai Press.

Latour, B. (1990). The force and reason of experiment. In H. E. Le Grand (Ed.), *Experimental inquiries* (pp. 49–80). Dordrecht: Kluwer.

Latour, B. (2005). *Reassembling the social: An introduction to actor-network-theory.* Oxford: Oxford University Press.

Leão, G. (2013). *A systemic-functional approach to the analysis of animation in film opening titles* (PhD Thesis). Sydney: University of Technology.

Leckner, S. (2012). Presentation factors affecting reading behaviour in readers of newspaper media: An eye-tracking perspective. *Visual Communication, 11*(2), 163–184.

Ledin, P., & Machin, D. (2016). Strategic diagrams and the technologization of culture. *Journal of Language and Politics, 15*(3), 321–336.

Lee, D. (1954). Linguistic reflections on Wintu thought. In E. Carpenter & M. McLuhan (Eds.), *Explorations: Studies in culture and communication* (Vol. 6., pp. 1–10). Eugene, OR: Wipf and Stock.

Lefsrud, L. M., Graves, H., & Phillips, N. (2013). Dirty oil, ethical oil: Categorical illegitimacy and the struggle over the Alberta Oil Sands. *Academy of Management Proceedings, 2013*(1). doi:10.5465/AMBPP.2013.13283abstract.

Lefsrud, L. M., Graves, H., & Phillips, N. (2018). Dirty oil or ethical oil? Visual rhetoric in legitimation struggles. *Research in the Sociology of Organizations, 54*(B), 101–142.

Lefsrud, L. M., & Meyer, R. E. (2012). Science or science fiction? Professionals' discursive construction of climate change. *Organization Studies, 33*(11), 1477–1506.

Lemke, J. (1995). *Textual politics.* London and Bristol: Taylor & Francis.

Lemke, J. (1998). Multiplying meaning: Visual and verbal semiotics in scientific text. In J. R. Martin & R. Veel (Eds.), *Reading science: Critical and functional perspectives on discourses of science* (pp. 87–113). London: Routledge.

Leonardi, P. M. (2012). Materiality, sociomateriality, and sociotechnical systems: What do these terms mean? How are they different? Do we need them? In

References

P. M. Leonardi, B. A. Nardi, & J. Kallinikos (Eds.), *Materiality and organizing: Social interaction in a technological world* (pp. 25–48). Oxford: Oxford University Press.

LeVine, P., & Scollon, R. (Eds.) (2004). *Discourse and technology: Multimodal discourse analysis*. Washington, DC: Georgetown University Press.

Lim Fei, V. (2004). Developing an integrative multi-semiotic model. In K. L. O'Halloran, *Multimodal discourse analysis* (pp. 220–247). London: Continuum.

Lima, M. (2011). *Visual complexity: Mapping patterns of information*. New York, NY: Princeton Architectural Press.

Lima, M. (2013). *The book of trees: Visualizing branches of knowledge*. New York, NY: Princeton Architectural Press.

Link, J. (1997). *Versuch über den Normalismus*. Opladen: Westdeutscher Verlag.

Liversedge, S. P., Rayner, K., White, S. J., Vergilino-Perez, D., Findlay, J. M., & Kentridge, R. W. (2004). Eye movements when reading disappearing text: Is there a gap effect in reading? *Vision Research*, 44(10), 1013–1024.

Livingstone, M. (2002). *Vision and art: The biology of seeing*. New York, NY: Harry A. Abrams.

Llewellyn, N., & Hindmarsh, J. (2013). The order problem: Inference and interaction in interactive service work. *Human Relations*, 66(11), 1401–1426.

Locke, J. (1972 [1706]). *An essay concerning human understanding* (Vol. II). London: Dent.

Loewenstein, J., Ocasio, W., & Jones, C. (2012). Vocabularies and vocabulary structure: A new approach linking categories, practices, and institutions. *The Academy of Management Annals*, 6(1), 41–86.

Luckmann, T. (2006). Die kommunikative Konstruktion der Wirklichkeit. In D. Tänzler, H. Knoblauch, & H.-G. Soeffner (Eds.), *Neue Perspektiven der Wissenssoziologie* (pp. 15–26). Konstanz: UVK Verl.-Ges.

Lueger, M., Sandner, K., Meyer, R. E., & Hammerschmid, G. (2005). Contextualizing influence activities: An objective hermeneutical approach. *Organization Studies*, 26(8), 1145–1168.

Lurie, N. H., & Mason, C. H. (2007). Visual representation: Implications for decision making. *Journal of Marketing*, 71(1), 160–177.

Maar, C., & Burda, H. (Eds.) (2004). *Iconic turn. Die neue Macht der Bilder*. Köln: DuMont.

Machin, D. (2004). Building the world's visual language: The increasing global importance of image banks in corporate media. *Visual Communication*, 3(32), 316–336.

Machin, D. (2007). *Introduction to multimodal analysis*. London: Hodder Arnold.

Machin, D. (2010). *Analyzing popular music*. London: Sage Publications.

Machin, D. (Ed.). (2013). Multimodal critical discourse studies (Special issue). *Critical Discourse Studies*, 10(4).

Machin, D., & van Leeuwen, T. (2007). *Global media discourse: A critical introduction*. London: Routledge.

Machin, D., & van Leeuwen, T. (Eds.). (2016). Multimodality, politics and ideology (Special issue). *Journal of Language and Politics*, 15(3), 243–258.

Maier, C. D. (2017). Exploring organizational heritage identity: The multimodal communication strategies. In O. Seizov & J. Wildfeuer (Eds.), *New studies in multimodality: Conceptual and methodological elaborations* (pp. 225–246). London: Bloomsbury.

Maier, C. D., & Andersen, M. A. (2014). Dynamic interplay of visual and textual identification strategies in employees' magazines. *International Journal of Strategic Communication, 8*(4), 250–275.
Malinowski, B. (1923). The problem of meaning in primitive languages. Supplement 1 to C. K. Ogden & I. A. Richards, *The meaning of meaning*. London and New York, NY: Harcourt, Brace, Jovanovic.
Malinowski, B. (1935). *Coral gardens and their magic* (Vol. 2). London: Allen and Unwin.
Margolis, E., & Pauwels, L. (Eds.) (2011). *The Sage handbook of visual research methods*. Los Angeles, CA: Sage Publications.
Margolis, J. D., & Walsh, J. P. (2003). Misery loves companies: Rethinking social initiatives by business. *Administrative Science Quarterly, 48*(2), 268–305.
Mariarcher, G., Ring, A., & Schneider, A. (2013). Same, same but different. How pictures influence emotional responses of users with different web search behaviours. In L. Cantoni & Z. Xiang (Eds.), *Information and communication technologies in tourism 2013. Proceedings of the international conference in Innsbruck, Austria, January 22–25, 2013* (pp. 375–387). Heidelberg: Springer.
Martin, J. R. (1992). *English text: System and structure*. Amsterdam: Benjamins.
Martinec, R. (1998). Cohesion in action. *Semiotica, 120*(1/2), 161–180.
Martinec, R. (2000). Types of processes in action. *Semiotica, 130*(3/4), 243–268.
Martinec, R. (2001). Interpersonal resources in action. *Semiotica, 135*(1/4), 117–145.
Martinec, R. (2004). Gestures that co-occur with speech as systematic resources: The realization of experiential meaning in indexes. *Social Semiotics, 14*(2), 193–213.
Martinec, R., & Salway, A. (2005). A system for image-text relations in new (and old) media. *Visual Communication, 4*(3), 337–372.
Martinec, R., & van Leeuwen, T. (2009). *The language of new media design: Theory and practice*. London: Routledge.
Massironi, M. (2002). *The psychology of graphic images: Seeing, drawing, communicating*. Mahwah, NJ: Erlbaum.
Matějka, L., & Titunik, I. R. (Eds.) (1976). *Semiotics of art: Prague school contributions* Cambridge, MA: MIT Press.
Matilal, S., & Höpfl, H. (2009). Accounting for the Bhopal disaster: Footnotes and photographs. *Accounting, Auditing & Accountability Journal, 22*(6), 953–972.
Matten, D., & Moon, J. (2008). 'Implicit' and 'explicit' CSR: A conceptual framework for a comparative understanding of corporate social responsibility. *Academy of Management Review, 33*(2), 404–424.
Matthiessen, C. (2015). Register in the round: Registerial cartography. *Functional Linguistics, 2*(9), 1–48.
McLuhan, M. (1963). *Understanding media*. New York, NY: Signet.
McMurtrie, R. (2017). *The semiotics of movement in space*. London: Routledge.
McQuail, D., & Windahl, S. (1982). *Communication models for the study of mass communication*. London: Longman.
McQuarrie, E. F., & Mick, D. G. (1999). Visual rhetoric in advertising: Text-interpretive, experimental, and reader-response analyses. *Journal of Consumer Research, 26*(1), 37–54.
McQuarrie, E. F., & Phillips, B. J. (2005). Indirect persuasion in advertising: How consumers process metaphors presented in pictures. *Journal of Advertising, 34*(2), 7–20.

Melander, R. (2016). Tre ting får kunderne til at flygte—og det er ikke højre priser. *Finans.dk*. Retrieved from http://finans.dk/live/erhverv/ECE8908707/tre-ting-faar-kunderne-til-at-flygte-og-det-er-ikke-hoeje-priser/.

Mengis, J., Nicolini, D., & Gorli, M. (2018). The video production of space: How different recording practices matter. *Organizational Research Methods*, 21(2), 288–315.

Merleau-Ponty, M. (1964). *The primacy of perception*. Evanston: Northwestern University Press.

Merleau-Ponty, M. (1968). *The visible and the invisible*. Evanston: Northwestern University Press.

Messaris, P. (1997). *Visual persuasion: The role of images in advertising*. Thousand Oaks, CA: Sage Publications.

Messaris, P., & Abraham, L. (2001). The role of images in framing news stories. In S. D. Reese, O. H. Gandy, Jr., & A. E. Grant (Eds.), *Framing public life: Perspectives on media and our understanding of the social world* (pp. 215–226). New York, NY and London: Routledge.

Metz, C. (1974). *Film language: A semiotics of the cinema*. New York, NY: Oxford University Press.

Meyer, A. D. (1991). Visual data in organizational research. *Organization Science*, 2(2), 218–236.

Meyer, J. W., & Rowan, B. (1977). Institutionalized organizations: Formal structure as myth and ceremony. *American Journal of Sociology*, 83(2), 340–363.

Meyer, R. E., & Höllerer, M. A. (2010). Meaning structures in a contested issue field: A topographic map of shareholder value in Austria. *Academy of Management Journal*, 53(6), 1241–1262.

Meyer, R. E., & Höllerer, M. A. (2016). Laying a smoke screen: Ambiguity and neutralization as strategic responses to intra-institutional complexity. *Strategic Organization*, 14(4), 373–406.

Meyer, R. E., Höllerer, M. A., Jancsary, D., & van Leeuwen, T. (2013). The visual dimension in organizing, organization, and organization research. *The Academy of Management Annals*, 7(1), 487–553.

Meyer, R. E., Jancsary, D. C., Höllerer, M. A., & Boxenbaum, E. (2018). The role of verbal and visual text in the process of institutionalization. *Academy of Management Review*, 43(3), 392–418.

Meyer, M., & Wodak, R. (Eds.) (2016). *Methods of critical discourse analysis* (3rd ed.). London: Sage Publications.

Milic, L. (1970). Connectives in Swift's prose style. In D. C. Freeman (Ed.), *Linguistics and literary style* (pp. 243–257). New York, NY: Holt, Rinehart and Winston.

Miller, D. (1998). *A theory of shopping*. Cambridge: Polity Press.

Mills, C. W. (1940). Situated actions and vocabularies of motive. *American Sociological Review*, 5(6), 904–913.

Mintzberg, H., & van der Heyden, L. (1999). Organigraphs: Drawing how companies really work. *Harvard Business Review*, September–October 1999.

Mitchell, A. A., & Olson, J. C. (1981). Are product attribute beliefs the only mediator of advertising effects on brand attitude? *Journal of Marketing Research*, 18, 318–322.

Mitchell, W. J. T. (1980). *The language of images*. Chicago, IL: Chicago University Press.

Mitchell, W. J. T. (1994). *Picture theory: Essays on verbal and visual representation*. Chicago, IL and London: The University of Chicago Press.

Moeran, B. (2013). Proposing fashion: The discourse of glossy magazines. *Comunicação e Sociedade*, 24, 120–142.

Mondada, L. (2008). Using video for a sequential and multimodal analysis of social interaction: Videotaping institutional telephone calls. *Forum: Qualitative Social Research* 9(3), article 39.

Morrow, D. G., Hier, C. M., Menard, W. E., & Leirer, V. O. (1998). Icons improve older and younger adults' comprehension of medication information. *Journal of Gerontology: Psychological Sciences*, 53B(4), 240–254.

Müller, M. G. (2011). Iconography and iconology as a visual method an approach. In E. Margolis & L. Pauwels (Eds.), *The Sage handbook of visual research methods* (pp. 283–297). London: Sage Publications.

Müller, M. G., & Kappas, A. (2010). Visual emotions—emotional visuals: Emotions, pathos formulae, and their relevance for communication research. In K. Döveling, C. Scheve, & E. A. Konijn (Eds.), *The Routledge handbook of emotions and mass media* (pp. 310–331). London and New York, NY: Routledge.

Müller-Doohm, S. (1997). Bildinterpretation als struktural-hermeneutische Symbolanalyse. In R. Hitzler & A. Honer (Eds.), *Sozialwissenschaftliche Hermeneutik* (pp. 81–108). Opladen: Leske + Budrich.

Mumby, D. K. (2004). Discourse, power and ideology: Unpacking the critical approach. In D. Grant, C. Hardy, C. Oswick, & L. Putnam (Eds.), *The Sage handbook of organizational discourse* (pp. 237–258). London: Sage Publications.

Newman, M. E. J. (2006). Modularity and community structure in networks. *Proceedings of the National Academy of Sciences*, 103(23), 8577–8582.

Nicolini, D., Mengis, J., & Swan, J. (2012). Understanding the role of objects in cross-disciplinary collaboration. *Organization Science*, 23(3), 597–906.

Norris, S. (2006). Multiparty interaction: A multimodal perspective on relevance. *Discourse Studies*, 8(3), 401–421.

Norris, S. (2009). Modal density and modal configurations: Multimodal actions. In C. Jewitt (Ed.), *The Routledge handbook of multimodal analysis* (pp. 86–99). London: Routledge.

Norris, S. (2016). *Multimodality* (Vols. 1–4). London: Routledge.

Norris, S. (Ed.) (2012). *Multimodality in practice: Investigating theory-in practice-through-methodology*. London: Routledge.

Norris, S., & Jones, R. (Eds.) (2005). *Discourse in action: Introducing mediated discourse analysis*. London: Routledge.

O'Halloran, K. (2004). Visual semiosis in film. In K. O'Halloran (Ed.), *Multimodal discourse analysis* (pp. 109–130). London: Continuum.

O'Halloran, K., & Smith, B. (Eds.) (2006). *Multimodal studies: Exploring issues and domains*. London: Routledge.

O'Toole, M. (1994). *The language of displayed art*. Leicester: Leicester University Press.

Oakley, M. (1985). *Our society and others*. Sydney: McGraw-Hill.

Oberg, A., Drori, G. S., & Delmestri, G. (2018). Where history, visuality, and identity meet: Institutional paths to visual diversity among organizations. *Research in the Sociology of Organizations*, 54(B), 71–99.

Ocasio, W. (1997). Towards an attention-based view of the firm. *Strategic Management Journal*, 18(S1), 187–206.

Oliveira, F. M., Islam, G., & Toraldo, M. L. (2018). Multimodal imaginaries and the 'big worm': Materialities, artefacts and analogies in São Paulo's urban renovation. *Research in the Sociology of Organizations*, 54(A), 27–62.

Oliver, D., & Roos, J. (2007). Beyond text: Constructing organizational identity multimodally. *British Journal of Management*, 18(4), 342–358.

Olk, B., & Kappas, A. (2011). Eye tracking as a tool for visual research. In E. Margolis & L. Pauwels (Eds.), *The Sage handbook of visual research methods* (pp. 433–451). London: Sage Publications.

Orlikowski, W. J., & Scott, S. V. (2008). Sociomateriality: Challenging the separation of technology, work and organization. *Academy of Management Annals*, 2(1), 433–474.

Painter, C., Martin, J. R., & Unsworth, L. (2013). *Reading visual narratives: Image analysis of children's picture books*. London: Equinox.

Panofsky, E. (1939). *Studies in iconology: Humanistic themes in the art of the renaissance*. New York, NY: Oxford University Press.

Panofsky, E. (1957). *Gothic architecture and scholasticism: An inquiry into the analogy of the arts, philosophy, and religion in the middle ages*. New York, NY: World Publishing.

Parry, K. (2010). A visual framing analysis of British press photography during the 2006 Israel-Lebanon conflict. *Media, War & Conflict*, 3(1), 67–85.

Pauwels, L. (2010). Visual sociology reframed: An analytical synthesis and discussion of visual methods in social and cultural research. *Sociological Methods & Research*, 38(4), 545–581.

Pershina, R., & Soppe, B. (2018). Let the games begin: Institutional complexity and the design of new products. *Research in the Sociology of Organizations*, 54(A), 219–254.

Phillips, B. J. (2000). The impact of verbal anchoring on consumer response to image ads. *Journal of Advertising*, 29(1), 15–24.

Phillips, N., Lawrence, T. B., & Hardy, C. (2004). Discourse and institutions. *Academy of Management Review*, 29(4), 635–652.

Phillips, N., & Oswick, C. (2012). Organizational discourse: Domains, debates, and directions. *The Academy of Management Annals*, 6(1), 435–481.

Pinch, T., & Bijsterveld, K. (Eds.) (2012). *The Oxford handbook of sound studies*. Oxford: Oxford University Press.

Pinch, T., & Swedberg, R. (2008). *Living in a material world: Economic sociology meets science and technology studies*. Boston, MA: MIT Press.

Pink, S. (2001). *Doing visual anthropology*. London: Sage Publications.

Pollock, G. (2006). *Psychoanalysis and the image: Transdisciplinary perspectives*. Malden, MA: Blackwell.

Powell, W. W., & Colyvas, J. A. (2008). Microfoundations of institutional theory. In R. Greenwood, C. Oliver, K. Sahlin, & R. Suddaby (Eds.), *The Sage handbook of organizational institutionalism* (pp. 276–298). Los Angeles, CA: Sage Publications.

Powell, W. W., Oberg, A., Korff, V., Oelberger, C., & Kloos, K. (2017). Institutional analysis in a digital era: Mechanisms and methods to understand emerging fields. In G. Krücken, C. Mazza, R. E. Meyer, & P. Walgenbach (Eds.), *New Themes in institutional analysis: Topics and issues form European research* (pp. 305–344). Cheltenham, UK and Northampton, MA: Edward Elgar.

References

Pratt, M. G., & Rafaeli, A. (1997). Organizational dress as a symbol of multilayered social identities. *Academy of Management Journal, 40*(4), 862–898.

Pratt, M. G., Schultz, M., Ashforth, B. E., & Ravasi, D. (2016). *The Oxford handbook of organizational identity.* Oxford: Oxford University Press.

Preston, A. M., Wright, C., & Young, J. J. (1996). Imag[in]ing annual reports. *Accounting, Organizations and Society, 21*(1), 113–137.

Preston, A. M., & Young, J. J. (2000). Constructing the global corporation and corporate constructions of the global: A picture essay. *Accounting, Organizations and Society, 25*(4–5), 427–449.

Pugh, D. S., & Hickson, D. J. (2007). *Writers on organizations.* Thousand Oaks, CA: Sage Publications.

Putnam, L. L., Phillips, N., & Chapman, P. (1996). Metaphors of communication and organization. In S. R. Clegg, C. Hardy, & W. R. Nord (Eds.), *Handbook of organization studies* (pp. 375–408). London: Sage Publications.

Puyou, F.-R., & Quattrone, P. (2018). The visual and material dimensions of legitimacy: Accounting and the search for socie-ties. *Organization Studies, 39*(5–6), 721–746.

Puyou, F.-R., Quattrone, P., McLean, C., & Thrift, N. (Eds.) (2012). *Imagining organizations: Performative imagery in business and beyond.* New York, NY and London: Routledge.

Quattrone, P. (2009). Books to be practiced: Memory, the power of the visual, and the success of accounting. *Accounting, Organizations and Society, 34*(1), 85–118.

Raab, J. (2008). *Visuelle Wissenssoziologie: Theoretische Konzeption und materiale Analysen.* Konstanz: UVK Verlagsgesellschaft.

Raaijmakers, A., Vermeulen, P. A. M., & Meeus, M. T. H. (2018). Children without bruised knees: Responding to material and ideational (mis)alignments. *Organization Studies, 39*(5–6), 811–830.

Rafaeli, A., & Pratt, M. G. (1993). Tailored meanings: On the meaning and impact of organizational dress. *Academy of Management Review, 18*(1), 32–55.

Rämö, H. (2011). Visualizing the phronetic organization: The case of photographs in CSR reports. *Journal of Business Ethics, 104*(3), 371–387.

Ravasi, D. (2017). Visualizing our way through theory building. *Journal of Management Inquiry, 26*(2), 240–243.

Ravelli, L. J., & McMurtrie, R. J. (2016). *Multimodality in the built environment.* London: Routledge.

Ray, J. L., & Smith, A. D. (2012). Using photographs to research organizations: Evidence, considerations, and application in a field study. *Organizational Research Methods, 15*(2), 288–315.

Reisigl, R., & Wodak, R. (2016). The discourse-historical approach (DHA). In R. Wodak & M. Meyer (Eds.), *Methods of critical discourse studies* (3rd ed., pp. 23–61). Los Angeles, CA: Sage Publications.

Riach, K., & Warren, S. (2015). Smell organization: Bodies and corporeal porosity in office work. *Human Relations, 68*(5), 789–809.

Roderick, I. (2016). The politics of office design: Translating neoliberalism into furnishing. *Journal of Language and Politics, 15*(3), 284–287.

Rodríguez, L., & Dimitrova, D. (2011). The levels of visual framing. *Journal of Visual Literacy, 30*(1), 48–65.

Rorty, R. (Ed.) (1967). *The linguistic turn: Recent essays in philosophical method.* Chicago, IL and London: University of Chicago Press.

References

Rose, G. (2012). *Visual methodologies: An introduction to researching with visual materials* (3rd ed.). Los Angeles, CA: Sage Publications.

Rowley-Jolivet, E. (2004). Different visions, different visuals: A social semiotic analysis of field-specific visual composition in scientific conference presentations. *Visual Communication*, 3(2), 145–175.

Rowlinson, M., Casey, A., Hansen, P. H., & Mills, A. J. (2014). Narratives and memory in organizations. *Organization*, 21(4), 441–446.

Saldanha, G., & O'Brien, S. (2013). *Research methodologies in translation studies*. London: Routledge.

Sartre, J.-P. (1940). *L'imaginaire: Psychologie phénoménologique de l'imagination*. Paris: Gallimard.

Saussure, F. de. (1949). *Cours de linguistique générale*. Paris: Payot.

Schegloff, E. A. (1996). Some practices for referring to persons in talk-in-interaction: A partial sketch of a systematics. In B. Fox (Ed.), *Studies in anaphora* (pp. 437–485). Amsterdam: John Benjamins Publishing Company.

Schramm-Klein, H., Swoboda, B., & Morschett, D. (2007). Internet vs brick-and-mortar stores: Analyzing the influence of shopping motives on retail channel choice among internet users. *Journal of Customer Behaviour*, 6(1), 19–36.

Schroeder, J. E. (2012). Style and strategy: Snapshot aesthetics in brand culture. In F.-R. Puyou, P. Quattrone, C. McLean, & N. Thrift (Eds.), *Imagining organizations: Performative imagery in business and beyond* (pp. 129–151). New York, NY and London: Routledge.

Schroeder, J. E., & Zwick, D. (2004). Mirrors of masculinity: Representation and identity in advertising images. *Consumption, Markets and Culture*, 7(1), 21–52.

Schwalbe, C. B., Silcock, B. W., & Keith, S. (2008). Visual framing of the early weeks of the U.S.-led invasion of Iraq: Applying the master war narrative to electronic and print images. *Journal of Broadcasting & Electronic Media*, 52(3), 448–456.

Scott, L. M. (1994). Images in advertising: The need for a theory of visual rhetoric. *Journal of Consumer Research*, 21(2), 252–273.

Scott, L. M., & Rajeev, B. (Eds.) (2003). *Persuasive imagery: A consumer response perspective*. Mahwah, NJ: Erlbaum.

Scott, L. M., & Vargas, P. (2007). Writing with pictures: Toward a unifying theory of consumer response to images. *Journal of Consumer Research*, 34(3), 341–356.

Shneiderman, B. (1997). *Designing the user interface: Strategies for effective human-computer interaction*. Reading, MA: Addison-Wesley.

Shortt, H. L. (2015). Liminality, space and the importance of 'transitory dwelling places' at work. *Human Relations*, 68(4), 633–658.

Shortt, H. L., & Warren, S. K. (2012). Fringe benefits: Valuing the visual in narratives of hairdressers' identities at work. *Visual Studies*, 27(1), 18–34.

Shortt, H. L., & Warren, S. K. (2017). Grounded visual pattern analysis: Photographs in organizational field studies. *Organizational Research Methods*. doi.org/10.1177/1094428117742495

Sillince, J. A. A., & Barker, J. R. (2012). A tropological theory of institutionalization. *Organization Studies*, 33(1), 7–38.

Slutskaya, N., Simpson, A., & Hughes, J. (2012). Lessons from photoelicitation: Encouraging working men to speak. *Qualitative Research in Organizations and Management: An International Journal*, 7(1), 16–33.

Smets, M., Burke, G., Jarzabkowski, P., & Spee, P. (2014). Charting new territory for organizational ethnography: Insights from a team-based video ethnography. *Journal of Organizational Ethnography*, 3(1), 10–26.
Smith, M., & Taffler, R. (1996). Improving the communication of accounting through cartoon graphics. *Accounting, Auditing & Accountability Journal*, 9(2), 68–85.
Spangenberg, E. R., Grohmann, B., & Sprott, D. E. (2005). It's beginning to smell (and sound) a lot like Christmas: The interactive effects of ambient scent and music in a retail setting. *Journal of Business Research*, 58(11), 1583–1589.
Stenglin, M. (2009). Space and communication in exhibitions: Unravelling the nexus. In C. Jewitt (Ed.), *The Routledge handbook of multimodal analysis* (pp. 419–430). London: Routledge.
Stigliani, I., & Ravasi, D. (2012). Organizing thoughts and connecting brains: Material practices and the transition from individual to group-level prospective sensemaking. *Academy of Management Journal*, 55(5), 1232–1259.
Stigliani, I., & Ravasi, D. (2018). The shaping of form: Exploring designers' use of aesthetic knowledge. *Organization Studies*, 39(5–6), 747–784.
Stiles, D. R. (2011). Disorganization, disidentification and ideological fragmentation: Verbal and pictorial evidence from a British business school. *Culture and Organization*, 17(1), 5–30.
Stowell, A. F., & Warren, S. (2018). The institutionalization of suffering: Embodied inhabitation and the maintenance of health and safety in e-waste recycling. *Organization Studies*, 39(5–6), 785–809.
Strang, D., & Meyer, J. W. (1993). Institutional conditions for diffusion. *Theory and Society*, 22(4), 487–511.
Streeck, J., Goodwin, C., & LeBaron, C. D. (Eds.) (2011). *Embodied interaction: Language and body in the material world*. Cambridge: Cambridge University Press.
Styhre, A. (2010). *Visual culture in organizations: Theory and cases*. London and New York, NY: Routledge.
Suchman, M. C. (1995). Managing legitimacy: Strategic and institutional approaches. *Academy of Management Review*, 20(3), 571–610.
Swedberg, R. (2016). Can you visualize theory? On the use of visual thinking in theory pictures, theorizing diagrams, and visual sketches. *Sociological Theory*, 34(3), 250–275.
Tagg, P. (1990). Music in mass media studies. Reading sounds for example. In K. Roe & U. Carlsson (Eds.), *Popular Music Research. Nordicom-Sweden*, 2, 103–115.
Thompson, L. J. (2008). Gender equity and corporate social responsibility in a post-feminist era. *Business Ethics: A European Review*, 17(1), 87–106.
Thompson, P., & Davenport, P. (1982). *The dictionary of visual language*. Harmondsworth, Middlesex and New York, NY: Penguin.
Thornton, P. H., Ocasio, W., & Lounsbury, M. (2012). *The institutional logics perspective: A new approach to culture, structure and process*. Oxford and New York, NY: Oxford University Press.
Thurlow, C., & Aiello, G. (2007). National pride, global capital: A social semiotic analysis of transnational visual branding in the airline industry. *Visual Communication*, 6(3), 305–344.
Tienari, J., & Vaara, E. (2016). Identity construction in mergers and acquisitions: A discursive sensemaking perspective. In M. Pratt, M. Schultz, B. E. Ashforth, &

References

D. Ravasi (Eds.), *Oxford handbook of organizational identity* (pp. 455–473). Oxford: Oxford University Press.
Tomperi, T. (2009). *Akateeminen kysymys? Yliopistolain kritiikki ja kiista uudesta yliopistosta* (Academic question? Criticism on the universities act and the dispute over the new university). Tampere: Vastapaino.
Toraldo, M. L., Islam, G., & Mangia, G. (2018). Modes of knowing: Video research and the problem of elusive knowledges. *Organizational Research Methods*, 21(2), 438–465.
Tracey, P. (2012). Religion and organization: A critical review of current trends and future directions. *The Academy of Management Annals*, 6(1), 87–134.
Tseng, C.-I. (2013). *Cohesion in film: Tracking film elements*. London: Palgrave Macmillan.
Tufte, E. R. (1983). *The visual display of quantitative information*. Cheshire, CT: Graphic Press.
Tufte, E. R. (1990). *Envisioning information*. Cheshire, CT: Graphic Press.
Tufte, E. R. (1997). *Visual explanations*. Cheshire, CT: Graphic Press.
Unsworth, L. (Ed.) (2008). *Multimodal semiotics*. London: Continuum.
Vaara, E. (2014). Struggles over legitimacy in the Eurozone crisis: Discursive legitimation strategies and their ideological underpinnings. *Discourse & Society*, 25(4), 500–518.
Vaara, E., Sonenshein, S., & Boje, D. (2016). Narratives as sources of stability and change in organizations: Approaches and directions for future research. *The Academy of Management Annals*, 10(1), 495–560.
Vaara, E., & Tienari, J. (2008). A discursive perspective on legitimation strategies in multinational corporations. *Academy of Management Review*, 33(4), 985–993.
Vaara, E., & Tienari, J. (2011). On the narrative construction of MNCs: An antenarrative analysis of legitimation and resistance in a cross-border merger. *Organization Science*, 22(2), 370–390.
Vaara, E., Tienari, J., & Irrmann, O. (2007). Crafting and international identity: The Nordea case. In L. Lerpold, D. Ravasi, J. van Rekom, & G. Soenen (Eds.), *Organizational identity in practice* (pp. 215–231). London: Routledge.
Vaara, E., & Whittington, R. (2012). Strategy-as-practice: Taking social practices seriously. *The Academy of Management Annals*, 6(1), 285–336.
Valdez, P., & Mehrabian, A. (1994). Effects of color on emotions. *Journal of Experimental Psychology: General*, 123(4), 394.
Van Leeuwen, T. (1999). *Speech, music, sound*. London: Palgrave Macmillan.
Van Leeuwen, T. (2001). Semiotics and iconography. In T. van Leeuwen & C. Jewitt (Eds.), *Handbook of visual analysis* (pp. 92–118). London: Sage Publications.
Van Leeuwen, T. (2005). *Introducing social semiotics*. London: Routledge.
Van Leeuwen, T. (2006). Towards a semiotics of typography. *Information Design Journal*, 14(2), 139–155
Van Leeuwen, T. (2007). Legitimation in discourse and communication. *Discourse & Communication*, 1(1), 91–112.
Van Leeuwen, T. (2008a). *Discourse and practice: New tools for critical discourse analysis*. New York, NY: Oxford University Press.
Van Leeuwen, T. (2008b). New forms of writing, new visual competences. *Visual Studies*, 23(2), 130–135.

Van Leeuwen, T. (2011). *The language of colour: An introduction*. London: Routledge.
Van Leeuwen, T. (2014). Parametric systems: The case of voice quality. In C. Jewitt (Ed.), *The Routledge handbook of multimodal analysis* (pp. 76–86). London: Routledge.
Van Leeuwen, T. (2015). Looking good: Aesthetics, multimodality and literacy studies. In J. Rowsell & K. Pahl (Eds.), *The Routledge handbook of literacy studies* (pp. 426–439) London: Routledge.
Van Leeuwen, T. (2016). A social semiotic theory of synesthesia? (A discussion paper). *Hermes—Journal of Language and Communication in Business*, 55, 105–119.
Van Leeuwen, T. (2017). Sonic logos. In L. Way & S. McKerrell (Eds.), *Music as multimodal discourse* (pp. 119–134). London: Bloomsbury.
Van Leeuwen, T. (2018a). Legitimation and multimodality. In R. Wodak & B. Forchtner (Eds.), *The Routledge handbook of language and politics* (pp. 218–232). Abingdon and New York, NY: Routledge.
Van Leeuwen, T. (2018b). Multimodality in organization studies: Afterword. *Research in the Sociology of Organizations*, 54(B), 235–242.
Van Leeuwen, T., & Caldas-Coulthard, C. (2004). The semiotics of kinetic design. In D. Banks (Ed.), *Text and texture: Systemic-functional viewpoints on the nature and structure of texts* (pp. 355–381). Paris: L'Harmattan.
Van Leeuwen, T., & Iversen, D. L. (2017). Semiotic technology and education—The case of Mathletics. In A. Akerfeldt & F. Lindstrand (Eds.), *Didactics after Vygotsky*. Stockholm: Liber.
Van Leeuwen, T., & Jewitt, C. (2001). *Handbook of visual analysis*. London: Sage Publications.
Van Leeuwen, T., & Wodak, R. (1999). Legitimizing immigration control: A discourse-historical analysis. *Discourse Studies*, 1(1), 83–118.
Vásquez, C., & Cooren, F. (2012). Imagining passion in action: An analysis of translation and treason. In F.-R. Puyou, P. Quattrone, C. McLean, & N. Thrift (Eds.), *Imagining organizations: Performative imagery in business and beyond* (pp. 191–212). New York, NY and London: Routledge.
Veltruský, J. (1964 [1940]). Man and object in the theatre. In P. L. Garvin (Ed.), *A Prague school reader on esthetics, literary structure and style* (pp. 83–91). Washington, DC: Georgetown University Press.
Venkatraman, M., & Nelson, T. (2008). From servicescape to consumptionscape: A photo-elicitation study of Starbucks in the new China. *Journal of International Business Studies*, 39(6), 1010–1026.
Ventola, E. (1987). *The structure of social interaction: A systemic approach to the semiotics of service encounters*. London: Frances Pinter.
Ventola, E., Charles, C., & Kaltenbacher, M. (Eds.) (2004). *Perspectives on multimodality*. London: Continuum.
Vesa, M., & Vaara, E. (2014). Strategic ethnography 2.0: Four methods for advancing strategy process and practice research. *Strategic Organization*, 12(4), 288–298.
Vince, R., & Broussine, M. (1996). Paradox, defense and attachment: Accessing and working with emotions and relations underlying organizational change. *Organization Studies*, 17(1), 1–21.

References 221

Voronov, M., & Vince, R. (2012). Integrating emotions into the analysis of institutional work. *Academy of Management Review*, 37(1), 58–81.

Wagner, J. (2002). Contrasting images, complementary trajectories: Sociology, visual sociology and visual research. *Visual Studies*, 17(2), 160–171.

Waller, M. J., & Kaplan, S. A. (2018). Systematic behavioral observation for emergent team phenomena: Key considerations for quantitative video-based approaches. *Organizational Research Methods*, 21(2), 500–515.

Warner, W. L., & Lunt, P. S. (1941). *The social life of a modern community*. New Haven, CT: Yale University.

Warren, S. (2002). 'Show me how it feels to work here': Using photography to research organizational aesthetics. *Ephemera*, 2(3), 224–245.

Warren, S. (2005). Photography and voice in critical qualitative management research. *Accounting, Auditing & Accountability Journal*, 18(6), 861–882.

Wasserman, V., & Frenkel, M. (2011). Organizational aesthetics: Caught between identity regulation and culture jamming. *Organization Science*, 22(2), 503–521.

Way, L. C. S., & McKerrell, S. (Eds.) (2017). *Music as multimodal discourse*. London: Bloomsbury.

Wedlin, L., & Sahlin, K. (2017). The imitation and translation of management ideas. In R. Greenwood, C. Oliver, T. B. Lawrence, & R. Meyer (Eds.), *The Sage handbook of organizational institutionalism* (pp. 102–127). London: Sage Publications.

Weick, K. E., Sutcliffe, K. M., & Obstfeld, D. (2005). Organizing and the process of sensemaking. *Organization Science*, 16(4), 409–421.

Wengeler, M. (2003). *Topos und Diskurs: Begründung einer argumentationsanalytischen Methode und ihre Anwendung auf den Migrationsdiskurs (1960–1985)*. Tübingen: Niemeyer.

Wenzel, M., & Koch, J. (2018). Strategy as staged performance: A critical discursive perspective on keynote speeches as a genre of strategic communication. *Strategic Management Journal*, 39(3), 639–663.

Westera, W. (2013). On the cybernetic arrangement of feedback in serious games: A systems-theoretical perspective. *Education and Information Technologies*, 20(1), 57–73.

Whiting, R., Symon, G., Roby, H., & Chamakiotis, P. (2018). Who's behind the lens? A reflexive analysis of roles in participatory video research. *Organizational Research Methods*, 21(2), 316–340.

Wildfeuer, J. (2013). *Film discourse interpretation: Towards a new paradigm for multimodal film analysis*. London: Routledge.

Wilhoit, E. D. (2017). Photo and video methods in organizational and managerial communication research. *Management Communication Quarterly*, 31(3), 447–466.

Williamson, J. (1979). *Decoding advertisements*. London: Marion Boyars.

Wingstedt, J. (2017). If you have nothing to say – sing it!: On the interplay of music, voice and lyrics in the advertising jingle. In L. C. S. Way & S. McKerrell (Eds.), *Music as multimodal discourse* (pp. 135–157). London: Bloomsbury.

Wodak, R., & Meyer, M. (Eds.) (2016). *Methods of critical discourse studies*. Los Angeles, CA: Sage Publications.

Yakura, E. K. (2002). Charting time: Timelines as temporal boundary objects. *Academy of Management Journal*, 45(5), 956–970.

Yantis, S. (Ed.) (2001). *Visual perception: Essential reading*. London: Taylor & Francis.

Zappavigna, M. (2016). Social media photography: Constructing subjectivity in Instagram images. *Visual Communication*, *15*(3), 271–292.

Zhao, S., Djonov, E., & van Leeuwen, T. (2014). Semiotic technology and practice: A multimodal social semiotic approach to PowerPoint. *Text & Talk*, *34*(3), 349–375.

Zhao, W. (2018). Protest in style: Exploring multimodal concision in rhetorical artifacts. *Research in the Sociology of Organizations*, *54*(A), 119–149.

Zijderveld, A. C. (1979). *On clichés: The supersedure of meaning by function in modernity*. London: Routledge.

Zilber, T. B. (2006). The work of the symbolic in institutional processes: Translations of rational myths in Israeli high tech. *Academy of Management Journal*, *49*(2), 281–303.

Index

Aalto University: merger 129, 132; reactions and use of logo 137–139; use of new logo in intentional identity construction 135–136; visual identity 133–135
abstraction 108–111
aestheticization 109
'affordances' 64, 186
analytical diagrams 115–117
archaeological approach: challenges 58–61; concept of 19–20, 49; core ideas 52–53; legitimation case study 178; methods 55–56; opportunities 60–61; organization 53–54; studies 56–57
arrows 30, 113–115, 117, 120, 123–125, 128
artefacts: abuse and manipulation of 138–139; 'agency' of 64; approaches to analysing modes of 61; codes 57; depiction of moral legitimacy in 163–164; 'inscription' of 64; materiality of 13–14; semiotic 164; visual 10–11, 17, 19, 49, 62–64, 91, 94–96; *see also* multimodal artefacts
art history 16
aural mode 60
authenticity 135–136, 185
authorization 163, 172–173

'bi-stratal' semiotic system 35
body language 69

case studies: corporate social responsibility 102, 162–179; diagrams 101–102, 104–128; logos 102, 129–139; online shopping 102, 140–161
category formation 57

Centre–Margin diagram 109, 118
city management 91
classification diagrams 115, 117
cognitive legitimacy 163
cognitive metaphor theory 77
colour 109–111
communication: characteristics of diagrammatic 105–111; metafunctions of 30–35, 40–41, 45; organization and 7; role in social construction of reality 4–5, 24
communication and media studies 18
'communication models' 7, 105, 113
'conative function' 34
conceptual diagrams 115–118
conduit model 7
'context of culture' 26–27
'context of situation' 25–27, 44
corporate reporting 56
corporate social responsibility (CSR): in Austrian Corporate Reporting 166–176; 'instantiation' of 20, 33; legitimation case study 102, 162–179; as a response issues of legitimacy 164–166
corporate sustainability 164
credibility 171–172
critical discourse analysis 8, 53, 55–56, 128
cultural memory 19, 52
cybernetic diagrams 113–114

de-personalization 107
'design' 38–39, 164
diagrams: *abstraction* 108–111; aesthetic embellishments 127; analysing 118–121; analytical 115–117; background elements 125–127; case study 101–102; Centre–Margin 109, 118;

characteristics of communication 105–111; characteristics of diagrammatic communication 105–111; classification 115, 117; *comprehensiveness* 108–111; conceptual 115–118; *context-dependency* 108; cybernetic 113–114; *de-personalization* 107; directional variation 125; dynamic 111–113; flowcharts 114–115; framing variations 125; grammar of 111–118; mind-mapping techniques 90, 109, 115, 118; narrative 113–115; *objectification* 107; resources for producing 122–127; social network 117–118; static 111–113; tables 115; templates 122–125; tree 117; types of 104; use for purposes of management and organization 105; use in *documenting* approach 90; *visual syntax* 105–107, 127
dialogical approach.: advantage of 85–86; challenges 85–86; concept of 21; core ideas 79–80; legitimation case study 178; methods 82–83; opportunities 86–87; organization 80–81; qualitative designs 86–87; studies 84–85
digitalization 10, 90
'discourse' 13, 38, 44, 164
discourse analysis: critical 8, 53, 55–56, 128; multimodal 9–10, 53; studies 6–7; teaching 121; use in analysis of visual-verbal composition 169; use in *archaeological* approach 55; use in study of multimodal legitimation 164; visual 17
'distribution' 39, 40
documenting approach: challenges 92–96; concept of 21–22; core ideas 88; opportunities 94–96; studies 90–92
durability 13
dynamic diagrams 111–113

'elusive knowledges' 96
emojis 36
ethnography 21, 88, 90–91
ethnomethodological conversation analysis (EMCA) 67
experimental research designs 73–74
'expressive function' 34
eye-tracking 74, 75, 77

field 37–38, 43
flowcharts 114–115
functional semiotics 30

Global Financial Crisis (GFC) 57
globalism 171, 173
'guide rhythm' 70

hermeneutics 169

ideational metafunction 30–32, 34, 38, 40–41
identity-building: logos in 130–132; in mergers and acquisitions 129–130; research 185; through sound and music 13; use of advertisements 61
'incipient' legitimation 163
indirect persuasion 74–75
'inscription' 64
'instantiation' 29
interpersonal metafunction 30, 32–33, 34, 40–41, 107

language: 'conative function' 34; 'expressive function' 34; functions of 34; materiality of 40; metafunctions of 32, 41; 'referential function' 34; 'restricted' 155; stratification of 35–39; verbal 42, 75, 105, 149–150, 161
'leadership' study 92–94
legitimacy 163–164
legitimation: conceptualizing as multimodal endeavour 162–179; multimodal 185; other research approaches to multimodal 178–179; strategies 171–176
lexicogrammar 35–38
linguistic turn 6–7
logos: Aalto University merger 132; Aalto University's visual identity 133–135; authenticity 135–136; case study 102, 129–139; distinctiveness 136; future orientation 137; in identity-building 130–132; identity-building in mergers and acquisitions 129–130; power structures 137; reactions and use of 137–139; self-esteem 136–137; sonic 58, 78; use in intentional identity construction 135–137

maps 108, 111, 115
marginalized groups 80–81

marketing 185
'marketization of discourse' 44
materiality 7, 12–14, 57–58, 67, 191
meaning 26–30, 67, 79–80, 109
meaning-making: actualization of 29–30, 42; inscribed in artefacts and texts 64; 'modal registers' as collective adaptations of resources 20, 24, 60, 92, 167, 186, 188–189; resources for 4; semiotics and 78; as social practice 27; use of 'semiotic technologies' as resources for 13, 97; in visual communication 39, 56; in Zalando's online shop 141–155
media 40, 164
mergers and acquisitions (M&As) 129–130
metafunctions 30–35, 40–41, 45, 52, 56, 61
metaphor clusters 7
Microsoft SmartArt 122–127
mind-mapping techniques 90, 109, 115, 118
modality 33, 107, 163
'modal registers' 77, 81, 152–153, 167, 186
mode: concept of 24, 37–38, 43, 45, 185–186; cultural construction of 189–190; definitions of 39–41; materiality of 39–41; methods for analysis of 56
'modern architecture' 57
'mood' 107
moral evaluation 163, 173
moral legitimacy 163
multimodal artefacts: approaches to analysing modes of 61; *archaeological* approach to study of 19–20, 49, 52–61; as cultural memory 19, 49, 52; *dialogical* approach to study of 21, 49–51, 79–87; *documenting* approach to study of 21–22, 49, 51, 88–96; methods for analysis of 17; *practice* approach to study of 20, 49, 62–70; role in organizational practices 64–65; as 'storage' of social stocks of knowledge 19; *strategic* approach to study of 20–21, 49, 71–78; as 'triggers' for *in situ* construction of social meaning 79–80, 86; use in interview situations 80–81; use to document research 88–91; *see also* artefacts, multimodality

multimodal conversation analysis 67–69
multimodal discourse analysis 9–10, 53
multimodality: analytical frameworks 8–9, 14–15; call for including additional modes in research 190–191; concept of 189; early approaches 4–5, 187–188; implications for organizational practice 192–194; legitimation research 162–179; methods 188–189; ongoing progress in research 183–187; organizational turn 8–9; potentials and avenues for future research 187–191; relevance of 186–187; role in constitution of meaning(s) and institutions 8; roots and inspirations for research 15–19; social semiotics approach 9, 41–44; status of research 98; *see also* multimodal artefacts
multimodal literacy 108
music 20, 28–30, 41, 77
mythopoesis 174

narrative diagrams 113–115
normative discourses 26, 44–45, 98

objectification 107
online shopping, Zalando case study 72, 102, 140–161
organizational communication 7, 27, 191
organizational legitimacy 164–166
organizational turn 8–9
organization research: areas of application of multimodal theory and data in 185; call for including additional modes in 190–191; cross-fertilization between multimodality research and 184; implications for practice 192–194; ongoing progress in multimodal 183–187; theory 3–4
organizations: making 'tangible' 12–14; making 'visible' 10–12

Paris School 4, 19
persuasion 74–75
philosophy 16
phonetics 35–38
phonology 35–38
photo elicitation 82–83, 85
photography 91

226 Index

photo interviews 82–83
PowerPoint 13, 41, 63, 69, 94, 97
power structures 80–81
practice approach: challenges 67–70; concept of 20; core ideas 62–63; legitimation case study 178–179; methods 65–66; mode 67–70; opportunities 69–70; organization 63–65; studies 66–67
Prague School 4, 18
product attributes 73–74
'*production*' 38–39, 40, 164
psychology 17
public discourse 13

qualitative designs 55, 86–87, 187
quantitative designs 55

'rank' 75
rationalization 163, 173
'recontextualization' 42–44
'referential function' 34
registers: advertising register 142, 149–150; catalogue register 142, 144; fashion magazine register 142, 150–154; product sheet register 142, 144–145; retail register 142, 146–149; in Zalando's online shop 142–155
resemiotization 11, 42–43, 67
'restricted languages,' 155
rhetorical model 7
rhythm 70
role structure 26

salience 70, 109
self-esteem 136–137
semantics 35–38
semiotic artefact 164
semiotics 18–19, 25–28; *see also* social semiotics
'semiotic technologies' 13, 14
sensemaking 80
'signs' 26, 27, 35, 80
'silenced' discourses 80
social action 26
social meaning 79–80
social network diagrams 115, 117–118
social practices 27, 43–45
social reality 52–53
social semiotics: approach to multimodality 4–5, 18–19; definition of 25; development phases 41–44; 'instantiation' 29; metafunctions 30–35; monomodal view 42; of music 28; polymodal view 42; 'semiotic' in 27–39; 'social' in 25–27; stratification 35–39; system 27–30
sociology 16–17
sociomateriality 13
sonic logos 58, 78
sound 20, 41, 70, 191
space 83
static diagrams 111–113
strategic approach: challenges 77–78; concept of 20–21; core ideas 71; legitimation case study 178; methods 73–74; opportunities 78; organization 71–73; studies 74–76
strategizing 185
strategy 64, 185
strategy-as-practice research 64
strategy development process 66
stratification 35–39, 164
'style' 155
subject positions 174–175
symbolic organization 26, 37–38
symbolization 109
'systemic functional linguistics' 42

technology 13, 14, 112–113
tenor 37–38, 43
textual metafunction 30, 33–34
theology 16
time 28
transferability 13
tree diagrams 117
'triggers' 79
'tri-stratal' semiotic system 35

'verbalization' 60
verbal language 42, 75, 105, 128, 149–150, 161
verbal mode 7–8, 58–59
video 91–92, 94–96
video data 66–67
visual anthropology 16–17, 21, 88
visual artefacts 10–11, 17, 19, 49, 62–64, 91, 94–96
visual communication 39
visual discourse analysis 17
visual field notes 88–89
visuality 10–12
visual methodologies 55
visual mode 52–53, 58–59
visual research 74
visual rhetoric 56, 71

visual syntax 105–107, 127
visual text 89–90

Zalando: advertising register 142, 149–150; catalogue register 142, 144; customer motivation 158–160; fashion magazine register 142, 150–154; multimodal meaning-making in 141–155, 160–161; online shopping 140–161; overview of 142; practice of shopping on 155–157; product sheet register 142, 144–145; register variation at 142; retail register 142, 146–149